CHOCOLATE
WARS

CHOCOLATE

WARS

THE 150-YEAR RIVALRY BETWEEN THE WORLD'S GREATEST CHOCOLATE MAKERS

DEBORAH CADBURY

PUBLICAFFAIRS
New York

Book Design by Trish Wilkinson
Set in 11.5 point Goudy Old Style

Library of Congress Cataloging-in-Publication Data

Cadbury, Deborah.
    Chocolate wars : the 150-year rivalry between the world's greatest chocolate
makers / Deborah Cadbury.—1st ed.
        p.   cm.
    Includes bibliographical references and index.
    ISBN 978-1-58648-820-8 (alk. paper)
    1. Chocolate industry—History. 2. Cadbury Ltd.—History. 3. Cadbury family.
I. Title.

HD9200.A2C33 2010
338.7'66392—dc22   2010022905

First Edition

10 9 8 7 6 5 4 3 2 1

For my mother and Martin
with love

Contents

Introduction

When I was a young child, the knowledge that a branch of my family had built a chocolate factory filled me with wonder. What sort of charmed life did such a possibility offer to my relatives? Each Christmas I had an insight when the most enormous case arrived from my uncle, Michael Cadbury, containing a large supply of mouthwatering chocolates. Even more memorable was the trip I made in the early 1960s to see how the chocolate was made. Opening the door to the factory at Bournville in Birmingham, I was greeted by a magical sight.

To a child's eyes, it was as though I had entered a cavernous interior that belonged to some benign, orderly, and highly productive wizard who had somehow saturated the very air with a chocolate aroma. My uncle and parents raised their voices against the whirr of machinery. But I did not hear them. All I could see was chocolate. It was all around me in every stage of the process. There was molten chocolate bubbling in vats towering above me, vats so huge that they had ladders running up their sides. Chocolate rivers flowed on a number of swiftly moving conveyers through gaps in the wall to mysterious chambers beyond. Solid chocolate shaped in a myriad of exciting confections travelled in neat soldierly processions towards the wrapping department. Such a miracle of clockwork precision and sensual extravagance was hard to take in. Even more puzzling to my young mind: How did this chocolate feast, which brought the idea of greed to a whole new level, fit with religion? For even though I did not yet understand the connection, I did know that the chocolate works were in some inexplicable way intimately connected with a little-known religious movement known as Quakerism. Was all this the hand of God?

My own father had left the Quaker movement just before the Second World War. He wanted, as he put it, to "join the fight against Hitler," a stance that was not compatible with Quaker pacifism. I was brought up in the Church of England, and as a child, when I joined my cousins for Quaker meetings, I felt as if I were on the outside looking in on a strange, even mystical tradition. Long silences endured in bare rooms, stripped of any sign that might excite the senses, where grown-ups contemplated the surrounding void, were incomprehensible to me. Equally incomprehensible: How did my rich chocolate relatives acquire that admirable restraint, that air of wholesome frugality? Even family picnics had a way of turning into long and chilly route marches, raindrops trickling down your back. The wealth and austerity seemed oddly incongruous. Did the one contribute to the other? Cheerful homilies from my father along the lines of "Every mickle makes a muckle" and "Look after the pennies and the pounds will look after themselves" did not supply a satisfactory answer. Even a five-year-old knew this was not the key to creating a chocolate factory.

A generation passed before I decided to retrace my steps up Bournville Lane. This time it was personal. I wanted to delve into the Bournville and family archives to uncover the whole story. Turning the corner in the lane in the autumn of 2007, my heart skipped a beat as I was taken back to that day when my father and uncle, both now much missed, had taken me round the factory. To my surprise, the chocolate works seemed even larger than I remembered. Imposing red brick blocks stood beside the neatly mowed lawn of the cricket pitch with Bournville village and green nestled behind. At the time, Cadbury was the largest confectioner in the world and the only independent British chocolate enterprise to survive from the nineteenth century. I wanted to understand the journey that took my deeply religious Quaker forebears from peddling tins of cocoa from a pony and trap around Birmingham to the Titan-like company that reached around the globe.

The story began five generations ago, when a farsighted forbear, Richard Tapper Cadbury, a draper in Birmingham in the early nineteenth century, sent his youngest son, John, to London to study a new tropical commodity that was attracting interest among the colonial brokers of Mincing Lane: cocoa. Was it something to eat or drink? Richard Tapper saw it primarily as a nutritious nonalcoholic drink in a world that relied on gin to wash away its troubles. Never could my abstemiously inclined ancestor have guessed what fortunes were entwined with the humble cocoa bean, although it seemed full of promise: a touch of the exotic.

His grandsons, George and Richard Cadbury, turned a struggling business into a chocolate empire in one generation. In the process, they took on their Quaker friends and rivals, Joseph Rowntree in York, and Francis Fry and his nephew Joseph in Bristol. The Cadbury, Fry, and Rowntree dynasties were built on values that form a striking contrast with business ethics today. Their approach to the creation of wealth was governed by an entire code of practice developed over generations since the Civil War by their Quaker elders and set out at yearly meetings and in Quaker books of discipline. This nineteenth-century "Quaker capitalism" was far removed from the excesses of the world's most recent financial crisis, in which business leaders see no harm in pocketing huge personal profits while their companies collapse.

For the Quaker capitalists of the nineteenth century, the idea that wealth creation was for personal gain only would have been offensive. Wealth creation was for the benefit of the workers, the local community, and society at large, as well as the entrepreneurs themselves. Reckless or irresponsible debt was also seen as shameful. Quaker directives ensured that no man should "launch into trading and worldly business beyond what they can manage honourably . . . so that they can keep their words with all men." Even advertising was dismissed as dishonest, mere "puffery": The quality of the product mattered far more than the message. Men like Joseph Rowntree and George Cadbury built chocolate empires at the same time as writing groundbreaking papers on poverty, publishing authoritative studies of the Bible, and campaigning against a multitude of heartrending human rights abuses in a world that seems straight out of Dickens. Puritanical hard work and sober austerity, with the senses in watchful restraint, were the guiding principles. Even art, literature, and theater were dismissed as too great an indulgence.

While it is easy to dismiss such values as antiquated notions that governed business life at a time before Darwin's ideas had taken root, Quaker capitalism proved extraordinary successful, and its puritanical work ethic generated a staggering amount of worldly wealth. In the early nineteenth century, around 4,000 Quaker families ran 74 Quaker British banks and more than 200 Quaker companies. As they came to grips with making money, these austere men of God helped to shape the course of the Industrial Revolution and the commercial world today.

The chocolate factories of George and Richard Cadbury and Joseph Rowntree inspired men in America such as Milton Hershey, the "King of Caramel," who took philanthropy to a new, all-American scale with the creation of the utopian town of Hershey in the cornfields of Pennsylvania. But with the growth of global trade, the appearance of international rivals, and the emergence of a tough breed of entrepreneurs in the twentieth century unshackled by religious conviction—men such as Frank and Forrest Mars—the chocolate wars that followed gradually eroded the values that shaped Quaker capitalism. Some Quaker firms did not survive the struggle, and those that did had to sacrifice their Puritan roots. In the process, ownership of the businesses passed from private Quaker dynasties to public shareholders. Little by little the implications of the transition from Quaker capitalism to shareholder capitalism began to take shape in the form of huge confectionery conglomerates that straddle the corporate world today. The story of four generations of Cadbury brothers and their rivals highlights different phases of this process. The Cadbury chocolate business came of age during the expansion of the British Empire in the Victorian era. It peaked a century later during the post–Cold War era when it became the world's largest confectionery company—only to be consumed in turn by global forces in the new millennium.

The end of an independent Cadbury began with an innocuous voice mail message. In late August 2009, Irene Rosenfeld, chairman of America's largest food company, Kraft Foods, requested a meeting with the Cadbury chairman, Roger Carr. Kraft Foods made a £10.2 billion ($16.3 billion) bid for the British chocolate company. The bid turned hostile. Five months later, after a long and bitter siege played out in the glare of the media, Kraft won over Cadbury's shareholders. Britain's last big chocolate enterprise fell to the American giant after 186 years of independence in one of the largest acquisitions in British corporate history.

Today the world's two largest food companies—the Swiss Nestlé and America's Kraft—circle the globe, feeding humanity's sweet tooth. The Americans spend £8 billion ($12 billion) on chocolate; the British spend £3.5 billion ($5.25 billion); and more than one in four people in America and Britain are obese. Yet these two behemoths are locked in a race to maintain market share in the developed world, while also selling their Western confections and other processed foods to emerging markets in the developing world. Somewhere along the way the four hundred-year-old English Puritanical ideal of self-denial and the Quaker vision of creating wholesome nourishment for a hungry and impoverished workforce have disappeared. Also vanished is a myriad of independent chocolate confectionery firms. In Britain alone: Mackintosh of Halifax and Rowntree of York are now owned by Nestlé, while Terry of York, Fry of Bristol, and Cadbury have become a division of Kraft.

My search was to explore how this happened. I wanted to unearth the true story of the original Quaker chocolate pioneers and the religious beliefs that shaped their business decisions and to discern how their values differ from today's corporate CEOs. At first sight, globalization has been profitable for all. It is hard to dispute economists who claim that the process has lifted billions of people across the world out of the poverty that was on the doorstep of the cocoa magnates of the nineteenth century. But the "process" has also come at a significant cost.

Bournville on a bitterly cold January day in 2010 provided a stark contrast to the peaceful charm of earlier visits. Outside the factory, staff members were parading with banners. "Kraft go to hell," said one. In a symbolic gesture, another protester set fire to a huge Kraft Toblerone bar. Unite, Britain's biggest trade union, had warned that thousands of jobs could be eliminated if Kraft merged with Cadbury. "Our members feel very angry and very betrayed," said Jennie Formby, Unite's national officer for food and drink industries. Kraft was borrowing an estimated £7 billion ($10.5 billion) to fund the takeover, and many feared Cadbury could become "nothing more than a workhorse used to pay off this debt," with assets stripped and jobs removed. The anger in the streets was palpable. My taxi driver, whose family was originally from Kashmir, spelled out the crisis. "The chocolate works are British," he told me firmly. It belongs to the workers and the local people—not just management and shareholders. "The factory should not be moved or closed," he said. He captured the mood of alienation and powerlessness in the local community, where Birmingham Members of Parliament spearheaded resistance to the takeover in Westminster.

The growing powerlessness of national governments in these international global deals is highlighted by the statements of British politicians during the Kraft takeover. Assurances from business secretary Lord Mandelson that Kraft "would face huge opposition" melted away. Prime Minister Gordon Brown, speaking at a press conference at Downing Street, declared, "We are determined that . . . jobs in Cadbury can be secure." But he had no powers to guarantee that security.

The British government's belief in an open-door policy on such foreign takeovers has been called into question as many British companies have recently slipped into foreign ownership, creating uncertainties about the British economy. The Swiss have always protected Nestlé, allowing their food and chocolate business to flourish. "In France, the loss of a 'Cadbury' would have been out of the question," says former Cadbury chairman Roger Carr. "Germany believes that strength at home is the first step to success abroad. In Japan selling a company over the heads of management is unthinkable. And in the United States, regulations exist to protect strategic assets." It is ironic that when Cadbury tried to buy the British firm of Rowntree in 1988—at the time one of the five largest confectionery firms in the world—it was stopped by the British government—which permitted the Swiss giant, Nestlé, to step in and buy it. "In Westminster they did not understand the global picture," says Sir Dominic Cadbury, the last family chairman.

Leaving aside the social and national issues, there are wider concerns raised by the Kraft takeover that bring the contrast between the Quaker values of the chocolate pioneers and today's shareholder capitalism sharply into focus. For the nineteenth-century Quaker, ownership of a business came with a deep sense of responsibility and accountability to all those involved. "The problem with the way we have developed our system of shareholder capitalism is that the shareholder is being divorced from his role in ownership," explains Dominic Cadbury.

The problem is highlighted most clearly by the role of hedge funds. By the end of Kraft's takeover battle in January 2010, 31 percent of Cadbury was owned by hedge funds. Although these funds held decision-making power that could affect the company's very survival, "They are not even *pretending* to operate as owners," continues Dominic. "They have no sense of obligation or responsibility for the company whatsoever. They are there purely for short-term gain. Their whole motivation was that the company did *not* survive. You try equating ownership with getting rid of a company! It is completely destructive." Apart from the short-term gains that flowed to the hedge funds, some £400 million ($600 million) was made from the deal in fees in the City of London. When the financial sector is motivated by such sizeable and immediate returns, what has happened to the goal of building long-term value?

For Timothy Phillips, chairman of The Quakers and Business Group, which aims to promote Quaker principles in business, there is another issue that comes with increasing size to create giants like Nestlé and Kraft. "What one is doing by supporting the argument that bigger is better all the time," he explains, "is creating essentially a global network of asset ownership on a vast scale." Nestlé, for example, has almost 500 factories in over 80 countries and sells a billion products worldwide every day. It has 250,000 employees and had annual sales in 2009 of over $100 billion providing income that exceeds the GNP of many small countries. It is also one of the world's most boycotted companies as a result of ethical questions raised over the marketing and promotion of a number of its brands. The sheer size of such global institutions presents a number of problems. "Wealth and power are concentrated into fewer and less accountable hands," says Phillips. The people running these institutions have extraordinary budgets and staff at their disposal and decision-making powers that transcend national barriers, yet they are accountable only to a narrow group of shareholders. "Is this process truly democratic?" asks Phillips. He argues that the global village of the twenty-first century requires tighter international regulation and accountability not just to shareholding owners but to all their stakeholders, including the workers, the customers, and the wider community.

For Sir Adrian Cadbury, whose life spans the period from family Quaker leadership to the Kraft takeover, there is another key issue. "The danger of Kraft taking over is that it is very easy for a larger firm effectively to destroy the *spirit* of the firm they take over." The indefinable qualities that make up the character and identity of a company, he argues, are built up over many years, and depend on history, reputation, international brands, and the quality of people who work for the company. "It is something that I believe has a life of its own and creates a very strong feeling about the company and the people that work in it. . . . A business should not get so big that you lose the sense of identity and belonging." From his years of practical experience as one of Cadbury's longest serving chairmen, he adds, "Speaking as an economist, I would say the limits of size are human; they are not economic. What is sadly only too likely to happen is that by becoming a subsidiary, losing its identity and spirit as a business—the orders come from head office which might even be in a different country—the danger is that people no longer see the reason for giving of their best. A business which in economic terms is doing very well can lose the drive of the very people that are in it."

That spirit of a business—so crucial to the motivation of its staff—is hard to define and measure. It is not to be found in the buildings or the balance sheet but is reflected in the myriad of different decisions taken by those at the helm of the business. The Quaker pioneers believed that "your own soul lived or perished according to its use of the gift of life." For them, spiritual wealth rather than the accumulation of possessions was the "enlarging force" that informed business decisions. But gone now, lost in another century, is that omnipotent all-seeing eye in the boardroom, reminding those Quaker patriarchs of the fleeting position of power. And what is there to replace it? Until the Kraft takeover, Cadbury had not quite severed its link with the vision of its founding pioneers. Sadly for some, the umbilical cord has been cut, and there is recognition that some of the indefinable guiding spirit of the founders appears to have been discarded as effortlessly as a candy wrapper. It is perhaps for this reason that so many in Britain spoke out against the loss of a cultural icon.

Irene Rosenfeld, commenting just before this book went to press, wrote, "Cadbury is a fantastic business, with a proud heritage and a long and distinguished history. This is something we respect and want to build on."

This book is a modest challenge to Rosenfeld and to Kraft. If her words are to be taken as anything more than platitudes, and if Kraft is truly to respect the values of Cadbury, it must understand its particular traditions and history. The story of Cadbury, in a way, is the story of a different kind of capitalism.

Irene Rosenfeld suggested that "the companies have very similar values. In fact I think if John Cadbury had met James Kraft, they could well have been friends." To be sure, Kraft was an inventive entrepreneur who, like Cadbury, began in a modest way. But as this book shows, the outcomes for the two firms are very different.

In setting out the history of the chocolate family dynasties, I have endeavored to be as objective as possible in exploring the gains and losses along the way and highlighting the steps that have taken us from the Quaker values of the nineteenth century to today's global village. Could the companies' founders have been friends? Are the goals of John Cadbury and his sons reflected in the modern global powerhouse?

I leave that to the reader to decide.

PART
I

1

A Nation of Shopkeepers

In mid-Victorian times, the English town of Birmingham was growing fast, devouring the surrounding villages and nearby woods and fields. The unstoppable engine of the Industrial Revolution had turned this modest market town into a great sprawling metropolis. Country dwellers hungry for work drove the population from 11,000 in 1720 to more than 200,000 by 1850. In the city they found towering chimneys that turned the skies thunder grey and taskmasters unbending in their demands. Machines, oblivious to the seasons, never stopped issuing the unspoken command: more labor, more work, and more toil to feed the looms, to fire the furnaces, and to drive the relentless wheels of commerce and industry far beyond English shores.

Birmingham was renowned across the country for innovation and invention. According to the reporter Walter White, writing about a visit to the city in *Chamber's Edinburgh Journal* in October 1852, "to walk from factory to factory, workshop to workshop and view the extraordinary mechanical contrivances and ingenious adaptations of means to ends produces an impress upon the mind of no common character." The town was a beacon of industrial might and muscle. This was where steam and fire forged with iron and coke, metal and clay to make miracles.

By the mid-nineteenth century, the foggy streets resounded with hammers and anvils fashioning metal, bronze, and iron into buttons, guns, coins, jewelry, buckles, and a host of other Victorian wonders. Walter White marvelled at the "huge smoky toyshop" and the "eager spirit of application manifested by the busy population." But he was evidently less taken with the sprawling town itself, which he considered "very ill arranged and ugly" and dismissed as "a spectacle of dismal streets."

At the heart of these dismal, foggy streets, opposite today's smartly paved Centenary Square, there was a road called Bridge Street, which in 1861 was the site of a Victorian novelty: a cocoa works. Approached down a dirt road, past busy stables, coach houses, and factories, it was surprisingly well hidden. But wafting through the grimy backstreets was a powerful aroma, redolent of rich living. Guided by this heady perfume, the visitor was drawn past the blackened exterior, through a narrow archway into a courtyard with an entrance leading off to the heart of the chocolate factory. And it was in this modest retreat that two young Cadbury brothers hurried one day early in 1861.

There was a crisis in the family. Twenty-five-year-old Richard and twenty-one-year-old George Cadbury knew the wonderful aroma of chocolate disguised the reality. The chocolate factory and its owner, their father, John Cadbury, were in decline. The family faced a turning point. The business could go under completely. John Cadbury turned to his sons for help.

Photographs of the time show George and Richard Cadbury soberly dressed as Quakers in characteristic plain dark Victorian suits with crisp white shirts and bow ties. Richard's softness of features contrasts with his younger brother, whose intensity of focus and air of concentration are not relaxed even for the photographer. "I fixed my eye on those who had won," George admitted. "It was no use studying failure." He had, said his friends, "boundless ambition." And he needed it. The family firm was hemorrhaging money.

By chance, Walter White toured the Bridge Street factory and has left a vivid account of what it was like in 1852. Leaving behind the storehouse crammed with sacks of cocoa beans from the Caribbean, White entered a room that blazed with heat and noise: the roasting chamber. With its four vast rotating ovens, "the prime mover in this comfortable process of roasting was a 20-horse steam engine." After this, "with a few turns of the whizzing apparatus," the husk was removed by the "ceaseless blast from a furious fan" and the cocoa, "now with a very tempting appearance," was taken for more "intimate treatment." This occurred in a room where "shafts, wheels and straps kept a number of strange looking machines in busy movement." After yet more pressing and pounding, a rich frothing chocolate mixture flowed, "leisurely like a stream of half-frozen treacle." This was formed into a rich cocoa cake, which was shaved to a coarse powder ready for mixing with liquid for drinking. Upstairs White found himself in a room where management "had put on its pleasantest expression." The girls, all dressed in clean white Holland pinafores, were "packing as busily as hands could work. No girl is employed," he added, "who is not of a known good moral character." Such a factory, he concluded, "was a school of morality and industry."

But almost ten years had passed since Walter White's visit, and the "school of morality and industry" had been quietly dying of neglect. Twenty-one-year-old George Cadbury was quick to appraise the desperate situation. "Only eleven girls were now employed. The consumption of raw cocoa was so small that what we now have on the premises would have lasted about 300 years," he wrote. "The business was rapidly vanishing."

During the spring of 1861, George and Richard wrestled with their options. Pacing the length of the roasting room in the evenings, the four giant rotating ovens motionless, the dying embers of the coke fire beneath them faintly glowing, the brothers could see no simple solution. George had harbored hopes of developing a career as a doctor. Should he now join his brother in the battle to save the family chocolate business? Or close the factory? Would they be able to succeed where their own father had failed?

It was their father, John, who had proudly shown Walter White around in 1852. But in the intervening years, he had been almost completely broken by the death of his wife, Candia. John had watched Candia's struggle against consumption for several years, her small frame helpless against the onslaught of microorganisms as yet unknown to Victorian science. Equipped only with prayers and willpower, he took her to the coast, hoping the fresh air would revive her, and brought in the best doctors.

But nothing could save her. By 1854, Candia had gratefully succumbed to her bath chair. Eventually she was unable to leave home and then she was confined to her room. "The last few months she was indeed sweet and precious," wrote John helplessly. When the end came in March 1855, "Death was robbed of all terror for her," he told his children. "It was swallowed up in victory and her last moments were sweet repose." Yet as the weeks following her death turned into months, John failed to recover from his overwhelming loss. He started to suffer from a painful and disabling form of arthritis and took long trips away from home in search of a cure. After years of diminishing interest in his cocoa business, Cadbury's products deteriorated, their workforce declined, and their reputation suffered.

Richard and George knew that their father's cocoa works was the smallest of some thirty manufacturers who were trying to develop a market in England for the exotic New World commodity. No one had yet uncovered the key to making a fortune from the bewitching little bean imported from the New World. There was no concept of mass-produced chocolate confectionary. In the mid-nineteenth century, the cocoa bean was almost invariably consumed as a drink. Since there was no easy way to separate the fatty cocoa oils, which made up to 50 percent of the bean, from the rest of the bean, it was visibly oily, the fats rising to the surface. Indeed it often seemed that the novelty of purchasing this strange product was more thrilling than drinking it.

Their father, like his rivals, followed the established convention of mixing cocoa with starchy ingredients to absorb the cocoa butter. As their business had declined, the volume of these cheaper materials had increased. "At the time we made a cocoa drink of which we were not very proud," recalls George Cadbury. "Only one fifth of it was cocoa—the rest was potato flour or sago and treacle: a comforting gruel."

This "gruel" sold to the public under names that were common at the time for cocoa dealers such as Cocoa Paste, Soluble Chocolate Powder, Best Chocolate Powder, Fine Crown, Best Plain, Plain, Rock Cocoa, Penny Chocolate, or even Penny Soluble Chocolate. Customers did not buy it in the form of a powder but as a fatty paste made into a block or cake. To make a drink at home, they chipped or flaked bits off the block into a cup and added hot water—or milk if they could afford it. It is a measure of how badly the Cadbury cocoa business was faring that three-quarters of their trade from the Bridge Street factory came from tea and coffee sales.

Although promoted as a health drink, cocoa had a mixed reputation. Unscrupulous traders sometimes colored it with brick dust and added other questionable products not entirely without problems for the digestive system: a pigment called umber, iron filings, or even poisons like vermilion and red lead. Such dishonest dealers also found that the expensive cocoa butter could be stretched a little further with the addition of olive or almond oil or even animal fats such as veal. The unwary customer could find himself purchasing a drink that could turn rancid and was actually harmful.

Although the prospects for the business in 1861 did not look hopeful, the alternatives for Richard and George were limited. As Quakers, higher education was not an option for them. Like all nonconformists, they were legally banned from Oxford and Cambridge, the only teaching universities in England at the time. As pacifists, Quakers could not join the armed services. Nor were they permitted to stand as members of Parliament, and they faced restrictions on other professions such as the law. As a result, many Quakers turned to the world of business, but here too the Society of Friends laid down strict guidelines.

In a Quaker community, a struggling business was a liability. Failing to honor a business agreement or falling into debt was seen as a form of theft and punished severely. If the cocoa works went under owing money to creditors, Richard and George would face the censure of the Quaker movement or, worse, they would be disowned completely and treated as outcasts within their circle. Quite apart from these strict Quaker rules, in Victorian society business failure and bankruptcy could lead to the debtors' prison or the dreaded poorhouse, either option raising the prospect of an early grave.

Ahead was a battle. Defeat was all too possible. The brothers did not have to dedicate themselves to this small space, with their offices scarcely bigger than a coffin. "It would have been far easier to start a new business, than to pull up a decayed one which had a bad name," George admitted. "The prospect seemed a hopeless one, but we were young and full of energy."

To the remaining employees who now had reason to fear for their jobs, "Mr. Richard" appeared jovial, relaxed, and "always smiling," while "Mr. George" was cut from a different cloth, "stern but very just." His unremitting self-discipline and his ability to focus every aspect of his life on one goal became legendary. "He was not a man," a colleague later observed, "but a *purpose*." And what George and Richard decided to do next would become the stuff of family legend.

Richard and George Cadbury were the third generation of Cadbury tradesmen in Birmingham. It was their grandfather, Richard Tapper Cadbury, who had been instrumental in breaking centuries of long association with the West Country and leading the family in a new direction as shopkeepers in the town. At the close of the eighteenth century, as Napoleon prepared for his long march over Europe, the Cadburys, like countless others at the time, exemplified the Britain that the French leader dismissed as a mere "nation of shopkeepers." And just as Napoleon's scathing remark underestimated his enemy's real wealth and capacity for war, so it was easy not to see the huge potential emerging from a new generation of shopkeepers whose connections were only just beginning to reach out across the world.

"Very little is known of his early life," writes Richard of his grandfather. "He left home in Exeter when he was fourteen on the top of the coach . . . to serve as an apprentice to a draper." The young Richard Tapper remembered the morning of his leaving: "My father and mother got up early to see me off by the stage . . . and I thought my heart would break."

Richard Tapper was apprenticed in 1782 to a draper 150 miles away in Kent who supplied army uniforms to troops fighting in the American War of Independence. Within a year the war ended, troops were demobilized, and the business went bankrupt. Richard

Tapper then secured another opening as an apprentice in Gloucester, where, by the age of nineteen, he was proud to receive wages of £20 a year. After "scrupulously and conscientiously" avoiding any "unnecessary gratification," he reassured his parents in Exeter, it was possible for him to pay for his own washing and "appear so respectable as to be invited as guest among the first families of Gloucester." His next move was to London to work for a linen draper and silk dealer in Gracechurch Street. His wages eventually rose to £40 a year, which not only enabled him "to maintain a respectable appearance" but also to "purchase many books."

After ten long years mastering the trade, Richard Tapper was longing to start a draper's business of his own. He was dissuaded from his youthful dream of sailing for America by a family friend who warned him "that the country is still far from settled." Nor could he seek adventures in Europe with France in the frenzied grip of Robespierre's Reign of Terror and at war with its neighbors. So in 1794, equipped with enthusiasm and, through the Quaker network, quite a few references, Richard Tapper took the stage to Birmingham with a friend, Joseph Rutter. They had heard of an opening for a "Linen Draper and Silk Mercer" in the town and seized their chance.

The draper's shop was soon successful enough for Richard Tapper to buy out his partner and start a family. He married Elizabeth Head in 1796 and seven children followed over the next seven years. Elizabeth still found time to help in the shop, dressing the windows with fine silks and linens and taking an interest in the changing fashions. One year, they were obliged to enlarge their front door to accommodate the fashion for puffed "gigot" sleeves, strengthened with feather pads or whalebone hoops. Records show that Richard Tapper's business was so successful that in 1816 a second shop at 85 Bull Street was also registered in his name.

Like many Victorians, the young Richard Cadbury had a fascination with family history and compiled a "family book" on his ancestors complete with news cuttings, sketches, and Quaker records. This provided a vivid portrait of his grandfather's life. One of the problems Richard Tapper had to deal with in his shop was theft. After repeatedly losing silk that cost up to twelve shillings a yard, he felt he had to take action but soon came to regret it. He stopped a woman in his shop who had two rolls of silk hidden under her cloak. When he went to court to hear the outcome, to his alarm the judge sentenced the woman to death. "I was appalled," Richard Tapper told his children years later, "for I never realised what the sentence would be. Without delay I posted to London, saw the Secretary of State and got the woman's sentence commuted to transportation."

As a Quaker, Richard Tapper became deeply involved in community affairs and served on the Board of Commissioners for Birmingham, a precursor to the Town Council. He also worked as an Overseer of the Poor, including during the troubled year of 1800 when the harvest failed. According to the *St. James Chronicle*, the price of bread on October 8 rose to nearly two shillings for one loaf. In the parish of Birmingham, the poor were in dread of starvation, "the distress in the town was great," and there was "an alarming disorder" in the workhouse. Richard Tapper was among those who tried to ensure that there was enough food.

Richard Tapper's shop prospered, and his garden in the back of Bull Street was "a favourite place" for his growing family "with currants in abundance, flowers and a vine." The accounts of Richard's children are of particular personal interest since my own branch of the family can be traced to his oldest son, Benjamin, born in 1798. According to the *Birmingham Daily Post*, Benjamin had a passion for philanthropy. Among the many benevolent causes he supported were the local Infant Schools, the Bible Society, and the Society for the Suppression of Cruelty to Animals. But like many Quakers, according to the *Post*, by far "his most laborious and anxious labours" were devoted to the antislavery movement, "which more or less occupied his time and unwearied attention for upwards of thirty-five years." Regardless of whether he possessed the same "unwearied attention" for business, it was the custom for the oldest son to inherit the father's business, and when Benjamin turned thirty, he duly inherited his father's successful draper's shop on Bull Street and was happily settled for many years.

Richard Tapper Cadbury's second son, Joel, was able to fulfill his father's dream of seeking his fortune in America and set sail in 1815 at the age of sixteen. The Atlantic crossing took eighty days in high winds and rough seas that washed a man overboard and prompted seasoned sailors to say they "not have seen such sea." Joel eventually settled in Philadelphia and became a cotton goods manufacturer. He had a family of eleven children and established a large branch of Quakers on the East Coast of America.

But Richard's third son, John—the father of Richard and George—born in 1801 above his father's draper's shop, was destined to have a very different fate. According to an account handed down through the generations, John's farsighted father, having passed on his business to his oldest son, Benjamin, asked John to investigate the new colonial market in Mincing Lane, London. He was curious about the new commodity, the cocoa bean, which was arriving from the New World.

Today, among the gleaming black facades of Mincing Lane in the City, there is little to give away its colorful past as one of London's thriving trading markets. But when John Cadbury visited in the 1820s, there was a teeming market where colonial brokers met to trade in different commodities from Britain's growing empire. There were salesrooms where frenetic auctions were taking place for tea, sugar, coffee, jute, gums, waxes, vegetable oils, spices, and cocoa. Prices and details of business were written on a black board. Samples of goods from warehouses in docks along the nearby Thames were on display. They included the cocoa bean or "nib" from South America, which looked like a huge chocolate-colored almond, still dusted with the dried pulp that surrounded it in the cocoa pod and baked by a tropical sun.

At a time when cocoa was purchased primarily to produce a novelty drink for the rich, John tried to ascertain whether there might be a future in the unpromising black bean.

John Cadbury, like his father before him, had set out as an apprentice to learn his trade at a young age. In 1816, aged fifteen and proudly dressed in the best-quality cloth from the family draper's shop, John took the hazardous coach journey to Leeds, where he was apprenticed to a Quaker tea dealer. It appears he made a good impression. His aunt, Sarah Cash, who visited the following year declared, "John is grown a fine youth, he possesses a fine open countenance, is vigorous of mind and body and desires to render himself useful." Others also commented that the plain Quaker boy formed a contrast to "some of the rough Yorkshire boys." He wore "a neat white linen collar and black ribbon round his throat tied in a bow at the front." It seems the owners were soon content to leave the care of their tea business with John when they had to travel, and he was rewarded on his departure after seven long years with a fine encyclopedia.

John went to London and apprenticed at the teahouse of Sanderson Fox and Company. While in London he had a chance to see the warehouses of the East India Company and witness the sale of commodities such as coffee and cocoa. The 23-year-old was soon able to tell his father that he was convinced there was potential in the new exotic bean, although he was not yet clear what that potential was.

In 1824 John returned to Birmingham and set up a tea and coffee shop of his own on Bull Street, right next to his brother Benjamin's draper's shop. John's father lent him a small sum of money and said "he must sink or swim," there were no further funds. John proudly announced the opening of his shop in the local paper, *Aris's Birmingham Gazette*, on March 1. After setting out his considerable experience "examining the teas in the East India Company's warehouses in London," he drew the public's attention to something new. He wished to bring "to particular notice" a substance "affording a most nutritious beverage for breakfast . . . Cocoa Nibs prepared by himself."

John Cadbury took advantage of the latest ideas to attract business to his shop, starting with the shop window. While most other shops had green-ribbed windows, John had a myriad of small squares of plate glass set in a mahogany frame that it is said he polished himself each morning. This design feature alone was such a novelty that "people would come from miles around." On peering through the windows, prospective customers were intrigued by the unusual, a touch of the Orient in the heart of smoky Birmingham. The many inviting delicacies were displayed among handsome blue Chinese vases, Asian figurines, and ornamental tea chests. Weaving his way through all the exotica was a Chinese worker in Oriental dress, weighing and measuring, promising something different, a promise that was assured on opening the door by the lingering aroma of chocolate and coffee. John ground the cocoa beans in the back of the shop with mortar and pestle.

Word of John Cadbury's quality teas and coffees soon spread among some of the wealthiest and best-known families in Birmingham; his customers included the Lloyds, Boultons, Watts, Galtons, and others. Meanwhile, through the Quaker network, John met Candia Barrow of Lancaster. The Lancashire Barrows and Birmingham Cadburys had developed very close ties through marriage. In 1823 John's older sister Sarah had married Candia Barrow's older brother. This was followed in 1829 by the marriage of John's older brother Benjamin to Candia's cousin Candia Wadkin. In June 1832, when John Cadbury married Candia Barrow, it was the third marriage in a generation to link the two Quaker families and proved to be a very happy union.

As John's shop prospered, he could see for himself the growing demand for cocoa nibs. He took advantage of the large cellars under the shop to experiment with different recipes and created several successful cocoa powder drinks. So confident was he of the popularity of this nutritious and wholesome drink that he decided to take a further step—into manufacturing.

In 1831, John rented a four-storey premises close by on Crooked Lane, a winding back street at the bottom of Bull Street, and began to produce cocoa on a larger scale. Using machines to help process food was in its infancy, so to help with the roasting and pressing of beans, he installed a steam engine, which evidently was a great family novelty. According to his admiring aunt, Sarah Cash, everyone in the family "had thoroughly seen John's steam engine." After ten years he had developed a wide variety of different types of cocoa for his shop: flakes, powders, cakes, and even the roasted and crushed nibs themselves.

Meanwhile, Candia and John started a family and moved to a house with a garden in the rural district of Edgbaston. Their first son, John, suffered intermittently from poor health. Richard Cadbury, their second child, was born on August 29, 1835, and was followed by a sister, Maria, and then George, born on November 19, 1839. To the boys' delight, their parents placed a strong emphasis on the pursuit of a healthy outdoor life. Their house had a square lawn, recalled Maria: "Our father measured it round, 21 times for a mile, where we used to run, one after another, with our hoops before breakfast, seldom letting them drop before reaching the mile, and sometimes a mile and a half, which Richard generally did." Only then were they allowed in for breakfast, "basins of milk . . . with delicious cream on top and toast to dip in." After this early morning ritual, their father, John, set off to work. "I can picture his rosy countenance full of vigour," says Maria, "his Quaker dress very neat with its clean white cravat."

Another memorable delight for the boys was the arrival of the railway in Birmingham. Britain was in the grip of railway fever. The first train line, the Grand Junction Railway, steamed into Birmingham from Manchester in 1837. Within a year, a line opened that covered the hundred miles between Birmingham and London. The treacherous two-day journey to London by horse and coach became a two-hour journey by steam train, opening up dramatic new possibilities for trade.

Although Richard and George were close, Richard was sent away at the age of eight to join his older brother, John, at boarding school. George studied with a local tutor who had a decidedly individualistic view on the best way to deal with boys. He aimed to instil mental and physical fortitude with a diet of classics and combative sports, including occasional games of Attack, which he devised himself and involved arming the boys with sticks. Somehow George came through the experience with a sound knowledge of French and Virgil—and a keen appreciation of home life. George's spartan childhood was "severe but happy" with an emphasis on "iron discipline." Their lifestyle was "bare of all self indulgence and luxury."

Both George and Richard formed vivid impressions of trips to see their mother's family at Lancaster. Their grandfather, George Barrow, in addition to running a draper's shop in Lancaster, had created a prosperous shipping business with trade to the West Indies. His grandchildren were allowed to climb the tower he had built on the grounds of his house, from where they had a stunning view of Morecambe Bay and on occasion his returning ships, sometimes banked up three at a time on the quayside. Sea captains came to visit and would invariably regale the children with tales of wide seas and foreign lands, the wonders of travel, and the horrors of the slave trade.

By 1847 John Cadbury's Crooked Lane warehouse had been demolished to make way for the new Great Western Railway. Undeterred, John expanded his manufacturing operation into the Bridge Street premises and was soon joined by his brother Benjamin. By 1852 the two brothers were in a position to open an office in London and later received a royal accolade as cocoa manufacturers to Queen Victoria. It was around this time that John and Benjamin dreamed up a plan to create a model village for their workers away from the grime of the city and even designated one of their brands of cocoa The Model Parish Cocoa.

In 1850, when he was almost fifteen, Richard joined his father and his uncle at Bridge Street and was doubtless aware of these grand ambitions. With his father often away, he threw himself into the business "with energy and devotion." Despite his commitment to work, Richard found time for his love of sport. He was passionately fond of skating and in winter would rise very early to enjoy an hour on the ice before work. "Richard used fairly to dazzle us with his skating," said one young friend of his sister, Maria. But events were conspiring against such relaxed pursuits.

Cocoa sales had begun to decline during the economic depression of the "Hungry Forties," when a slump in trade, rising unemployment, bad harvests, and a potato blight in England and Scotland in 1845 combined to create widespread hardship. Many small businesses struggled, but for the Cadburys, the irrevocable blow came in the early 1850s when Candia was diagnosed with tuberculosis.

These painful years left their mark on Richard and George. They witnessed the inexorable decline, first of their mother, then of their father, then the neglect of the factory as though it too were burdened with a malady for which there could be no happy conclusion. John still occasionally walked through the factory in his starched white choker and neat black ribbon tied in a bow, but the enthusiasm that had prompted him to grow the venture over a period of 30 years was gone. He paid scant attention to the piles of cocoa beans accumulating in the stockroom. His hard-won accolade as cocoa manufacturer to Queen Victoria no longer excited him. A year after Candia's death, he dissolved the partnership with his brother Benjamin. Gradually his absences became more prolonged as he searched for a cure for his arthritis, and the family firm began to lose its good name.

These were the pressing concerns in young George Cadbury's mind when at the age of seventeen, in 1857, like his father and grandfather before him, he too was sent away to learn his trade as an apprentice. His sister, Maria, had taken his mother's place in the home looking after the younger children. His older brother Richard was taking on more responsibility for his father's business. George was keen to master the trade by working in a grocery shop in York run by another Quaker, Joseph Rowntree.

Once past York's famous city walls, seventeen-year-old George Cadbury found himself in a maze of winding streets with irregular gabled houses, the overhang of their upper storeys making the streets feel narrow and dark. As he crossed the center of town, the road opened onto a busy thoroughfare called Pavement. Almost directly opposite, he found the Rowntrees' shop at No. 28, a handsome eighteenth-century terraced house, tall and narrow, with subsidence that made it appear crooked. The colorful thoroughfare outside disguised the austerity and long hours that awaited George inside the shop.

Joseph Rowntree issued a memorandum that clearly set out the strict rules of conduct that he expected his numerous apprentices to follow. "The object of the Pavement establishment is *business* [his italics]. The young men who enter it as journey men or apprentices are expected to contribute . . . in making it successful. . . . It affords . . . a full opportunity for any painstaking, intelligent young man to obtain a good practical acquaintance with the tea and grocery trades. . . . The place is *not* suitable for the indolent and the way ward." The memorandum specified every detail of the boys' lives: no more than twenty minutes for a meal break, only one trip home a year, and the exact hour at which the young men were to return each night. In June and July they were allowed to walk outside in the evenings until ten o'clock; during all other months the curfew was earlier.

Living at the house were Joseph Rowntree's sons, including twenty-one-year-old Joseph and nineteen-year-old Henry Isaac. Joseph was tall and dark with an intensity of features, the natural severity of his own character complemented by years of Quaker upbringing. His father had taken him to Ireland on a Quaker relief mission in 1850 during the Irish potato famine, and the experience had left a lasting impression. Joseph remembered the look of death as starvation slowly turned the young and comely into the walking dead. Numberless unknown dead lay in open trenches or where they had fallen by the side of the road, alongside those still living, their faces showing their terror. For the serious-minded Joseph, it had been a formative experience and a shocking lesson on the effects of poverty. His younger brother, Henry, formed a contrast to Joseph's austerity. Somehow the full Puritan weight of Quaker training did not sit quite so readily on his young shoulders; he had a sense of fun and could be relied upon to lighten the mood.

By 1860 George Cadbury had returned to Birmingham, although he had barely completed three years as an apprentice. Whether his father recognized his ability and recalled him to help at home or whether the move was instigated by George because he was hungry to get started is not known.

To the employees at Bridge Street, the two young Cadbury brothers were curiously "alike and unalike." Richard was seen as "bright and happy with a sunny disposition." He claimed he would be happy simply to rescue the business and turn it around to make a few hundred pounds a year. George was much more driven. In the words of his biographer, Alfred Gardiner, he "had more of an adventurer's instinct. . . . The channel of his mind was narrower and the current swifter." Despite his ambition, he could see no simple solution. As the brothers deliberated during the spring of 1861 in the gloomy Bridge Street factory, the prospect seemed a dismal one. From their cramped office, they could see the empty carts banked up in the yard awaiting orders. It was not immediately obvious what they could do together that their father and uncle had not already tried and that would make the crucial difference.

The great hope, of course, was to come up with a breakthrough product. They did in fact have something in mind that their father had been working on before family difficulties drained his energy. It was a product very much of the moment, with healthful overtones, called Iceland Moss. The manufacturing process involved blending the fatty chocolate bean with an ingredient that was thought to improve health: lichen. It was fashioned into a bar of cocoa that could then be grated to form a nutritious drink. Richard had a flair for design. He could see the possibilities for launching Iceland Moss. It would be eye-catchingly displayed in bright yellow packaging with black letters that boldly proclaimed the addition of lichen, complete with the image of a reindeer to show how different it was. They aimed to promote the health properties of Iceland Moss, but would the untried combination of fluffy-textured lichen and the very fatty cocoa bean appeal to the English palate?

Apart from developing new products, the brothers also had to find new customers. Their father had only one salesperson, known at the time as a "traveller." His name was Dixon Hadaway and he alone covered a vast swathe of the country from Rugby in the south high up to the Scottish highlands, visiting grocers' shops to promote their line of cocoa wares. He took advantage of the new trains to cover the long distances between towns but was also obliged to travel by pony and trap or even on foot. Despite the challenges of getting around, Dixon Hadaway was evidently determined to keep up appearances, smartly attired with a tall top hat and dark tweed coat, although it was invariably crumpled from long hours of travelling. It seems he was appreciated by his customers, who claimed that he was so punctual that they could set their clocks by his visits. But punctuality and enthusiasm alone were not enough to secure new orders. People could not be expected to buy Cadbury's goods if they had never heard of them. George was clear. They needed more capital to fund a sales team.

To finance the extra staffing, they discussed how to manage the business more efficiently. The brothers' solution was to return to their puritanical roots: "work, and again work, and always more work." George enthusiastically planned to cut all indulgence from his life: games, outings, music, every luxury would go. Every penny he earned would be ploughed back into the business. This was harder for Richard. He was planning to marry in July.

A photograph survives of Richard's fiancée, Elizabeth Adlington, whose classic good looks are evident in spite of her serious expression and the limitation imposed on any enhancement of feminine Quaker beauty. Her face appears unadorned, her hair parted down the middle and pulled back severely. She wears a full skirt and crinoline, covered by a long black cloak and dark bonnet—the Quaker forefathers having deemed this quite enough excitement to attract a male. Richard was drawn to her "bright and vivacious" manner. In preparation for bringing home a wife, he had purchased a house on Wheeley's Road, about two miles from the factory. Spare moments were spent preparing the garden, transferring cuttings of his favorite plants from the rockery in his father's garden. "My little home is beginning to look quite charming now it is nearly completed," he told his youngest brother, Henry. There was just the furniture to buy before his wedding in July.

During the spring of 1861, the tone of the brothers' discussion changed. As Quakers they were accustomed to finding answers in silent prayer. They had a duty to the workforce, and there were family obligations to consider. Since their mother died, their sister Maria had taken her place, caring for the younger members of the family. Now their father was in urgent need of help. They too must listen to the clear voice of conscience, mindful of a debt to man and God. They too must endeavour to do their best. Whatever their misgivings, they had no real choice. They made their decision. In April the two young brothers took over the running of the factory.

There was one last hope. They each had inherited £4,000 from their mother. Determined to save the family dream of a chocolate factory, they staked their inheritance down to the last penny. If they failed to turn the business around before the capital was gone, they would close the factory.

2

Food of the Gods

Richard and George soon found they were running down their inheritance fast just to keep afloat. The first year was worrying. By the end of 1861, Richard's share of the loss was recorded at 226 pounds and George registered a similar figure. More capital from their inheritance would be needed. Richard, who had the added responsibilities of married life, imagined the next year's losses. Perhaps they were not businessmen. Was this the beginning of a slow and inevitable decline to bankruptcy?

The brothers tried to calculate how long their capital would last. In the absence of any other source of funds, they had to make further cutbacks. Even basic pleasures such as drinking tea and reading the morning paper were now sacrificed. Each day started at six in the morning and did not end until late in the evening, with a supper of bread and butter eaten at the factory. "This stern martyrdom of the senses," observed one of George's colleagues years later, "drove all the energy of his nature into certain swift, deep channels," creating an extraordinary "concentration of purpose." Any small diversion or treat was dismissed as a "snare" that might "appeal to the senses" or absorb precious funds.

While George focused on purchasing, policy, and development, Richard tackled sales. The infrequent office visits by Dixon Hadaway, their Northern traveller, made a vivid impression on the staff. "It was a red letter day," said one office worker. "It was real fun to listen to his broad Scotch, as we could only understand a sentence here and there." Hadaway loved his worn Scotch tweed coat, which he had worn since the Crimean War, "and I can still remember him extolling the beauties of the cloth and its wearing qualities." Richard joined Hadaway and frequently took out the pony and trap to drum up business. He also hired additional full-time travellers. Samuel Gordon was to target Liverpool and Manchester. John Clark, recommended through a Quaker cousin, was hired to take on the whole of England south of Birmingham. Richard sent him first to London, but in a matter of weeks, Clark found business there so bad he begged to be transferred back to Birmingham. He feared he was wasting both his and the firm's time. A letter survives from Richard, urging Clark not to give up on London and its suburbs:

> We do *particularly* wish this *well worked*, as we believe it will ultimately repay both us and thyself to do so, and thou may depend if thou dost *thoroughly* work it, we will see nothing is lost to thee whether with or with out success. . . . [Richard's italics] It is important for us both to pull together for we have so much to do to conquer reserve and prejudice, and thou may be assured we will do our part in this in the way of improvements in style and quality of our goods.

To cover more ground, George also began to travel, and letters from Richard's young wife show that his journeys away from home became more frequent. "We have come nearly to the end of another day and think of thee as that much nearer returning," Elizabeth wrote to her husband in Glasgow a year after their marriage in July 1862. "We shall all be happy together if thou hast had a prosperous time." In his enthusiasm to increase turnover, Richard himself would go into the warehouse to package the orders, "not only in the early days when hands were few, but even in his later years."

During 1862, since both brothers were often away, they hired more office staff. One young worker who showed great promise was William Tallis. Orphaned as a child, he had had very little education but impressed everyone with his ability and enthusiasm. They also employed their first clerk, George Truman, who recalls "working, as did Mr. George, till eight or nine every night, Saturdays included." George Truman evidently also tried his hand at selling to the shops in Birmingham. A novice salesman, he generously offered samples for customers to try. The free chocolate goodies proved popular. He soon ran out and returned "in great distress" because "one customer had eaten half his samples!" He was reassured when "Mr. George said he could have as many samples as he wanted and he went out the next day quite happy."

To address the problem of the product getting eaten before it left the factory, a system known as "Pledge Money" was put into effect. At the end of each day, a penny was awarded to any worker who successfully managed not to succumb to temptation. Every three months the pledge money was paid out, and one particularly abstemious employee remembers he accumulated so much that he was able to buy a pair of boots. Workers were also rewarded for punctuality. For those who arrived promptly at 6:00 AM, there was a breakfast of hot coffee or milk, bread, and buns.

Despite long sales trips away from home, the brothers soon found a lack of public enthusiasm for Iceland Moss, the product in which they had invested their early hopes. They continued to develop new lines of higher quality. They introduced a superior Breakfast Cocoa, as shown in their detailed sales brochure of 1862. This was followed a year later by Pearl Cocoa and then Chocolate du Mexique, a spiced vanilla-flavored cake chocolate. They improved existing brands such as Queen's Own Chocolate, Crystal Palace Chocolate, Dietetic Cocoa, Trinidad Rock Cocoa, and Churchman's Cocoa—a sustaining beverage for the sick. "So numerous are the sorts," reported the *Grocer* magazine, "the purchaser is much puzzled in his choice." So puzzled in fact that nothing seemed to excite the palate of Birmingham's growing population.

Richard was keen to find new ways to promote the company's range of nutritious beverages. Apart from notifying the trade through the *Grocer*, in 1862 he designed a stall to exhibit their products at the permanent exhibition in the Crystal Palace at Sydenham in South London. The brothers also paid for a stall exhibiting their wares in the Manchester Corn Exchange. But these efforts were not enough. An elusive, appetizing "something" was missing from their products, deepening their worries and underscoring the risky nature of exploiting the delicious cocoa bean. The travellers returned with disappointing orders, putting the struggling cocoa business in still further jeopardy.

In battling to save the Bridge Street factory, there was one issue that the brothers had failed to tackle. However inventive their new recipes, and however adventurous the palate of the English public, by turning cocoa beans into a drink, they were faithfully following centuries of tradition. Despite its long and colorful history of cultivation, by the mid-nineteenth century the dark cocoa bean was mostly consumed in liquid form, largely unprocessed and unrefined. The Cadbury brothers were still thinking along lines rooted in ancient history.

Like many Victorians, Richard Cadbury had a passion for foreign culture and history. With his life circumscribed by long hours of labor in provincial English towns, he longed to travel beyond Europe and had been brought up on vivid tales of the foreign lands where cocoa originated and the exotic history of its cultivation. "It was one of the dreams of our childhood," he wrote, "to sail on the bosom of that mighty river whose watershed drains the greater part of the northern portion of the continent of South America, and to explore the secrets of its thousand tributaries that penetrate forests untrodden by the foot of man." He was particularly interested in the long and colorful history of cocoa in South America and Mexico, a history that gave intriguing glimpses as to how it might best be cultivated and consumed.

Richard had never seen a cocoa plantation and exercised his curiosity by collecting stories of explorers. While the traders he met in Mincing Lane were never short on anecdotal accounts, he could learn more by corresponding with experts at the tropical botanical gardens in Jamaica and the Pamplemousse Botanic Gardens in Mauritius. Closer to home, knowledge of tropical species was increasing through the iconic glasshouses at the Royal Botanic Gardens at Kew. The magnificent Palm House had recently been completed, and in the early 1860s, work was just beginning on the Temperate House. Botanists knew cocoa by its scientific name, *Theobroma cacao* or food of the Gods, a label assigned to the plant in 1753 by the Swedish naturalist Carl von Linnaeus.

"This inestimable plant," Richard wrote, "is evergreen, has drooping bright green leaves . . . and bears flowers and fruit at all seasons of the year." He knew it flourished in humid tropical regions close to the equator and was acutely sensitive to slight changes in climate. The cocoa pod itself he described accurately as an oval pointed shape, "something like a vegetable marrow . . . only more elongated and pointed at the end." In contrast to European fruit trees, the pods grow directly off the trunk and thickest boughs from very short stalks rather than from finer branches. The outer rind of the pod is thick and when ripened becomes a firm shell. Inside, embedded in a soft, pinkish-white acid pulp are the seeds or beans—as many as thirty to forty within each pod.

Richard's romantic idea of cocoa plantations also came from reading travel narratives that were occasionally featured in fashionable magazines, such as the *Belgravia*. One such article described a magical tropical paradise, a million miles from Victorian Birmingham. "The vista is like a miniature forest hung with thousands of golden lamps," enthused a report in *Belgravia*, "anything more lovely cannot be imagined." Taller trees such as the coral tree were planted around the cocoa trees to provide shade. In March, the coral tree becomes covered in crimson flowers, and "at this season, an extensive plain covered with cocoa plantations is a magnificent object," declared the *Belgravia*. "The tops of the coral tree present the appearance of being clothed in flames." Passing through the shady walkways of the plantation was like being "within the spacious aisles of some grand natural temple."

To harvest the marrow-like cocoa pods, the plantation workers would break them open with a long knife or cutlass. The seeds or beans were scooped out with a wooden spoon, the fleshy pulp scraped off, and the beans dried in the sun until the pale crimson seed turned a rich almond brown.

Richard could not know just how far into the past the history of cultivating cocoa beans extended. Recent research has revealed three millennia have elapsed since the Olmec, the oldest civilization in the Americas, first domesticated the wild cacao tree. Eking out an existence in the humid lowland forests and savannahs of the Mexican Gulf coast around 1500 to 400 BC, little survives of Olmec culture. Evidence that these early Mexicans consumed cocoa comes principally from studies in historical linguistics. Their word *ka ka wa* is thought to be the earliest pronunciation of cacao.

When the Maya became the dominant culture of Mexico, they extended the cultivation of cocoa across the plains of Guatemala and beyond. In Mayan culture, the rich enjoyed a foaming hot spicy drink. The poor took their cocoa with maize as a starchy porridge-like cold soup that provided easily prepared high-energy food. It could be laced with chili pepper, giving a distinct afterburn, or enhanced with milder flavorings such as vanilla.

Mayan art reveals that cocoa was highly prized. Archaeologists have found images decorating Mayan pottery of a "Cacao God" seated on his throne adorned with cocoa pods. There is evidence suggesting that Mayan aristocrats were buried with lavish amounts of food for the afterlife, including ornate painted jars for cocoa and cocoa flavorings. The earliest image of the preparation of a chocolate drink appears on a Mayan vase from around the eighth century AD, which curiously also depicts a human sacrifice. Two masked figures are beheading their victim, while a woman calmly pours a cocoa drink from one jar to another in order to enhance the much-favored frothy foam.

"European knowledge of cocoa as an article of diet," Richard found in his survey, "dates from the discovery of the Western world by Christopher Columbus." On August 15, 1502, during Columbus's fourth trip to the New World, he reached the island of Guanaja near the Honduran mainland. Two very large canoes suddenly appeared on the horizon. The Spanish captured them and found they were Mayan trading ships laden with cotton, clothing, and maize. According to Columbus's son, Ferdinand, there were a great many strange-looking "almonds" on board. "They held these almonds at great price," he observed. "When any of these almonds fell, they all rushed to pick it up, as if an eye had fallen." The Europeans could not understand how these little brown pellets could be so valued.

Spanish conquistadors, who arrived in Mexico in 1519, realized that cocoa was highly prized. The bean had special value in Aztec society since it was used as coinage—an idea that gave rise to the expression, "Money doesn't grow on trees." The Spanish saw that the Aztec people in the provinces paid tributes to their emperor, Montezuma, with large baskets of cocoa beans. The emperor kept a vast store in the royal coffers in the capital city of Tenochtitlan of no less than 40,000 loads: almost 1000 million cocoa beans. The Spanish soon worked out its value. According to one Spanish chronicler, "A tolerably good slave" was worth around one hundred beans, a rabbit cost ten beans, and a prostitute could be procured for as few as eight.

It is now known that the Aztecs, like the Mayans, used their favorite drink in a number of religious rituals, including human sacrifice. The Aztecs believed that their most powerful gods required appeasement, and prisoners of war had to be sacrificed each day to sustain the universe. In one macabre ritual, the heart of a slave was required to be cut out while he was still alive. The slave was selected for his physical perfection because until the time of his sacrifice, he represented the Aztec gods on earth and was treated with reverence. According to the Spanish Dominican friar Diego de Duran, who wrote *The History of the Indies of New Spain* in 1581, as the ritual approached its climax and the true fate of the victim was made known, the slave was required to offer himself for death with heroic courage and joy. Should his bravery falter, he could be "bewitched" by a special cocktail to embolden him, prepared from chocolate and mixed with the blood of former victims and other ingredients that rendered him nearly unconscious.

The cocoa bean found its way to Europe, where it was introduced to the Spanish royal household. The Spanish court initially consumed cocoa the South American way, as a drink in a small bowl, and then gradually replaced the corn and chilies with sugar and sometimes vanilla or cinnamon. In time elaborate chocolate pots were developed to skim and settle the heavy liquid before pouring, but the Spanish essentially ground the beans in the same way as the South American Indians, crushing them between stones or grinding them with stone and mortar to produce a coarse powder.

Richard Cadbury found one written account of cocoa preparation in Madrid from 1664 in which one hundred cocoa beans, toasted and ground to a powder, were mixed with a similar weight of sugar, twelve ground vanilla pods, two grains of chili pepper, aniseed, six white roses, cinnamon, two dozen almonds and hazelnuts, and achiote powder to lend a red hue. The resulting paste was used to make a cake or block of cocoa, which could be ground to form a drink. But whether mixed with maize or corn to absorb the fatty cocoa oils the Mexican way, or blended with sugar, the cocoa oils made the drink heavy and coarse, and cocoa continued to receive mixed reviews in Spain. Josephus Acosta, a Spanish writer at the turn of the seventeenth century, considered the chocolate drink much overrated, "foolishly and without reason, for it is loathsome . . . having a skum or frothe that is very unpleasant to taste."

For many years, the Spanish dominated South American cocoa cultivation. They introduced it to the West Indies and to islands such as Trinidad, where it soon became a staple crop. At first, English pirates raiding Spanish ships did not know what the bean was for. In 1648 the English chronicler Thomas Gage observed in his *New Survey of the West Indies* that when the English or Dutch seized a ship loaded with cocoa beans, "In anger and wrath we have hurled overboard this good commodity, not regarding the worth of it."

Gradually, however, during the seventeenth and eighteenth centuries, the cocoa bean found its way into the coffee houses of Europe. Its first mention in England appears in an advertisement in the *Public Advertiser* on June 22 1657: "At a Frenchman's house in Queensgate Alley is an excellent West India drink called Chocolate to be sold, where you may have it ready at any time at reasonable rates." In the 1660s, the diarist Samuel Pepys describes enjoying his drink of "chocolatte" or "Jocolatte" so much that he was soon "slabbering for another." Henry Stubbe, royal physician to King Charles II, published *A Discourse Concerning Chocolata* in 1662, in which he surveyed the "nature of the cacao-nut" and extolled the health benefits of the drink. Taken with spices it could relieve coughs and colds and strengthen heart and stomach. For anyone "tyred through business," Stubbes heartily recommended chocolate twice a day. It could even serve as an aphrodisiac. Word of the exotic new drink spread across England. White's famous Chocolate House, named after its Italian owner, Francis White, opened in 1693 in St. James, London.

Cocoa continued to gain in popularity principally as a drink prepared in the Mexican way, but it also was added as a flavoring to meat dishes, soups, and puddings. In Italy a recipe for chocolate sorbet survives from 1794. Once the mixture was prepared, "The vase is buried in snow layered with salt and frozen." For the more adventurous palate, Italian recipes from the period listed cocoa as an ingredient in lasagne or added it to fried liver. While most European preparations "were rough . . . and produced poor results," according to Richard Cadbury, "France developed a better system for roasting and grinding." The French *confiseurs* got straight on with the sweet course; no messing with chilies, curries, and fried liver. By the nineteenth century, they were winning a reputation for their exquisite handcrafted sweets made from chocolate: delicious mousses, cakes, crèmes, dragées, and chocolate-coated nuts.

With the wheels of European commerce and consumerism driving demand, in the Americas the cultivation of the cocoa bean was gradually extended beyond Mexico and Guatemala, reaching south to the lower slopes of the Andes in Ecuador, the rolling plains of Venezuela, and into the fringes of the Amazon rain forest of Brazil. In the Caribbean, cocoa plantations were established in Jamaica, St. Lucia, and Granada as well as Trinidad, which became a British colony in 1802.

By the mid-nineteenth century, despite the growing interest in the cocoa bean in Europe, it remained expensive and principally a novelty for the wealthy. "When we take into account the indifferent means of preparation," concluded Richard Cadbury, "we can hardly be surprised that it did not come into general favour with the public." As Richard and George struggled to launch their business, the full potential of *Theobroma cacao* had yet to be revealed. The unprepossessing little bean offered the mere tantalizing promise of prosperity.

In the early 1860s, George and Richard hardly needed to undertake the charade of stocktaking, which they did as a matter of course twice a year. They knew their business was not thriving. Cadbury Brothers did not excite the nation's taste buds. "We determined that we would close the business when we were unable to pay 20 shillings in the pound," George said, committed to honoring all financial agreements in full. He admitted the stocktaking was "depressing" but nonetheless thrived on the challenge. "We went back again to our work with renewed vigour and were probably happier than most successful men."

The struggle brought the brothers closer together. Quite apart from sharing the responsibility and the burden, Richard proved to be a delight as a partner. He was "very good natured and constantly up to practical jokes and fun of various kinds," George wrote, "so that one almost doubts whether immediate success in a business is a blessing." Workers too recalled Mr. George and Mr. Richard with a "cheery smile," although they knew "the Firm was in low water and losing money." They were aware of how dire things were and "at one stage expected any day to hear that the works were to be shut."

As losses mounted, Richard formed a list of everything he owned, noting the price each item would fetch if it had to be sold at auction. In 1862, his young wife, Elizabeth, was pregnant, and on September 27, the arrival of his first son, Barrow (named after Richard's mother's family), was great cause for celebration. But Richard knew the financial security of his young family was uncertain. Both brothers planned to shut the business rather than risk defaulting on any money owed and accruing debt. The stocktaking at the end of the second year was particularly gloomy. By Christmas 1862, the Cadbury brothers' losses had escalated to a further 304 pounds each.

But for George and Richard, there was another motive that went well beyond personal considerations. Business was not an end in itself; it was a means to an end. As Quakers, through their still failing business, they had a far greater goal to fulfill.

3

Wretched Little Victims
of the Workhouses

For George and Richard, the chocolate factory was to be much more than a commercial enterprise. As Quakers they shared a vision of social justice and reform: a new world in which the poor and needy would be lifted from the "ruin of deprivation." For generations, Cadburys had been members of the Society of Friends or Quakers, a spiritual movement originally started by George Fox in the seventeenth century. In a curious irony, the very religion that inspired Quakers to act charitably towards the poor also produced a set of codes and practices that placed a few thousand close-knit families like the Cadburys in pole position to generate astounding material rewards at the start of the industrial age.

Richard and George had been brought up on stories of George Fox, and many of the values, aspirations, and disciplines that shaped their lives stemmed from Fox's teachings. Born in 1624, the son of a weaver from Fenny Drayton, Leicestershire, Fox grew up with a passionate interest in religion at a time when the country had seen years of religious turmoil. Fox went "to many a priest looking for comfort, but found no comfort from them." He was appalled at the inhumanity carried out in the name of religion: people imprisoned, hung, or even beheaded for their faith. Disregarding the danger following the outbreak of civil war in 1642, he left home the following year and set out on foot for London. At just nineteen years old, Fox embarked on a personal quest for greater understanding.

During his years of travels, "when my hopes . . . in all men were gone," he had an epiphany. The key to religion was not to be found in the sermons of preachers but in an individual's inner experience. Inspired, he began to speak out, urging people to listen to their own conscience. Because "God dwelleth in the hearts of obedient people," he reasoned, it followed that an individual could find "the spirit of Christ within" to guide them, instead of taking orders from others. But his simple interpretation of Christianity put him in direct opposition to the authorities. If an individual was listening to the voice of God within himself, it followed that priests and religious authorities were a needless intermediary between man and God.

Fox was perceived as dangerous and his preaching blasphemous to established churches. Even the like-minded Puritans objected. They too adhered to a rigorous moral code and high standards of self-discipline, and they disdained worldly pursuits. But Fox's emphasis on the direct relationship between a believer and God went far beyond what most Puritans deemed tolerable. In emphasizing the primary importance of an individual's experience, Fox appeared contemptuous of the authorities and mocked their petty regulations. For example, he would not swear on oath. If there was only one absolute truth, he reasoned, what was the point of a double standard, differentiating between "truth" and "truth on oath"?

By 1649 Fox had crossed one magistrate too many. He was thrown into jail in Nottingham, "a pitiful stinking place, where the wind brought in all the stench of the house." The following year he was jailed in Derby prison for blasphemy. A justice in Derby in 1650 is believed to be the first to use the term "Quaker" to mock George Fox and his followers. He scoffed at the idea expressed in their meetings in which they were "silent before God" until moved to speak, "trembling at the word of the God." Despite its origins as a term of abuse, the name Quaker soon became widespread.

Fox was imprisoned sixty times, but the Quaker movement continued to gain momentum. It is estimated that during the reign of

Charles II, 198 Quakers were transported overseas as slaves, 338 died from injuries received defending their faith, and 13,562 were imprisoned. Among them were Richard and George's forebears on their father's side, including Richard Tapper Cadbury, a "woolcomber" who was held in Southgate prison in Exeter in 1683 and again in 1684.

By the end of Fox's life in 1691, there were 100,000 Quakers, and the movement had spread to America, parts of Europe, and even the West Indies. Fox established a series of meetings for Friends to discuss issues and formalize business: regional Monthly Meeting, county Quarterly Meeting, and a national Yearly Meeting. Key decisions at these meetings were written down and became known as the Advices. By 1738 these writings had been collated by clerks, transcribed in elegant longhand, and bound in a green manuscript, *Christian and Brotherly Advices*, which was made available to Friends Meetings across the country. It set out codes of personal conduct for Friends, under such headings as "Love," "Covetousness," and "Discipline." A section on "Plainness," for example, encouraged Quakers to cultivate "plainness of speech, behaviour and apparel." A Friend's clothing should be dark and unadorned; even collars were removed from jackets as they were deemed too decorative.

The strict rules of the Quakers also dictated that anyone who married outside the society had to leave. As a result, Quaker families tended to intermarry, resulting in a close-knit community across England of several thousand Quaker families. Generations of Quakers had emerged from years of persecution with a sense of solidarity and bonds forged by friendship, marriage, apprenticeships, and business. As the Industrial Revolution was gathering speed, this same solidarity and self-reliance generated a new spirit of enterprise. At a time when there was no such thing as a national newspaper, the Quakers—meeting regularly in different regions across Britain—enjoyed a unique forum in which to exchange ideas.

In 1709 Abraham Darby, a Quaker from Shropshire, pioneered a method of smelting high-grade iron using coke rather than charcoal. His son, Abraham Darby II, improved the process, changing the traditional horse pumps for steam engines to recycle water and refining techniques for making quality wrought iron. The Darbys built the world's first iron bridge and first major railway to ferry coal and ore at their iron foundry in Coalbrookdale in Shropshire. Their roaring furnaces drew visitors from miles around to see the awesome spectacle of flame, smoke, and machine. The younger Darby's daughter found the noise alone of "the stupendous bellows whose alternate roars, like foaming billows, was awful to hear."

Such advances fuelled the development of the iron industry, which powered the Industrial Revolution. In Sheffield, the Quaker inventor Benjamin Huntsman developed a purer and stronger form of cast steel. The Lloyds, a Welsh Quaker family, moved to Birmingham to create a factory for making iron rods and nails. In Bristol, a Quaker cooperative launched the Bristol Brass Foundry. By the early eighteenth century, Quakers managed approximately two-thirds of all British ironworks.

Railways accelerated the pace of change, and a Quaker was responsible for the world's first passenger train. In 1814, a meeting with engineer George Stevenson inspired Edward Pease, a Quaker businessman, to build the Stockton and Darlington Railway. On September 27, 1825, the first steam-hauled passenger train travelled twelve miles to Stockton on what became known as the "Quaker Line." Numerous Quakers were involved in financing and directing railway companies. Even the railway ticket and stamping machine was devised by a Quaker, Thomas Edmonson, as was the railway timetable itself, *Bradshaw's Railway Times*, created by George Bradshaw.

There seemed no limit to the number of new ideas generated by Quaker businessmen. Chinaware originally imported by the East India Company sparked developments in pottery and porcelain. In Plymouth, William Cookworthy introduced a new way to make fine china using Cornish china clay. In Staffordshire, Josiah Wedgwood launched a pottery business. Enduring shoe businesses were founded by Quakers: John Somervell opened K Shoes in Kendall, and James Clark in the village of Street in Somerset established the firm that still bears his name. The Reckitts started their business in household goods, while the Crosfields were soap and chemical manufacturers whose company evolved into Lever Brothers. The roll call of Quaker entrepreneurs resounds through the centuries with names like Bryant and May, who designed a safer form of matches; Huntley and Palmer, who started a biscuit business in Reading; and Allen and Hanbury, who developed pharmaceuticals.

Banking too was built on Quaker virtue. At a time of little financial regulation, according to the writer Daniel Defoe, the activities of many eighteenth-century financiers were seen as "founded in Fraud, born of Deceit, nourished by Trick, Cheat, Wheedle, Forgeries, Falsehood"—not totally dissimilar to some twenty-first-century banks. The Quaker traders stood apart. Customers learned to rely on typical Quaker attributes: skilled bookkeeping, integrity, and honesty served up by sober Bible-reading men in plain dark clothes. In the seventeenth and eighteenth centuries, local Quaker businesses began providing a counter in their offices that offered banking services. By the early nineteenth century, this practice had blossomed to seventy-four Quaker banks, one for almost every large city in Britain. James Barclay formed Barclays Bank in London, Henry Gurney established Gurney's Bank in Norwich, Edward Pease formed the Pease Bank in Darlington, Lloyds Bank was started in Birmingham, Backhouse's Bank grew across the north, Birkbeck flourished in Yorkshire, the Foxes set up in Falmouth, the Sparkes operated in Exeter, and many more. By the time Richard and George were born, Quaker banks, founded on a unique and trusted set of values, formed a solid network across the country.

As their banks and other businesses flourished, the Society of Friends continued to exchange views in Quaker meetings across the country, and the stoic independence, self-discipline, and questioning rebelliousness fashioned over a century in England was now channelled into the spirit of enterprise that fuelled the furnaces and mills of the Industrial Revolution.

But there was something else unique that guided Quakers in business from the earliest days of the Industrial Revolution. The original

Christian and Brotherly Advices of 1738 also included a section on "Trading." This highlighted key issues that a Friend might encounter in business and how to deal with them. It marks the foundation of business ethics built on truth, honesty, and justice—values that would form the basis of Quaker capitalism.

Central to the advice was that a Quaker must always honor his word:

> That none launch forth into trading and worldly business beyond what they can manage honourably and with reputation among the Sons of Men, so that they may keep their word with all Men; that their yea may prove their yea indeed, and their nay, may be nay indeed; for whatever is otherwise cometh of the Evil One . . . and brings Dishonour to the Truth of God.

Quakers entering into business were therefore encouraged to keep written accounts since accurate and thorough bookkeeping helped avoid errors of judgment.

> It is advised that all Friends that are entering into Trade and have not stock sufficient of their own to answer the Trade they aim at be very cautious of running themselves into Debt without advising with some of their Ancient and Experienced Friends among whom they live.

Above all else, Quaker elders, many of whom were in trade themselves, were keen "to Prevent the Great Reproach and Scandal" that might damage the reputation of the Society:

> It is advised . . . that all Friends concerned be very careful not to contract Extravagant Debts to the endangering and wronging of others and their families, which some have done to the Grieving Hearts of the upright, nor to break promises, contracts and agreements in the Buying and Selling or in any other lawful Affairs, to the injuring themselves and others, occasioning Strife and Contention and Reproach to Truth and Friends.

The local Monthly Meetings across the country were a forum for exchanging ideas, and Quakers were urged "to have a Watchful Eye over all their Members." If they found anyone "Deficient in Discharging their Contracts and just Debts," they were charged with "launching an Inspection into their Circumstances." Should "the Transgressor" fail to heed honest advice, "Friends justifiably may and ought to testify against such offenders." Accordingly, Friends collaborated in their local communities to help one another achieve high standards of integrity in trade.

As early as 1738, Quakers had a set of specific guidelines for business, which endeavored to apply the teachings of Christ to the workplace. Straight dealing, fair play, honesty, accuracy, and truth would form the basis of Quaker capitalism, and for those who fell short, there were rules of discipline. These guidelines were supplied to clerks in the Monthly and Quarterly Meetings and refined and formally updated every generation. They provide a snapshot of changing ethical concerns as the Industrial Revolution gathered momentum. For example, when the trading guidelines were updated in 1783 in the *Book of Extracts*, Friends were warned against a "most pernicious practice," which could lead to "utter ruin": the use of paper credit. This was considered "highly unbecoming," falling far short of "that uprightness that ought to appear in every member of our religious society." The 1783 *Extracts* warned unequivocally that this practice was "absolutely inconsistent with the truth."

Discipline could be severe for any members who were unable to meet the ethical standards required or acted imprudently in business. With the astonishing success of Quaker businesses and banks during the Industrial Revolution, protecting the good name of the Society became critically important. Those who repeatedly failed to demonstrate the high ethical conduct required of a Quaker tradesman could be disowned by the Society. This was seen as a harsh punishment, with the offender excluded from the local Quaker community and recognized publicly as a thief or a cheat.

As the nineteenth century progressed, the 1738 *Advices* and 1782 *Extracts* were updated once again into the more formal *Rules of Discipline* in 1833. By this time, material prosperity presented another issue for the Quaker elders. Was it right for a religious person cultivating plainness and simplicity to accumulate wealth? "We do not condemn industry, which we believe to be not only praiseworthy but indispensable," noted the *Rules of Discipline*, but "the love of money is said in Scripture to be 'the root of all Evil.'" The guidelines urged, "Dear Friends who are favoured with outward prosperity, when riches increase not to set your hearts upon them." The work ethic was entirely acceptable, but accumulating riches for oneself was not.

As Richard and George Cadbury embarked on their business life, Quaker guidelines were updated yet again, in *Doctrine, Practice and Discipline* of 1861. By now the section on trade had become a sophisticated set of rules under the heading "Advice in Relation to the Affairs of Life." The section covered a wide range of issues: honesty and truthfulness, plain dealing, fair trading, debt, seeking advice from fellow Friends, inappropriate speculation, discipline, and much more. With an increased number of Quakers experiencing worldly success, there was even a section for the children of rich Quakers to ensure they were not corrupted but fixed "their hopes of happiness on that which is substantial and eternal." The love of money "was a snare, which is apt to increase imperceptibly . . . and gradually withdraw the heart from God."

Richard and George Cadbury's entire worldview was shaped by Quaker values. This outlook molded their early childhood experiences, their learning as apprentices, their social and marriage opportunities, their choice of career, and their deeper understanding of the wider purpose of their chocolate business.

From their earliest years, they had seen their father endeavor to apply Quaker ideals in the community. According to Alfred Gardiner, John Cadbury was deeply concerned about "the savage indifference to the child." This was before Charles Dickens made Victorian society take notice of the plight of the "parish boy" and the "little workus" in his description of the recruitment of child criminals in *Oliver Twist* in 1838. In the 1820s, when John Cadbury was developing his shop on Bull Street, it was not uncommon for children in the workhouses to be carted off "like slaves to the cotton mills of Lancashire or to the mines."

John's greatest outrage was reserved for the practice of using young boys as chimney sweeps: on May 13, 1889, the *Daily Gazette* describes how he "vigorously condemned the barbarous practice." He discovered that children as young as five were being taken from workhouses and forced to climb chimneys to clean out the soot. Some chimneys were as narrow as seven inches square, and the children could only be induced to climb up when straw was lit beneath them or they were prodded with pins. Before they grew too big to be useful, many suffered twisted spines or damaged joints, or they were maimed by falls or burns. John was informed of a machine that could clean chimneys and "had the courage to call a meeting of Master Sweeps in the Town Hall," reported the *Gazette*. But his demonstration of the new machine met with strong opposition, mostly from the sweeps themselves, who were convinced they got a better result using boys.

A letter survives from John Cadbury to the Duke of Sutherland, who was chairing a House of Lords investigation into the use of climbing boys. John explained that in Birmingham he tried to win the sweeps over by supplying them with the machines himself. But still his campaign did not go smoothly. "Much prejudice against the machine has been raised," John informed the duke, because the master sweeps "have very improperly worked the machine and said and done all they could to prejudice . . . minds against them." John was so concerned he sent a signed petition to the House of Commons lobbying for a change in the law. He was delighted when legislation was eventually introduced banning the use of climbing boys.

George and Richard watched their parents become passionately involved in another major social issue of the time: alcoholism. The consumption of gin had become widespread in the eighteenth century. Many traditional pubs and alehouses were replaced by gin shops, which promised sweet oblivion with the tantalizing slogan: "Drunk for a penny. Dead drunk for two pence. Clean straw for nothing." This "liquid fire," in the words of (London magistrate) John Fielding, led to nothing less than "hell." The painter and social critic William Hogarth wrote of "Distress even to madness and death." Reports of children dying of neglect from drunken parents were commonplace. There were even accounts of children killed by their parents; their clothes provided a pittance for more gin.

John Cadbury's estimates suggested that one in thirteen households in Birmingham were somehow involved in the drink trade, and the majority of applicants for Poor Rate relief (a subsistence provided by the parish) were drawn from families with alcohol problems.

Candia and John were keen supporters of the Temperance Movement. In 1834, John publicly signed up to become a total abstainer, and he and Candia vigorously took on the town's drinkers and even the "Moderation Society," which tolerated modest drinking, with a "Total Abstinence Plan." According to an account on April 22, 1854, in *The Journal*, John's talks were packed with information. On this particular occasion, he told a concerned gathering in the town hall that he and his friends had "travelled through every street in Birmingham" and established that there were "593 licensed victuellers and 975 beer houses, amongst 45,844 inhabited houses, with around one house in every thirty dedicated to the sale of intoxicating drinks. His research had also led him to believe that there were 6,593 drunkards in Birmingham, of which an estimated 10 percent—659 people—died each year.

Another sad tale recorded in Richard Cadbury's family book concerns the formidable old Birmingham workhouse, which was then at the bottom of Lichfield Street and Steel House Lane. When John arrived for his first meeting as an Overseer of the Poor, he was dismayed to discover the distinguished committee, in true Dickensian style, met once a month for a "sumptuous repast" in which members filled themselves with "the choicest delicacies," washed down with brandy, before "attending to the shivering paupers outside." Bubbling over with righteous anger, John set out to expose "the illegality and iniquity" of holding such banquets. Evidently his enthusiasm "incurred much disfavour." In the heated debate that followed, one old gentleman who had never been known to speak on any former occasion was stirred to rise to make a brief but pithy point: "I spakes for the dinners!" Needless to say, John managed to get this practice stopped.

John also served on the wonderfully named Steam Engine Committee, which was responsible for tackling what he saw as "the serious evil" of smog and smoke. As chairman in the 1840s, he gathered data on the Birmingham chimneys that were emitting the greatest volume of dense black smoke per hour and put pressure on proprietors to take action. As chair of the Markets and Fairs Committee, he dealt with unwholesome meats and fraudulent trading. And he won funds as governor of the Birmingham General to develop the hospital. There was, declared the *Daily Gazette* on May 13, 1889, a widespread belief "that the poor were operated on for the sake of medical science," and John would periodically attend surgeries "to prevent any unnecessary cruelty to patients of the poorest class."

Their parents' example of patient and helpful concern towards society's less privileged members was a mantle that George and Richard accepted as an essential Quaker duty. They saw it as their moral responsibility to improve the plight of those in the industrial slums. Quaker idealism lay at the very heart of their business goals. Saving the chocolate factory held out the promise of providing employment, helping the workforce, and by extension the entire community. Even more fundamental, by developing and promoting cocoa as a drink that everyone could afford, they aimed to provide nutritious alternatives to alcohol and stop the spread of "mother's ruin."

Despite their diminishing inheritance, George and Richard persevered with reforming zeal. George saw the relationship with the employees as key. Sitting in the stockroom at 6:00 AM over breakfast, he encouraged workers to discuss issues in their lives, or he tried to help with their education, reading aloud to them and exchanging views on topics of interest or stories from the Bible. By today's standards, such actions seem paternalistic and even intrusive, but at a time when people could not read, it was valued. Many staff members spoke of their enjoyment of these small meetings, which "were more like family gatherings." One youth named Edward Thackray recalled how honoured he felt when Mr. George called him into his office "and they knelt together in prayer over some weighty business question."

The brothers' interest in the workers was also very practical. In spite of their losses, George and Richard pressed ahead with plans to increase wages with a new payment structure that tripled women's pay. A staff fire brigade was organized, which fortunately was never tested by a serious fire in the chocolate works. The brothers introduced the novel idea of a "sick club" to help pay for staff who had to take leave for illness. There was an evening sewing class once a week at the factory, during which George read to the group. The "boneshaker" bicycle—with iron-rimmed wheels, no springs, and no ball bearings—was extremely popular, and anyone could take it home if they could learn to ride it. Richard and George were among the first employers in Birmingham to introduce half days on Saturday and bank holidays. They even took the staff on leisure outings.

According to the *Daily Post* on June 21, 1864, "On Thursday last, Messrs Cadbury brothers . . . with commendable liberality took the whole of their male employees on a delightful trip to Sutton Park. The afternoon was spent by some in playing cricket . . . and others rambling through the park enjoying the invigorating air." At five o'clock, the whole company "sat down to a substantial tea which was duly appreciated." There was cricket in the summer, and during the winter, "when work was a bit slack," reports office worker George Brice, "the appearance of Mr George with his skates was a sure sign that we were to be the recipients of his favour in the shape of a half day's skating."

As the business experience grew, George and Richard were conscious that a paternal responsibility for the firm's employees was falling gently on their shoulders, quite naturally from friendly daily contact. The welfare of the staff was woven into the brothers' lives. The factory was not just a business. It was a world in miniature. It was a way to improve society. It provided them with a means to create an ideal world that would benefit others right in the middle of the big sinful city. They would create a "model chocolate factory."

But first they had to learn how to make a profit.

4

They Did Not
Show Us Any Mercy

No amount of prayers or hymns could solve one very particular problem. The Cadbury brothers faced stiff competition. The English manufacturers "showed no mercy," claimed George, although they spoke with a friendly face and a reasonable voice. From the cramped offices of the Cadbury brothers' modest factory, their rivals looked unassailable. Expertly they sailed on the great seas of commerce. They made it look easy, inviting, like an adventure.

In London the Taylor Brothers claimed to be the largest cocoa and mustard manufacturers in Europe. A picture of their Spitalfield works in the east end, proudly depicted on their sales brochure, showed a vast complex of factories, mills, and smoking chimneys with horses and carriages gaily travelling to and fro and giving an impression of grandeur. In addition to mustard and chicory, their sales list boasted more than fifty different types of drinking cocoas, including all the familiar lines in Victorian England. Established in 1817, they had gained considerable expertise in cocoa preparation. They claimed their technical know-how guaranteed the removal of any noxious, greasy oiliness from their delicious products. The firm was huge and, surrounded by the ever-growing London population, continued to grow with seemingly unstoppable success.

But the Taylors were not the only competition in the capital. They had rivals such as Messrs. Dunn and Hewett of Pentonville, who also sold an enterprising range of cocoas that included Vanilla Shilling Chocolate sold "unwrapped," various types of Chocolate Sticks wrapped in tin foil, and a curious Patent Lentilized Chocolate sold in "half pound cannisters." The early chocolate drinks made with powdered lentils, tapioca, dried peas, or sago to mop up the cocoa fats were possibly not for connoisseurs, but these thick, rich cocoa soups did satisfy the untried taste buds of many a Londoner. And for the really hard up, they promoted a slightly fatty "Plain Chocolate Sold in Drab Paper."

In addition to the commercial activity in London, there were regional centers of chocolate production, notably at York. As an apprentice, George Cadbury had witnessed the daring and confidence of Henry Rowntree on his entry into the world of the chocolatier. In 1860 Henry went to work in the cocoa and chicory business of the Tuke family, Quakers who were friends with the Rowntrees. Samuel Tuke had run the business, but after his death, his sons were not interested in taking charge of the family concern. Within two years, Henry was able to buy out the cocoa division of Tuke & Company. Henry could see that the Tuke premises, situated in the narrow, winding Castlegate in the heart of the old city of York, were too cramped and he set out to expand his cocoa works.

In buccaneer spirit he bought for £1000 what he called a "wonderful new machine" for grinding beans. Included in the sale were a motley collection of old buildings, which he optimistically described as his chocolate factory—an ironworks, a tavern, and several cottages in various stages of disrepair at Tanner's Moat—the whole enterprise practically falling into the putrid-smelling River Ouse. Henry explored the larger premises with enthusiasm, smelling only chocolate as he glimpsed the river's black and treacherous water.

The company's leading brand had been Tuke's Superior Rock Cocoa, which Henry duly relabelled Rowntree's Prize Medal Rock Cocoa after it won a prize at a local fair. To keep customers loyal, Henry extolled the virtues of his Rowntree's Rock Cocoa compared to rival brands. He evidently had a sense of humor and would raise a smile with a quip from Deuteronomy, no doubt appreciated by listeners who

knew their Bible: "For their Rock is not as our Rock, even our enemies themselves being judges." As he embarked on transforming
Tanner's Moat works into a modern factory that could churn out
Rowntree's Rock Cocoa to sell across England, Henry could smell the
future. He had the support of his older brother, Joseph, who was running the Rowntree's grocery shop in the center of York. George Cadbury knew that the Rowntrees had the determination to succeed.

There were other firms in York poised to benefit from the arrival of
the railway. By the middle of the nineteenth century, some twelve
trains a day leaving London could deliver 250,000 visitors to York over
the year. Joseph Terry and his brothers, who had inherited their father's
confectionery business in 1854, took advantage of the new opportunities. Starting back in 1767, their forebears had sold boiled sweets and
candied peel to the rich. Over the generations, the Terrys established
a reputation for a range of sugar-based confections sold in their enticing sweet shop not far from Rowntree's grocery shop. Just to open the
shop door invited the unwary customer into a magical Hansel and
Gretel world of sugared strawberries, raspberries, lemons, and oranges.

With the arrival of the railways, Joseph Terry was soon selling to
customers in more than seventy-five towns across the Midlands and
the north of England. To meet rising demand, he moved his manufacturing in 1862 to a larger site just outside the city walls. Here the
twice-weekly steam packet brought exotic fruits and cocoa. In the
1860s, Joseph Terry was looking closely at how to diversify his range
of sweetmeats to make more use of cocoa in chocolate-covered nuts
and sweets.

But the Cadburys—and the other chocolate manufacturers—
faced their stiffest competition in a giant Quaker concern in Bristol:
Fry and Sons. The Frys ran the largest cocoa works in the world, so
large that it was fast shaping the city of Bristol. Their factory was
the size of a small town, and their sprawling works easily accommo-
dated the varied processes of production. This was cocoa making for
England. The Cadburys' little plant could not compete.

George Cadbury was intrigued. "I never looked at the small people
or the people who had failed," he declared. "I wanted to know how

men succeeded, and it was their methods I examined, and if I thought them good, applied." Through the Quaker network, George was able to approach the Frys in Bristol and found a partner, Francis James Fry, who was prepared to take him under his wing. Francis Fry and George Cadbury formed a loose alliance of English cocoa makers, which met for convenience in the London offices of the Taylor brothers. "I suppose we had some energy," George recalled years later. "For Francis James Fry elected to go round with me to see the Cocoa and Chocolate Manufacturers." George was surprised, remarking, "I was a young man in a small business compared to his." A year older than George, Francis James was the fourth generation in his family's firm. With Fry's sales approaching a colossal £100,000 a year, Francis was secure in the knowledge that the young Cadbury brothers were no threat.

George Cadbury had everything to learn about the development of a family firm from his Fry counterpart—and learn he did. The Bristol firm, he noted, from the earliest years had an outstanding reputation for innovation.

The story of the House of Fry opens in Bristol at a time when the city had more in common with the Tudor period than the modern world. Born in 1728 into a Quaker Wiltshire family, Francis James Fry's great-grandfather, Joseph Fry, who had trained as an apothecary, came to Bristol as a young man seeking an opportunity.

At the time, Bristol was the West Country hub for trade and as a port was second only to London. On the quayside, the harbor opened onto a forest of rigging and sails from a multitude of ships arriving from the New World. The port was packed with sailors, slaves, and merchants, the air heavy with the scent of rum and tar; and marvels from the New World, such as sugar and cocoa, were unloaded into wagons and warehouses. In the eighteenth century, the Flying Coach was the fastest public transport from Bristol to London. With relays of fresh horses staged down the line, it was possible to reach the capital in two days.

Joseph Fry, a sober figure in his dark Quaker clothes, took a tiny shop in Small Street and began his apothecary business in 1753, when it was still customary to keep jars of leeches in the window. As a sideline to his pills and potions, he sold cocoa, which he promoted as a health drink because he was convinced it was a highly nutritious alternative to alcohol. Fry's chocolate drink became popular in the fashionable nearby town of Bath, known as "the first city of pleasure in the kingdom." Smart coffeehouses appeared overnight, promoting the chocolate drink to the aristocracy.

In just eight years, Joseph Fry was in a position to take over the leading cocoa manufacturer in the area, Walter Churchman. Fry's cocoa consisted of the oily cocoa flakes and powder in suspension in liquid, and Churchman's drink was clearly superior. Churchman's secret rested on a patent he had taken out in 1729 for "an invention and new method for the better making of chocolate by an engine." It was a water-powered machine that enabled him to create a much finer cocoa powder than anyone else. Once Fry secured the recipe, his Churchman's Chocolate became very popular.

Joseph Fry was inventive and seized his chance to develop the business. By 1764, he had agents promoting his products in no less than fifty-three towns and was in a position to open a warehouse in London. In 1777, he moved his cocoa factory to larger premises on the fashionable Union Street, then on the banks of the River Frome, and he used water power to drive the cocoa-grinding mills. His business interests were many and varied, and under his concerned gaze and industrial "green fingers," everything he touched flourished. He also owned a share in the Bristol China Works, created a type foundry in London, was a partner in a large soap- and candle-making business in Bristol, and bought a share of a chemical works in Battersea. Some feat for a businessman before the age of railways, telegraphs, and telephones and with little support beyond the Flying Coach and the Penny Post.

In 1795, Joseph's son, Joseph Storr Fry, inherited the cocoa business and continued to develop the Union Street works. Since the water flow from the River Frome was not reliable, he took the remarkable step of installing one of James Watt's first steam engines. To the astonishment of the workers, this clanking, hissing, mechanical marvel transformed cocoa production and was soon regarded as "one of the wonders of the World." According to Fry's records, the steam power from this engine was diverted "by means of a vertical shaft carried up through the factory" to the third floor, where it turned Britain's first "mechanically driven machine for grinding Cocoa Nibs." News that someone was using a Watt steam engine for food manufacture elicited comments from across the country. "We are credibly informed," marvelled the *Bury and Norwich Post* on June 6, 1798, that "Mr. Fry of Bristol has one of these Engines—improved by an ingenious Millwright of the city—for the *sole purpose* of manufacturing Cocoa. It is astonishing to what variety of manufactures this useful machine has been applied!"

Apart from installing a steam engine to grind the beans, Joseph Storrs Fry received a patent from King George III to build a new kind of machine to roast the beans, which he installed in the factory next door. Doubtless he was gratified to find *The Times* full of praise on August 8, 1801, for the "excellent articles produced from his celebrated manufactory." By the time George Cadbury's father was opening his tea and chocolate shop in Birmingham in 1824, the Frys were using nearly 40 percent of the cocoa imported into Britain and enjoying annual sales of £12,000.

In 1835 the business passed to the third generation of Frys. Brothers Joseph II, Francis, and Richard continued to develop the site on Union Street and pioneered new brands. They launched Pearl Cocoa, which countered the heavy oiliness of their cocoa drinks with the addition of arrowroot that absorbed the cocoa oils. Since Pearl Cocoa contained less costly ingredients like molasses and sugar, it could be cheaply priced to attract poorer households and it became a huge seller. Homeopathic Cocoa took advantage of the burgeoning interest in health. For the upmarket consumer, they introduced a finely ground Soluble Cocoa, which was slightly less gritty. All these products cost a fraction of what it cost to manufacture them a hundred years earlier, when their grandfather's best cocoas, at over seven shillings per pound, cost as much as the average farmworker received for his weekly wage. These new variations cost around one shilling per pound while their workers were earning ten shillings per week.

Fry was noted not only for its innovation but also for the austerity of its Quaker founders. One worker who recorded the atmosphere of the firm in the mid-nineteenth century recalls "primitive and paternalistic" conditions. "The quiet of Union Street was even more marked between 9:00 to 9:20 when all employees attended a morning meeting," he records. "It was not uncommon to see passers stop to listen admiringly to the peaceful strains of a hymn sung by our girls and workmen as a prelude to the working day."

As Richard and George were struggling to establish their firm in Birmingham during the 1860s, according to *Fry's Works Magazine*, "so great had become the expansion of our trade," that the factory was inadequate to deal with "orders pouring into the House from every quarter." Fry had travelling salesmen in no less than fifty towns at a time when Cadbury's only traveller, Dixon Hadaway, covered the whole of the north of England and Scotland in his pony and trap. George learned that a single Fry traveller with a flair for sales managed to secure ninety-five accounts in just four towns: Cheltenham, Stroud, Worcester, and Gloucester. Gloucester alone bought £10,000 of goods. In the age of the steamship, Fry also benefited from the Bristol docks that linked the company to Queen Victoria's burgeoning empire and an ever-expanding horizon. To cap it all, they took advantage of Bristol as a leading naval base and won a contract to supply the British Navy—almost doubling their orders overnight. For the military, cocoa was valuable because it was easy to transport in tins and warm and filling for the troops.

From the Cadbury brothers' loss-making warehouse in Birmingham, the Frys appeared invincible. George knew he had a great deal to learn, and travelling with Francis James Fry gave him the chance to find out more about their latest pioneering inventions.

In 1847 the Fry brothers introduced a novelty into the Victorian market. They had experimented with mixing their cocoa powder with its by-product, the excess cocoa fat. Whether by accident or design, they hit upon a way of blending the two ingredients with sugar to make a rich creamy paste. This concoction was then pressed into a mold and left to set. The result: the first solid chocolate bar in Britain. It was a breakthrough: a way of mass-producing a chocolate product that could be eaten instead of being consumed as drink. This made chocolate portable and turned it into a totally new kind of snack—to carry on the railways or to bring to work. They called it Chocolat Delicieux a Manger.

Fry's new product, however, did not appeal to anyone with a really sweet tooth. It was bitter, coarse, and heavy and probably only of interest to the dedicated few who also possessed a strong jaw. Initially sales were slow. Undeterred, the Fry brothers had glimpsed a sweeter, more solid future. They set to work on more recipes for chocolate confectionery that could be produced in bulk. Secretly they experimented with a new kind of white minty cream. This was made by boiling sugar in an open pan, whipping it to an opaque creamy consistency, and adding mint flavoring to give a fresh taste. After the minty cream had cooled and been cut into sticks, these were dipped in luxurious dark chocolate. By 1853, Fry's frock-coated travellers were opening their sample cases to reveal a brand new product: Fry's delectable chocolate-coated Cream Sticks. Shopkeepers were amazed when they tasted the first chocolate confectionery produced on a factory scale; it was rich and satisfying, a real treat. Better still, mass production meant that the price was significantly lower than handmade confections.

The recipe proved to be a success, and within a few years it was brilliantly reformulated as a new type of chocolate bar. The chocolate for these "morsels of delight" according to Fry's literature, was formed into a thin, light paste. The mint cream was set in hundreds of tiny molds and taken to covering rooms, where "scores of young damsels" with chocolate trays coated the batches. In 1866 the first wagonloads of Fry's Chocolate Cream found their way throughout Britain to the grocers and sweetshops. Preliminary sales of Fry's minty chocolate sensation may have been modest, but there was growing interest— and not just from customers.

French chocolatiers, who had long held a reputation for exquisite handmade confections, were also exploring ways to produce them in bulk. Just outside Paris at his chocolate works on the River Marne in Noisiel, Emile Menier hit upon a process not dissimilar to Fry's. He inherited his business from his father, a chemist, who had originally used cocoa sweetened with sugar as a coating for his pills. Emile developed the cocoa side of his father's business and by the mid-nineteenth century, he had created a method for pressing dark chocolate into a mold. Wrapped in chrome yellow paper, it was the first solid chocolate bar made in France, and it proved so successful that Menier's output quadrupled in ten years, reaching 2,500 tonnes in the mid-1860s, a quarter of the country's total output. Emile was able to invest more funds in his factory at Noisiel. Originally powered by a humble water mill, the factory was now equipped with shining new steam turbines, creating such a splendid spectacle that the locals called it "the cathedral." Much of Menier's chocolate was exported, and like many Europeans, he had his eye on the dense populations in Britain's industrial towns. Soon he was in a position to open a factory of his own on Southwark Street in London.

To improve the texture of his chocolate and increase his production, Menier needed extra cocoa butter, the fatty part of the bean. He found a ready supplier in Holland—in Weesp, near Amsterdam, where a cocoa-making family firm was run by Coenraad van Houten. Somehow the Van Houtens had managed to solve a problem that had eluded everyone else: how to mechanize the separation of the fat content from the rest of the cocoa bean. As a result, his cocoa was purer and more refined than anything else on the market, and he had cocoa butter, as a by-product, for sale. Exactly how he achieved this was a trade secret, but there was no secret about his sales. Van Houten had agents building up a sales list in London; Edinburgh, Scotland; and Dublin, Ireland.

A regular traveller to London, George Cadbury could not fail to notice the new products: a purer form of cocoa made by the Dutch and eating chocolate manufactured as solid bars in bulk. In the 1860s, sales of eating chocolate were modest—nothing compared to the established drinking cocoa brands in England. Even so, like a flag planted on new territory beating against the wind, it pointed the way to unlock the potential hidden inside the little chocolate bean.

George was at a loss. He recognized that the Fry family was better placed than anyone else in Britain to take on the foreign competition. Although none of their cocoas matched the quality of Van Houten's pure Dutch cocoa, Fry of Bristol was the cocoa metropolis of the world. Their four factories on Union Street, towering eight stories high, seemed as secure as their granite and concrete exteriors. Just as their towering citadel dominated the town, so the bounty within dominated the market. The variety and sheer abundance of Fry's chocolate temptations put them in a class of their own. They were indeed a beacon, a light to follow.

The Cadbury brothers did not have the money to invest in the molding machinery that would mass-produce such luxurious temptations as a chocolate bar. Their inability to produce a popular product and make a profit was becoming critical. With no significant funds for investment, Richard and George struggled on producing cocoa as a drink mixed with the questionable starches to absorb the fat. Their new products, Iceland Moss, Pearl Cocoa, Breakfast Cocoa, and others, had failed to make an impact, and their losses continued to mount.

In response to yet another grim stocktaking, it fell to Richard to tackle overdue accounts. "We made the lowest class of goods," George wrote later, and consequently they had some of the "least desirable custom" who were not always ready or willing to settle their debts. "The small shopkeepers were constantly failing," he continued. Some went under without paying—putting Cadbury at risk of going under as well.

The brothers had resolved, whatever happened, not to take on any liabilities that they could not meet and not to turn to their father for additional funds. In Victorian tradition, their only sister, Maria, now in her thirties, had postponed any thoughts of marriage to devote herself to caring for their father. The oldest brother, John, after a brief attempt at farming in the West Country, had made the bold decision to immigrate to Australia. He sailed from the East India Docks in London on December 17, 1863, on the ninety-day journey for Brisbane. Their younger brother Edward was embarking on a home-decorating business and the youngest, Henry, was still in his final years at school.

Richard and George determined that rather than assume the risk of taking on a debt, they would shut the business if they spent their entire inheritance. They continued to work relentlessly, spending long days on the road selling their cocoas to reluctant grocers and returning to the warehouse to pack the orders themselves if hands were short. The shortage of money was proving a strain at home. Richard's oldest son, Barrow, later recalled an outing when the family had gone to Pebble Mill. His mother, Elizabeth, suddenly felt unwell, but both his parents elected "to tramp all the way back again when his father would have given so much, had he been able, to take her home in a cab."

Unfortunately, the brothers' industry and virtue made no difference. At the end of four years, they were facing disaster. "All my brother's money had disappeared," George admitted. "I had but 1,500 left—not having married." There were insufficient funds left in their inheritance to develop a business desperate for capital. George knew the enterprise was dying for want of mechanization but they dared not risk additional loss. "I was preparing to go out to the Himalayas as a tea planter," said George. "Richard was intending to be a surveyor."

The Cadbury business was all but dead.

5

Absolutely Pure, Therefore Best

BIRMINGHAM 1866

George Cadbury was considering one final reckless gamble. It would consume every last penny of his inheritance. As long as he did not fall into debt or risk the great disgrace of bankruptcy, he believed it was a risk that had to be taken.

The more George learned about the Dutch manufacturer Coenraad van Houten, the more intrigued he became. Van Houten was having great success exporting his refined, defatted cocoa to Britain from his steam factory in Weesp. Dixon Hadaway told him that Van Houten's cocoa was so popular it was on sale in regional towns like Leeds and Liverpool as well as in the capital. Gradually George began to realize that this was the model he should follow. Refined cocoa surely held the key to the future.

George discovered that the key to Van Houten's success lay with an invention Coenraad had developed with his father, Casparus, more than thirty years earlier. The Van Houtens recognized that established methods of boiling and skimming the bean resulted in an indigestible cocoa consisting of over 50 percent cocoa butter. After experimenting with different designs of mechanical grinders and presses, they eventually perfected a hydraulic press that reduced the cocoa fat to less than 30 percent. The flour and other less appealing extras that had been used to sop up the fat were no longer required. The result: a purer, smoother drink that tasted more like chocolate and less like potato flour.

The Dutch process was a trade secret and no one in England, not even Fry, had discovered a way to manufacture a purer cocoa. George pondered: Could this be the way to best their English rivals? Would the Dutch be prepared to sell their machine? If they had such a machine, could the brothers turn the factory around using the spare cocoa butter to create fancy chocolates like the French? Suddenly George could see a business future that made sense. Instead of using the cocoa bean to create one type of product, a fatty and adulterated cocoa, he could create two distinctly different products—pure cocoa and eating chocolate—using the most appropriate bit of the bean for each. A whole new set of possibilities opened up—if he could get hold of the machine.

"I went off to Holland without knowing a word of Dutch," said George, "saw the manufacturer with whom I had to talk entirely by signs and the dictionary." They were locked in discussion in Van Houten's factory: George, plainly dressed, earnest, frustrated by the language, and absolutely sure that the odd-looking machine would save the Cadbury factory, was desperate to charm and persuade and take home the prize.

Mr. Van Houten succumbed. The defatting machine was sold to the Quaker gentleman. The records do not reveal the agreed-upon price, but it is likely that the purchase used up much of George's remaining funds—around £1000. George made shipping arrangements to get the monstrous prize back to Bridge Street. It arrived by canal, and the sturdy cast-iron apparatus, a full ten feet tall, was hard to maneuver into position from the wharf into the chocolate works. Worse, the thing was very greedy; to make it economical, George had to feed the giant hopper with a large amount of beans. They had to find a way to increase volume, and fast.

The preparations to launch their new product were further constrained by a double tragedy in the family. In January 1866, their younger brother, twenty-two-year-old Edward, died unexpectedly after a short illness. When John, their thirty-two-year-old brother, wrote home in May from Brisbane to express his grief at the loss, Maria was alarmed to see that his writing appeared unsteady and his letter was unsigned. Doctors in Australia confirmed that John was suffering from "colonial fever," a form of typhus. News of John's death on May 28 followed almost immediately.

The unexpected loss of two brothers in such quick succession made Richard and George feel their responsibilities ever more keenly. The survival of the family business rested with them. Hopes of future family prosperity depended on this last throw of the dice. In the coming months, they streamlined production of the new drink. By the autumn, Richard was ready to start designing the artwork for the packaging. At last, in the weeks before Christmas 1866, Cocoa Essence was launched.

It soon became apparent that there was a problem. Unlike competitors whose cocoa went further with the addition of cheaper ingredients, such as starch and flour, Cocoa Essence was pure and by far the most expensive cocoa drink on sale. The launch faltered. Customers were scarce. The strain on the brothers was beginning to exact a toll.

To the Frys, watching their competition from Bristol, the Cadbury brothers' move hinted at desperation. Under the management of Francis Fry, sales reached a staggering £102,747 during 1867. Following Fry's contract with the Navy, their workforce rose to two hundred. With the Fry name established across England, "it was an extremely hard struggle," George Cadbury admitted. "We had ourselves to induce shopkeepers to stock our cocoa and induce the public to ask for it." It looked as though George's gamble had failed.

In 1867, George and Richard made one last effort, exploiting something that Quaker rivals such as the Rowntrees in York spurned on principle: advertising. Plain Quakers, like the Rowntrees, believed that the business should be built on the quality and value of their goods. Nothing else should be needed if the product was honest. Advertising one's goods was like advertising oneself—abhorrent to a man of God. To Joseph Rowntree, who was proudly settled as "Master Grocer" in his shop in York, advertising seemed a slightly shabby and unprincipled enterprise, in which promotion was somehow elevated above the quality of the product. Even though he could see that his younger brother Henry's cocoa works at Tanner's Moat was not taking off as hoped, nonetheless he did not consider advertising to be the answer. He dismissed it as mere "puffery"; he even objected to fancy packaging and was content to alert his customers to a new product with a restrained and dignified letter. His deeply religious sensibility was offended by the idea of hyped-up claims or exaggeration of any kind.

The Frys had similar Quaker sensibilities when it came to excessive promotion. With the confidence that comes with over a hundred and fifty years as a successful family business, Francis Fry saw little need for change. "Our early advertisements had a certain coy primness about them," conceded Fry's management in the company's 1928 *Bicentenary Report*. Their "venerable announcements" of their original drink in the eighteenth century, Churchman's Chocolate, consisted of long-winded essays trying to explain why the product was unique and how to obtain it—by Penny Post or in "the hands of errand boys." This progressed in the early nineteenth century to little homilies that advised the public on how to prepare the drink and why it was good for them. Even the language was old-fashioned, describing the firm as an apothecary. "We were full of innocent pride in that period," wrote the management. Certainly they had nothing that would stop you in your tracks. No gorgeous girl of forthright demeanor with glossy lips and an unmistakable message in her eyes as she sipped her cocoa. Nothing to actually hit you in the eye or stimulate the taste buds: just a message, hardly readable in small typeface, telling of Churchman's Chocolate.

To the Cadbury brothers, however, it seemed that advertising could do more. Another company, Pears, was taking advertising to new levels. In 1862, Thomas Barratt had married into the Pears family and saw a way of turning a little-known, quality product, Pears soap, into a household name. Barratt broke through with a simple, attention-grabbing message. He began by enlisting the help of eminent medical men such as Sir Erasmus Wilson, president of the Royal College of Surgeons, as well as members of the Pharmaceutical Society of Great Britain. At a time when many soap products actually contained damaging ingredients, the medical men were happy to endorse Pears because it was "without any of the objectionable qualities of the old soaps." Barratt created posters and packaging adorned with eye-catching images of healthy children and beautiful women with the brand name boldly written across the package. For the consumer, the message was immediate and simple: use this soap and you will be healthy and beautiful. Barratt is often described as the father of modern advertising.

Desperation drove the Cadbury brothers to a different decision from their Quaker rivals. They knew they had to change public perception of their pure new drink. Shrugging off their Quaker scruples, they took a gamble and committed to another investment. Like the Pears team, they asked their salesmen to visit doctors in London with samples of their new product. To the delight of the brothers, they too won the support of the obliging medical press. "Cocoa treated thus will, we expect, prove to be one of the most nutritious, digestible and restorative of drinks," enthused the *British Medical Journal*. Noting the brothers' claim that their product was three times the strength of ordinary cocoas and free from "excess fatty matter," the *Lancet* concurred. The product is "genuine. . . . Essence of Cocoa is just what it is declared to be by Messrs Cadbury brothers."

The Cadburys' timing was excellent because during the 1860s, purity of manufactured foods was a growing concern for the public. There was very little regulation of the food market. Even staples like bread could be contaminated. The public had first been warned in 1820 when the chemist Frederick Accum published *A Treatise on Adulterations of Food and Culinary Poisons*, which argued that processed food could be dangerous. By the 1850s, Dr. Arthur Hassall had written a series of reports in the *Lancet* exposing typical scams in cocoa production: brick dust, red lead, and iron compounds to add color; animal fat or starches such as corn, tapioca, or potato flour to add bulk. By 1860, in response to public pressure, the government introduced the first regulations to prevent adulteration of food.

Yet still the scams continued. In one government investigation, more than half the cocoa samples tested were contaminated with red ochre from brick dust. Consumer guides appeared teaching customers how to test their cocoa and warning that a slimy texture and cheesy or rancid taste indicated the presence of animal fat. If the cocoa thickened in hot water or milk, this was evidence that starches had been added, something you could confirm if your comfort drink turned blue in the presence of iodine. Most worrying of all was the continued use of contaminants, including poisons such as red lead, which were injurious to the public's health but which enhanced a product's color or texture. It was small wonder then that the *Grocer* hurried to follow the lead of the medical press and sang the praises of the Cadbury brothers' pure new product: "There will be thousands of shop keepers who will be glad of an opportunity to retail cocoa guaranteed to contain nothing but the natural constituents of the bean!"

With this support, in 1867 the Cadburys planned the largest advertising campaign they had yet undertaken. There was no longer a question mark over advertising. They would use it with confidence and really make the Cadbury name stand out. And best of all, the product was honest. They could shout it from the roof tops. They were, in essence, rebranding their new cocoa product—and with it, the whole image of cocoa.

Richard Cadbury came up with a slogan that capitalized on the strengths of their new product: "Absolutely Pure, Therefore Best." They took out full-page advertisements in newspapers and put posters in shop fronts and on London omnibuses. Since the London General Omnibus Company had amalgamated more than six hundred horse-drawn buses in the capital into one fleet, it was feasible to create a unified poster campaign across the city. Soon the Cadbury name, synonymous with the purity of the product, was everywhere. It was unavoidable, rippling through the city like a refrain from a song. Given half a chance, the Cadbury brothers would have covered the dome of St. Paul's, protested one writer. But at the chocolate works, everyone caught the mood of excitement.

The public got the message. By the autumn of 1868, the campaign was gaining momentum. The staff on Bridge Street grew to almost fifty. David Jones, a former railway goods porter who longed to be a traveller, vividly recalled his first day: "George put a sample in my hand and told me to go wherever I wanted for a week, the only stipulation being that I should not trespass on the grounds of another traveller." Jones chose North Wales and soon had reason to regret his decision. No one had tasted anything like Cocoa Essence before. "I gave hundreds of shopkeepers a taste," he remembered, "only to watch their faces lose their customary shape as though they had taken vinegar or wood worm." But Jones would not give up. He managed to secure thirty-five orders and was gratified to find the Cadbury brothers were "highly pleased." Another traveller, John Penberthy, also felt the thrill of winning orders. "The delight of travelling in those ancient days, working towns not previously visited by a Cadbury traveller, surpassed in my opinion . . . the discoveries of Shackleton, Peary or Dr. Cook!"

While pressing on with the launch of Cocoa Essence, the Cadbury brothers also followed Fry's lead with experimental types of eating chocolate. Their father, John Cadbury, had tested out a French eating chocolate before, but now that they had a large volume of creamy cocoa butter as a by-product of their pure cocoa drink, they could dramatically scale the manufacture of eating chocolate. Rather than mimic Fry's rough chocolate bar, the Cadbury brothers were after something altogether more luxurious. They found that when the cocoa butter was mixed with sugar and then cocoa liquor was folded back into the mix, it produced a superior dark chocolate bar. Then they went one step further. They wanted to launch a new concept that would bring the exotic qualities of the French chocolatier to the popular market. Richard called it the Fancy Box.

Had they not been in charge of a chocolate factory, still faltering slightly, the lavish contents of the Fancy Box would undoubtedly have violated their principles. It represented the most un-Quakerly immoderation and extravagance. Generations of Quakers before them had maintained a beady-eyed vigilance in the pursuit of "truth and plainness." The senses on no account were to be indulged; the path to God demanded a numbing restraint and self-denial. But Richard and George, the apparently devout Quakers, had come up with the ultimate in wanton and idle pleasure.

The lid of each Fancy Box opened to release the richest of scents—the chocolate fumes inviting the recipient with overwhelming urgency to trifle among the decadent contents as a whiff of almond marzipan, a hint of orange, rich chocolate truffle, and strawberries from a June garden bathed in thick chocolate beguiled the very air, all begging to be crushed between tongue and palate. Each one had a French-sounding name, adding more forbidden naughtiness: Chocolat du Mexique, Chocolat des Delices aux Fruits, and more.

It is ironic that George and Richard dreamed up these chocolate indulgences at a point when their own lives had become most spartan. "At that time I was spending about 25 pounds a year for travelling, clothes, charities and everything else," George wrote. "My brother had married, and at the end of five years he only had 150 pounds. If I had married, there would have been no Bournville today, it was just the money I saved by living so sparely that carried us over the crisis." It is arguable, therefore, that their unremitting self-denial fuelled their appreciation of sensual extravagance.

In the pursuit of plainness, the Quakers also spurned most artistic endeavor. The arts were a worldly distraction that could divert a Quaker from the inner calm that led to God. As a result, George and Richard's father never allowed a piano in the house and had given up learning his treasured flute. As for painting, this was considered a superfluous indulgence that could lead a Quaker astray with a false appreciation of something "worthless and base." But just as he had ignored the criticisms against advertising, Richard chose to ignore the rigid rules against making art. Revelling in exuberant splashes of color, he began a series of paintings to paste on the covers of the Fancy Box.

He chose pictures that appealed to Victorian sentimentality. He had travelled to Switzerland and made sketches of the Alpine scenery. Now these drawings, along with postcard images of the seaside and even his own children formed the basis of his designs. "Among the pictorial novelties introduced to the trade this season, few if any excel the illustration on Messrs Cadburys' four-ounce box of chocolate crèmes," enthused the *Birmingham Gazette* on January 8, 1869. "It is chaste yet simple, and consists of a blue eyed maiden some six summers old, neatly dressed in a muslin frock, trimmed with lace, nursing a cat." It was Richard's own daughter, Jessie, with her favorite kitten. To strike a real note of luxury, Richard decided that some of the Fancy Boxes should be covered in velvet and lined with silk and a mirror. In every way, Cadbury's chocolate was to stand for quality. The reviewer writing for the *Chemist and Druggist* magazine on December 15, 1870, was certainly won over. "Divine," he declared. "The most exquisite chocolate ever to come under our notice."

It was one thing to dream up recipes for the Fancy Box but quite another to mass-produce them. "When I think how we were cramped up in small rooms at Bridge Street," recalled Bertha Fackrell of the top crème room, "the wonder is to me now that we turned out the work as well as we did." A lack of space was the least of their problems. "Oh the job we had to cool the work!" Bertha continued. Although there were small cupboards with ventilators around the room, all too often when staff from the box room came to collect the crèmes and chocolate balls, they were still too warm. "I remember once we girls put our work on the window sill to cool when someone accidentally knocked the whole lot down into the yard below."

Sales of the Fancy Box increased and gradually more staff was hired. One new worker, the crème beater, T. J. O'Brien, was amazed to find the owners grafting with the workers. "During these trying times I never knew men to work harder than our masters who indeed were more like fathers to us," he wrote. "Sometimes they were working in the manufactory, then packing in the warehouse, then again all over the country getting orders." O'Brien's work beating the crèmes was heavy and "often Mr. George and Mr. Richard would come and give me a help."

But for all their hard work, reward was not to come easily to the Cadbury brothers. For Richard, busy pouring all his energy into the factory, the enjoyment of success, so longed for, so hard won, was wiped away. His adored wife, Elizabeth, died at Christmastime in 1868, ten days after giving birth to his fourth child. Suddenly their achievements seemed as nothing. The very center of his family was gone, but he knew that for a Quaker, numbing grief must be borne with stoicism.

Richard, at thirty-two, was left with four very young children under his care. Barrow was the oldest at six, followed by Jessie, who was three, one-year-old William, and the new baby, who had been named after Richard. "He was everything to our baby lives," says Jessie of her father. "I can well remember riding on his shoulders and going to him with all our troubles." However pressed Richard was at work, she recalls, "he was so much to us always." The loss of his wife, in a Quaker household, required "humble submission to God's will." The children learned fortitude from their father. For Jessie, the certainty of her own father's love made her feel "it was worth braving anything."

Perhaps because Richard grew much closer to his children at this time, during the spring of 1869, he found the time to set up a nursery for poor or abandoned children and infants in the neighborhood. He rented a house for them and enlisted the help of a friend, the maternal and highly competent Emma Wilson. Mrs. Wilson had been widowed seven years earlier and had managed to earn an income and raise seven children on her own. She became indispensable, not only in the nursery but also by helping out with Richard's children at Wheeley's Road.

Sometimes Richard's children accompanied him to his office. Barrow remembers coming to Bridge Street with his father and delighting in watching boxes as they were unloaded from the colonies. "One day a large boa constrictor emerged and was chased by two men who held it down with sugar and cocoa bags," Barrow recalled. "It was a revelation that the boa constrictor could bend its body with such force whatever the strain." When the frightened boy fled to the Cocoa Essence sieving room, he was soon discovered "and given a lecture on the impropriety of being there." Hygiene was all-important; no leniency was given, even when hiding from a boa constrictor.

Although the Cadbury brothers' position had improved, they did not yet feel secure. No capital remained. Their livelihood and their future depended on the public drinking their cocoa, charmed by a blonde blue-eyed girl holding a kitten and smiling sweetly from the lid of a chocolate box.

In York, the Rowntrees appeared to thrive with a quality grocer's shop in the center of town and a big chocolate factory by the river. But Joseph Rowntree, successful purveyor of superior foods, was worried. The problem was his brother, Henry, and the chocolate factory at Tanner's Moat, which looked like a medieval castle with its forbidding high walls and blackened windows. It was becoming apparent that Henry had optimistically overreached himself by investing in the rambling complex on the River Ouse. By 1869, after a seven-year struggle, his cocoa was still struggling to find a market and the firm's future looked uncertain. The prospect of his brother failing was real.

The lesson of years of stern homilies about honoring debt, plain dealing, and trustworthiness began to preoccupy Joseph. He knew perfectly well from the family's much thumbed copy of the *Rules of Discipline* that a good Quaker should "have a watchful eye over all their members and those heading for commercial trouble should be warned and if required, helped in their difficulties." Joseph knew Henry was in trouble, running his business in a most eccentric manner with equally eccentric accounts. Their father had died shortly after setting Henry up in the cocoa business, and as his older brother, Joseph felt keenly aware of his duty. Much though he delighted in his role as Master Grocer in his shop, he could not allow himself to put self-interest first when his brother was in need of help.

Even at thirty-three, Joseph Rowntree had already earned a reputation as a man who took his Quaker responsibilities seriously. Having witnessed the horror of the Irish Potato Famine, he had made time while running the grocery shop to undertake an exhaustive study on poverty in England. His study had attempted to investigate not just the effects but also the causes of poverty. Researching back to the time of the Black Death, he had carefully gathered facts on pauperism, illiteracy, crime, and education. He had begun to uncover the complex web of connections that can trap a family in poverty. He published his findings as a paper, *British Civilisation*, which he hoped to present at an Adult School Conference in Bristol in 1864, only to find that fellow Quakers, such as Francis Fry's nephew, Joseph Storrs Fry II, who was running the conference, urged him to modify his language. The following year, Joseph Rowntree published a more measured paper, *Pauperism in England and Wales*, a landmark study that set out the figures and questioned the role of church and state in perpetuating social injustice.

Rowntree's studies were thought-provoking and they gave him confidence in his ability to collect data and analyze problems—traits that he reasoned could help him stabilize his brother's business. In 1868 he took a bold step. He withdrew his inheritance from the security of the Pavement grocery shop to invest with Henry, hoping to bring order to the bohemian chocolate factory by the river while Henry was put in charge of production. There was every reason to believe that properly run, the factory could turn the corner. After all, other firms were making a profit from cocoa.

But for Joseph, who had a great eye for detail, there was much to vex him as he embarked upon a painstaking examination of his brother's accounts. Henry liked informality, and a number of irregular and unbusinesslike practices blossomed undisturbed in his factory. It seemed each room, each account book or order book, each pile of receipts offered a fatal flaw. Joseph was confronted by a parrot in the workroom and an obstinate donkey with a predilection for steam baths. The parrot distracted the workers, and the donkey failed to meet Joseph's exacting calculations for the firm's transport, stubbornly refusing to budge from the warmth of steam pipes that emerged from the factory walls. The donkey had to go—to be replaced with a much more versatile handcart.

As for the accounts, Joseph's detailed notebooks from that time reveal long columns as he tried to get to the bottom of debts to York Glass, York Gas, and even to staff, such as the saddler and the parcel delivery service. To resolve discrepancies in the accounts, Joseph was obliged to resort to hearsay to work out liabilities: "Beaumont says he *thinks* [underlined] Epps gave a 7% discount upon his lowest whole sale quotation." Henry's staff, as well as Henry, it was clear, were a trifle hazy when it came to the details of the deals they had made. Perhaps that was not surprising with staff that had been pared down to the bone. Seven workers managed the key processes of grinding, roasting, rubbing, and carrying sacks from the warehouse. There were definitely no spare funds to squander on something that Joseph viewed as disreputable as advertising.

As a small antidote to the Mad Hatter logic of the castle, Joseph Rowntree cast a discerning eye over the competition. Recognizing Cadbury's potential breakthrough with Cocoa Essence, he began to make discreet enquiries as to where he could purchase machinery to make a purer form of cocoa.

At Bridge Street, Richard and George Cadbury were beginning to find their wilderness years were behind them. "The first sign of upward movement," reported Thomas Little in the packing room, came from a traveller in the Black Country. "The weight of the goods had broken the springs of his van, and he had had to run it into a customer's cart house for repair and ride home on a horse." It was one of many clues that they were turning the corner. Skillful use of technology and advertising were winning customers. And once the Cadbury brothers knew what they were doing, the ideas kept coming. Records for the Birmingham patent office show that on November 3, 1869, they sealed a patent for one of the first kinds of chocolate biscuit: "A new improved description of biscuit manufactured from the cocoa bean," and the search was on for new forms of luxury products.

This amount of progress was not enough for George Cadbury. Seizing the initiative from his rivals, he went on the offensive to promote Cadbury's pure new cocoa. Aware of the public's growing sensitivity to food adulteration, he lobbied the government to take action. The addition of other substances made an inferior and less digestible form of cocoa, he argued, and the consuming public should know what they are buying. Eventually he was summoned to a government committee to give evidence. In a troubling move for his competitors, he insisted that only an absolutely pure product, such as Cadbury's Cocoa Essence, should be called "cocoa." All other preparations mixed with additional ingredients should be sold under a different name.

The Frys and other cocoa manufacturers woke up to the threat. They began to promote their cocoas, arguing that they only used nutritious additives. It was a bitter battle in which Cadbury benefited greatly from the free publicity, much of it at the hands of their rivals who were protesting the proposed new regulations and insisting that they added only the best ingredients.

The victory, however, went to George Cadbury. The government introduced the Adulteration of Food Acts in 1872 and 1875. Under the new legislation, all ingredients in cocoa had to be listed. The public could see for themselves that Cadbury's Cocoa Essence was the purist form of cocoa. Worse still, grocers who stocked adulterated cocoas without proper labelling could be prosecuted. Records show the Marylebone police prosecuted a Master Grocer by the name of Mr. Kirby of 212 High Street in Camden after he sold to the inspector two samples of cocoa that were adulterated: One "was manufactured by Messrs Taylor Bros . . . and the other by Messrs Dunn and Hewett and Co."

As sales of Cocoa Essence rocketed in the early 1870s, the number of employees at the Bridge Street works grew rapidly. For Richard and George, the view from their office windows formed a stark contrast to the view they had ten years earlier. Then an air of neglect was unmistakable surrounding the dying firm. Now, all was bustle and busyness and the applause of horses' hooves from the crowded courtyard, where carts and carriages waited to transport stock.

The early 1870s for the very upright Joseph Rowntree and his brother, Henry, were markedly different: They were still struggling to survive. Joseph meticulously pasted into his notebook some Cadbury's flyers that were full of exasperating claims: Cadbury's cocoa went "three times as far" as the best of the other adulterated cocoas and just one halfpenny will "secure a delicious cup of breakfast cocoa." But Joseph Rowntree was not in a position to take them on. Quite the reverse. He was having such a hard time that the passionate and indignant author of *Poverty in England and Wales* found that he was able to relax his Quakerly ideals—just a little. The Rowntrees needed a shortcut, a little know-how, some real expertise for turning the unlovely-looking cocoa bean into something deliciously edible in a charming package.

Joseph's private notebook reveals that in March 1872, he went to London to recruit new employees and did not see anything wrong in conducting a little industrial espionage at the same time. He leased an address in central London at 314 Camden Road and placed advertisements in the London papers, some in the vicinity of Taylor's Spitalfield works:

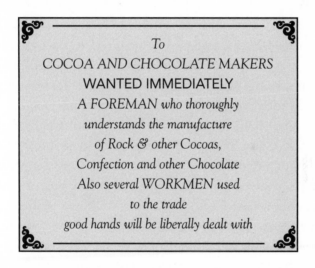

To
COCOA AND CHOCOLATE MAKERS
WANTED IMMEDIATELY
A FOREMAN *who thoroughly
understands the manufacture
of Rock & other Cocoas,
Confection and other Chocolate
Also several* WORKMEN *used
to the trade
good hands will be liberally dealt with*

Aware of the need for discretion, the Rowntree name did not appear on the advertisements. Applicants were advised to "Apply by letter only to: 'G.F., 12 Bishopsgate St EC.'"

Recording every exacting detail in his elegant longhand, Joseph Rowntree found that the Taylor brothers' employees were a willing mine of information. He soon received eager replies from a number of their employees such as the mixer and foreman, James French:

Gentlemen

In answer to an Advertisement in the Clerkenwell News, I beg leave most respectfully to offer my services as a Mixer, having been in Messrs Taylor Bros factory for Two years, and understand making

Rock Cocoa and others, but not Confection, wishing to better myself.

The favour of a reply will be immediately attended to by

Gentlemen

Your obedient servant

James French

Joseph Rowntree came to London to conduct interviews between March 7 and March 12. His records reveal that the interviews went far beyond discussions of the applicant's experience. Workers were willing to discuss every aspect of the Taylor brothers' business, details of manufacturing, and even precious recipes—for a sum. One of the first men Joseph hired was James French, who had his fare to York paid, was offered twenty shillings a week, and, most important, given a welcoming "present of 5 pounds" for his Taylor recipes.

James French introduced Rowntree to other workers, such as Robert Pearce of Whitechapel, who claimed to manufacture "all of Taylor's Chocolate, Chocolate Sticks, and Confection Chocolate." Pearce was also invited to come to the York factory during his three-week holiday, where he would receive two pounds a week "for imparting all his knowledge." Other successes followed. William Garrett, who had worked for twelve years at Taylors, received two shillings and six pence for, among other things, a recipe for Unsworth's Cream Cocoa. Rowntree learned about the technology used by the Taylor brothers from Henry Watkins, a man described as "the cleverest man on Taylor's Flake Floor," who could "take a mill to pieces and put it together again." And after meeting with James Mead of Taylor's Flake Floor, who received ten shillings, Rowntree was able to set out pages of detail covering Taylor's manufacturing processes. To prepare Rock Cocoa, Rowntree knew the exact order in which the Taylors added the ingredients, the ratios of different types of beans, and even the temperature of the mixer: "as hot as the hand can comfortably bear and sometimes [by accident] gets hotter." Equally important, he gleaned that Taylor's Rock Mills were made by a Thomas Neal and made an appointment to meet him.

Quietly, almost unnoticed, Taylor's men were relieved of valuable knowledge and years of exacting work judging different processes in the making of chocolate. All their labor and expertise was fed to, gobbled up, and digested by the dark, rather religious man with the worried look. Joseph Rowntree was, with a modest sum, the repository of enough information to duplicate key processes in Taylor's factory.

It seems that Rowntree was not overly troubled by his conscience, for in April, he was back for more information, before a brief trip to Germany, where he gathered price lists and technical information about companies such as the Stollwerck Brothers of Cologne. June 1872 brought the intrepid traveller back to London. In the interim, more advertisements appeared in local London papers, such as the following in the *Stoke Newington* press. Having gleaned all he could about Taylor's Rock Cocoa on his first visit, this time he wanted to learn more about Soluble Cocoa.

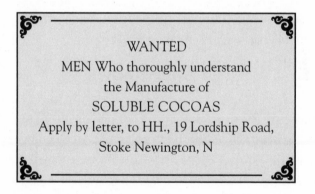

WANTED
MEN Who thoroughly understand
the Manufacture of
SOLUBLE COCOAS
Apply by letter, to HH., 19 Lordship Road,
Stoke Newington, N

Word was spreading. Henry Richard Thompson had been at the chocolate firm of Dunn and Hewitt in Pentonville for thirty years. Thompson was offered an opportunity "to come down for at least 4 weeks to teach all he knows, wages 2 pound per week. One pound to be allowed for each railway journey to York and a lump sum of 10 pounds to be given for the receipts and the knowledge."

Joseph Rowntree also decided to take a closer look at his Quaker rivals. He took the train to Bristol and met Fry's workers, including men such as J. Charles Hanks. Hanks claimed to have all of Fry's recipes. When he arrived in Birmingham, Joseph Rowntree was particularly keen to make contact with French workers involved in the manufacture of Cadbury's Fancy Box. Soon after, he went to Paris. The "object of this journey," he wrote, was to make enquiries of certain French chocolatiers, such as Emile Menier at Noisiel sur Marne.

It speaks volumes about the struggle to survive the intense competition that Joseph Rowntree, a man who in public epitomized Quaker virtue, a man whose principles led him to spurn advertising as dishonest, would engage in such subterfuge. Bribing workers to elicit his rivals' secrets fell far short of the ideals of honesty and plain dealing required of Quakers, but if he wrestled with his conscience, there is no record of it in his notes. Remarkably, even as he was engaged in this discreet espionage of his Quaker competitors, he also wrote to both Fry and Cadbury to suggest that they collaborate. He proposed that the Quaker firms unite on price and discounts to help them all deal with the foreign competition. Such unified action, he argued, would enable Quaker values to survive.

Meanwhile in Birmingham, the Cadbury brothers realized they were making headway. After the introduction of the new legislation, orders began pouring in for Cocoa Essence. It slowly dawned on them that the factory, for so long a millstone that imprisoned them in a rigid regime of work, was making a profit. The future need not be as spartan as the past.

Richard was ready for some warmth and charm in his life. He met and fell in love with Emma, the daughter of Mrs. Wilson, who ran the nursery. He bought the perfect home that backed onto the canal. "Every time I come into the house I think of you," he told Emma. "It seems like one real step to having you here, to have a home for you. . . . I have given you all my heart, and I have not much else to give you, but all that I have seems to belong to you quite as much as to me." They married in July 1871.

Even George, whose horizons had been so narrowed by work, fell under the hypnotic spell of their modest success. He met twenty-two-year-old Mary Tyler through his cousin, and a relationship soon developed. Ten years of ruthless self-denial and austerity made it hard for him to express his emotions. "A Spartan severity," writes his biographer, Alfred Gardiner, "was the key note and the senses were kept in rigorous and watchful restraint." The reserve of his letter of proposal contrasts with that of his brother: "I feel that thou dost love the Saviour," he wrote to his prospective fiancée. "And that if we were united together it would be in Him, and that thus united we should calmly, peacefully & joyously pass through life's journey."

Mary Tyler was so confused by George's formality and unromantic approach that she consulted her mother, who was equally baffled. "We are quite at a loss how to council thee. . . . It certainly struck us the letter was written without ardour, and in a businesslike manner," Mrs. Tyler replied to her daughter, "without even saying that he felt a strong preference for thee."

George may not have realized just how much his austerity and re-straint, which had served him so well in business, threatened this delicate opportunity. Mr. and Mrs. Tyler sensed that their daughter was unsure. "Are we not right in judging that thy feelings on the subject are a little doubtful and mingled?" inquired her mother. She went on, "If looking to the future thou feels pretty sure thou couldst not really enjoy his companionship in the very nearest of relations, why the best way is to send him a positive refusal."

Mary could not bring herself to this point. Later that summer, Mary's parents arranged to meet George for a short break in South-end. Away from the confines of the factory, George's feelings were more in evidence. Abandoning his ingrained sense of discipline and restraint, when he arrived in the town and found that Mary was not at the arranged meeting place, "He set off to run like a boy, running all the way to our lodgings," to find her. Over the following few days, the restrained and saintly George found a way to express his love, and Mary had a "sweet look of quiet joy."

The couple married in April 1872. An extensive honeymoon in Switzerland, France, and Rome was planned. For the first time in more than a decade, George abandoned the shackles of business for a tour of Europe with his young bride. As he boarded the train for departure to France, the world of the factory faded—but not by much.

PART
II

6

Chocolate That Could
Melt in the Mouth

VEVEY, SWITZERLAND, 1870s

Unknown to the Cadbury brothers, who at last appeared to have
success in their sights, two Swiss entrepreneurs were secretly working on a breakthrough so critical it would transform the destiny of
the "food of the gods." In doing so, they had the potential to destroy
the English manufacturers.

The legend began in a small way when a young entrepreneur, Daniel Peter, completed his apprenticeship with a candlemaker in Alsace
and came to the picturesque town of Vevey nestled in the Swiss Alps.
But his plan to set up shop as a candlemaker with his brother, Julian,
was overtaken by events. In the mid-nineteenth century, a method of
distilling kerosene from oil was found. This was swiftly followed by
the development of the kerosene lamp with a clean-burning light,
making the old flickering tallow candles and whale oil lamps of the
past obsolete. The future looked lighter and brighter, but not for a
candlemaker.

Daniel Peter continued to run the Frères Peter Candle Company
with his brother, but he also found time to pursue his keen interest
in the manufacture of food. With breakthroughs in food processing,
canned meat, pea soup, and bottled fruit were just some of the novelties being dished up by man and machine. The centuries-stale

ship's biscuit was being transformed into a miracle of standardized temptations; even condiments were getting a modern makeover. The days when convenience food tended to be soup or hot eels from a street vendor were over. "Without a doubt, industrial products intended as food offer manufacturers the best prospects for success," observed Peter. "These processed foods are consumed every day and unlike other products, there is a constant demand for them that is not subject to the whims of fashion."

Peter's opportunity to move into the food business proved to be right on his doorstep, when he fell in love with a local girl, Fanny Cailler, and married her in 1863. Her father had created a chocolate factory, the first in Switzerland to mechanize the process of grinding cocoa beans. For Daniel Peter, his father-in-law's chocolate business was an inspiration. The more he learned about cocoa, the more convinced he was that it had an exciting future. Cocoa, he predicted, would become a regular part of people's diet like coffee. Full of optimism, he set off to Lyon to work in a chocolate factory and master the exotic craft of the French chocolatier.

In 1867, the year that the Cadbury brothers' Cocoa Essence was taking off in Britain, thirty-one-year-old Peter returned to Vevey in Switzerland to start a chocolate business of his own. He and Fanny settled at 13 Rue des Bosquets, and next door at No. 12, he proudly attached his nameplate to his second company: Peter-Cailler et Compagnie. In this picturesque setting, nestled into the foothills of snowcapped mountains, he hoped to create the perfect chocolate.

According to one family story, it took a crisis to lead Peter to the breakthrough that would transform chocolate across the world. On September 30, Fanny gave birth to a baby daughter named Rose Georgina Peter, but there was a problem. Rose rejected her mother's breast milk. With each hour slipping by and their baby unable to feed, the young parents became distraught. Peter appealed for help from a neighbor, a trader who was something of a local celebrity. For the man he turned to was none other than the acclaimed German inventor Henry Nestlé.

Henri Nestlé looks out from his sepia Victorian photograph, his dark, slightly hooded eyes betraying an intensity and air of concentration. His thinning hair is neatly swept back from a broad forehead; the customary beard, a little unruly, the only hint of disorder. This imposing figure was known locally as a merchant, but he had real flair as a scientist and entrepreneur.

When Peter arrived on his doorstep looking for help, Henri Nestlé was on the verge of a life-changing advance. He had just begun selling a special type of "milk flour" for babies, using his own formula for creating powdered milk. Peter and his wife were desperate for baby Rose to try Nestlé's special formula.

Born in Frankfurt in 1814, Heinrich Nestlé left Germany as a young man to travel, and like Peter, he chose to settle by the beautiful shores of Lake Geneva in Vevey. Changing his name to Henri Nestlé, he rapidly demonstrated his versatility as an entrepreneur, a maverick, and a scientist. Quite apart from his trade as a druggist, selling medicines, seeds, and mustard, his interest in oil lamps flourished into a business for the manufacture of liquid gas. His small company lit a dozen or so of the gas lamps in Vevey and also manufactured fertilizer. Like Peter, Henri Nestlé was intrigued by developments in food manufacture, and by 1847, he had begun to research infant feeding. This was an era still plagued by infant mortality. In Switzerland, one in five babies died before their first birthday. The challenge for Henri Nestlé was to create a new type of food for babies whose mothers were unable to breast-feed.

Since milk turned rancid so quickly, the puzzle was how to keep milk fresh. Using his own kitchen as a laboratory, Nestlé experimented with different ways of preserving whole milk. By 1866 he had a solution. He found a way to create a milk powder concentrated by an air pump at low temperature that he believed was as "fresh and wholesome" as Swiss milk "straight from the cow's udder." To this he added a cereal, "baked by a special process of my invention," to create a unique formula he called *farine lactée*.

By chance in September 1867, Henri Nestlé was approached by a friend who was treating a premature baby boy. The baby was convulsive and could not breast-feed or keep down any alternative; his

mother was very ill as well. After fifteen days, the baby's survival
hung in the balance, but to the family's delight, they discovered that
he was able to digest Nestlé's formula. News of this "miracle" spread
across town.

It was an anxious moment when Daniel and Fanny Peter tried to
coax baby Rose to drink Henry Nestlé's formula. The baby was fret-
ful, hungry but unable to keep food down. After a few moments
came the sounds the distraught parents had so longed to hear: normal suckling from a contented baby. The milk lived up to its promise. Rose recovered and began to put on weight.

Doctors tested the product and reached the same result. Mothers
began to ask for it. Despite sceptics who insisted it was no more than
a "sack of flour," Nestlé was full of confidence in his new invention.
"My discovery has tremendous value," he declared, "for there is not
another food comparable to my baby food." In 1868 after successful
launches in Vevey and Lausanne in Switzerland and his hometown
of Frankfurt, demand continued to rise. Certain of success, he dispatched a sales team in France and ventured to England to open an
office in London. "Believe me it's no small matter to market an invention in four countries simultaneously," he said. He installed a
large new vacuum pump and was able to manufacture more than
a half-ton of dried infant milk a day. Even with the outbreak of the
Franco-Prussian War in July 1870, which made it harder to move
goods around Europe, the company's growth seemed unstoppable.

Through his friendship with Henry Nestlé, Daniel Peter began to
see an opportunity. It occurred to him that his chocolate products and
Henri Nestlé's technology for creating powdered milk might be combined to create a creamy milk chocolate drink. After all, people were
accustomed to mixing cocoa powder with milk or water to make a
beverage. So why not mix the two directly to form a ready-made milk
chocolate powder. And why stop at a drink? If milk and chocolate
could be combined into a solid tablet or bar, it would be far sweeter
and smoother than the slightly bitter dark chocolates on the market.

From his small warehouse by the lakeside, Daniel Peter experimented with adding Nestlé's dried milk to cocoa and sugar. After his

initial optimism, he hit upon a problem. When cocoa was combined with Nestlé's milk powder, the resulting drink was coarse and grainy. Yet when he processed the milk himself, the water in the milk did not blend well with the oil in the cocoa bean. In addition, the water reacted with the sugar to alter the texture. He had to find a way to dry the milk without spoiling it.

Peter became obsessed with the challenge. His plant was open round the clock; he made his dark chocolate confections during the day, and at night he experimented with different ratios of milk powder and cocoa powder. Friends told him it was impossible. The water in the milk would never mix with the fat in the cocoa bean. He could afford only one member of staff, apart from his wife. Using very basic water-powered machines, he tried every variation of evaporating the water from the milk before blending it with the chocolate. At one stage he thought he had succeeded. "I was happy," he said later, "but a few weeks later as I examined the contents an odor of bad cheese or rancid butter came to my nose. I was desperate, but what was I to do?" Whether using milk or milk powder, the chocolate was a gritty, gravely pulp, best consumed quickly before it turned rancid. "I did not lose courage," he said, "but continued to work as long as circumstances allowed."

Meanwhile, Henri Nestlé's company continued to grow. By 1871 around 1,000 yellow cans rolled off his production line each day. Three years later, the number had risen to half a million cans of infant cereal a year that were being sold on five continents. With all the problems of manufacture, distribution, shipping, and sales, managing the firm was becoming too demanding for Nestlé, who was approaching sixty. In 1875 he sold his company for one million Swiss francs to a Swiss businessman, who bought everything, including the rights to Nestlé's name. One of the witnesses to the sale was Henri's friend and neighbor, Daniel Peter.

Henri Nestlé understood the difficulties of managing the production of milk products in bulk and advised his struggling friend to approach his leading competitor, the Anglo Swiss Condensed Milk Company, which had found a way to mass-produce condensed milk.

If Peter started with condensed milk, there would be less water to evaporate, and it might prove easier to remove the excess with the technology he had.

Peter set out to meet with the managers at Anglo Swiss. It appears that he was reluctant to reveal too much of his new idea. He was making "a new product for which I am sure there will soon exist great demand," he said, adding that it was in their mutual interest for him "to order the milk I need from you." But when he repeated his experiments, adding condensed milk to the cocoa powder, sugar, and cocoa butter, the result, although improved, was still not reliable. So Peter created a special "drying room," where the milk and chocolate mixture was turned into flakes, spread on trays, and heated still further. Finally, in 1875, he hit upon a formula that produced a silky smooth chocolate. It was the world's first ready-made milk chocolate drink, and he called it Chocolats au Lait Gala Peter.

The latter part of the nineteenth century was the heyday of English tourism in Switzerland. It was common practice for the wealthy to send their daughters to Swiss finishing schools or to take a tour of the Alps for the spectacular scenery. One English grocer who made his way to Vevey was so struck by the new product that he placed an order for one hundred pounds of milk chocolate to try back home. Vevey was also on the route of the Orient Express. Soon Peter's invention, in its colorful copper wrapper, was making its way east.

Daniel Peter seized every opportunity to promote his new product. In 1878 he took his invention to the International Exhibition in Paris, organized to celebrate France's recovery after the Franco-Prussian War. The largest exhibition ever held, it attracted 13 million visitors over several months, many of them from across the Channel. A world of wonders awaited inspection, including strange novelties like Graham Bell's telephone and Thomas Edison's megaphone. Among such feats of ingenuity was Le Premier des Chocolats au Lait, the new chocolate drink emblazoned with a gratifying Silver Award. Daniel Peter had arrived.

Better still, the English loved his milk chocolate, allowing Peter to dream of a secure future. "If a town of 8,000 inhabitants can consume more than 100 pounds in a year," he calculated, "then the six million inhabitants of London could easily consume 40 tons." Full of enthusiasm, the inventor of milk chocolate set off to England. He wanted to challenge the Quaker firms and their pure dark cocoas with his sweeter, milkier brand. And why stop there? Was there a future, he wondered, in turning his novelty drink into a solid form for enjoyment as a milk chocolate bar?

BERNE, SWITZERLAND, 1870s

Peter's breakthrough milk chocolate drink was swiftly followed by another Swiss technical advance. One hundred kilometers from Vevey, in the town of Berne, was a small water mill run by an aspiring chocolatier named Rodolphe Lindt. Lindt had trained as a confectioner and was keen to try his hand at creating chocolate.

According to one probably apocryphal story, Rodolphe Lindt, the gentleman entrepreneur, had a greater appreciation for the pleasures of life than dedicating himself to the hard disciplines of business. On one occasion, he left for his weekend entertainment in such a hurry, he failed to stop his roller grinder. Consequently the roller pressed the beans for a full three days.

On Monday morning, when he entered his factory, he found that the resulting mixture, far from being ruined, was silken and smooth. Pounded and churned to an exquisitely fine texture, the result was an irresistible velvety chocolate rich with subtle aromas. Whether Lindt's famous recipe really had its origins in a happy accident is not known, but there is no doubt that the bon vivant was soon experimenting with a unique method of preparing chocolate.

After consultations with his brother, August, a pharmacist, he tried variations in temperature and timing to see which yielded the best results and enabled him to fold extra cocoa butter into the mix. Cocoa butter, unlike other fats, melts at body temperature. After several days, folding in as much cocoa butter as possible, Lindt found he had a rich velvet chocolate that could melt in the mouth. Encouraged by the possibilities, he developed a special machine that he called a conch, due to its shell-like shape. It was a wrought-iron trough, firmly embedded in a granite base, with sides that curved inwards to prevent spills. A heavy granite roller attached to a steel arm passed repeatedly back and forth over the chocolate paste. As the chocolate slapped against the sides of the trough and over the granite rollers that drew air into the mix, it became lighter, airier, finer, and more liquid. After three days of "conching," Lindt found still more cocoa butter could be folded into the mix, making the chocolate silky smooth. He proudly called it his *Chocolat Fondant.*

Another benefit of conching was that it facilitated the manufacturing process. Rather than creating a solid dough that was hard to press into the molds, Lindt could simply pour his liquid chocolate into molds to set. A dark chocolate bar was no longer a gritty and toffee-like substance that just might break your teeth. The news spread fast among the genteel ladies in the nearby finishing schools at Berne and Neuchâtel, who sampled the results of his experiments, Rodolphe Lindt's fondant "could melt in the mouth."

Surprisingly, Lindt was in no hurry to exploit his chocolate speciality. Without a sales team, he relied on word of mouth to promote his product, and local connoisseurs were eager to test this new sensory delight. Across town in Berne, Jean Tobler was impressed with Lindt's chocolate and tried to create something similar for his own shop, the *Confiserie Speciale.* It proved hard to fathom the key to Lindt's success, so Tobler approached him directly in the hopes of joining forces. News of the breakthrough spread to other Swiss chocolate entrepreneurs, such as Philippe Suchard, who had opened sweetshops in Serrières, Lörrach, and Neuchâtel. The Sprüngli family, owners of a successful chocolate business in Zurich, were equally amazed at the quality of chocolate produced by such a novice. All the Swiss firms were keen to crack his formula.

But Rodolphe Lindt was so determined to safeguard the secrets of his unique conching process that he installed his new technology in a separate building. The machinery was protected as though it were the Crown Jewels. The key that guarded it was guarded itself. The fabled recipe that had apparently come into being by a careless accident was firmly locked in the mind of Rodolphe Lindt.

Switzerland was fast establishing a reputation as the land of chocolate. Both Rodolphe Lindt and Daniel Peter had created recipes that set them apart. Recipes so mouthwatering they could destroy a rival—not just in Switzerland but across the continent. And after several trips to England, Peter had no doubt that there was an appreciative foreign market waiting for his wonderful new milk chocolate invention—especially in Britain's booming industrial cities.

CHAPTER
7

Machinery Creates
Wealth but Destroys Men

BIRMINGHAM, ENGLAND, 1870s

In England, George Cadbury, like his older brother, Richard, was more focused on his ideals than the competition. He loathed the fast-growing slums and the dark and ugly spread of industrialization over unspoiled countryside. Why, he asked, should progress and the "triumph of machinery" lead to a reduction in quality of life? "Machinery," he declared, "creates wealth but destroys men."

George and Richard saw the mean slum dwellings as a cause of workers' continuing misery, driving them to drink to escape the squalor of their lives. They saw the very worst of it in Birmingham firsthand through their work for the Adult School movement. Before the Education Act of 1870, there was no compulsory elementary education, and the vast majority of adults in the slums were illiterate. The aim of the Adult Schools was to help them learn to read and write.

Every Sunday from the age of twenty, George rose early to ride to one of the roughest districts at Severn Street to meet the other teachers before school started at 7:00 AM. The dedication of his fellow teachers proved an inspiration. The former mayor of Birmingham and a Quaker, William White, taught every week at the Adult School until his death at the age of eighty. On one occasion, George learned that seventy-five-year-old William White had walked "a mile and half through untrodden drifts of snow up to two feet depth" to get to his class on time.

The pupils were equally inspiring. They emerged from the slums, the drinking houses, even the prison gate. Any absentees were invariably routed out by a party of former thieves and drunks who knew their way around the vicious gangland of dark alleys and hovels in the slums. From a life of rags and filth and poverty, they came to learn and to escape the badge of failure and desperation that went with illiteracy. George's class size swelled to three hundred students, and he taught more than 4,000 men over a period of fifty years.

For those who stayed the course, there were rewards. One woman rose during George's lesson and declared she had had "more happiness in the one year since her husband joined the class than she had had in the twenty-nine years of her married life before." This kind of experience fuelled George's conviction that the best way to improve a man's lot is to raise his ideals. But how, he reasoned, "can a man cultivate ideals when his home is a slum and his only place of recreation is a public house?" George and Richard knew that the adults in their classes were tyrannized by "the sweater, the rack renter and the publican"—the unscrupulous employers of sweated labor, overcharging landlords, and managers of public houses who exploited people's addictions and helped to drive them to ruin. Their outspoken opposition to these groups made them enemies. "It is unreasonable," George declared at a meeting in Manchester, "to expect a man to lead a healthy, holy life in a back street or a sunless slum." Was it necessary, he continued, that the factory system should "narrow the lives" of the workers to such an extent, "belittling and oppressing" them with hideous conditions of life? But since it was clear that the factory system was there to stay, secured by the country's growing prosperity, what was the solution?

The idea of social welfare and reform was still in its infancy. Apart from the dreaded workhouses, there was little means of support. It was survive or die. Victorians managed to turn a blind eye to the full horror of poverty on their doorstep, until writers like Charles

Dickens forced them to look. Driven by his own experiences as a child in a blacking factory, he reinforced the message that poverty causes misery through stories such as the parish child, Oliver Twist: "the humble, half-starved drudge, to be cuffed and buffeted through the world, despised by all and pitied by none." Dickens believed passionately that "the reform of habitations of the people must precede all other reforms, and that without it all other reforms must fail."

In a Cadbury photo album from the period, after pages of neatly displayed sepia pictures of family members, there are images of influential thinkers of the day, doubtless used as a talking point for visitors. Included in these photos, besides Charles Dickens, Charles Darwin, and Thomas Carlyle, is the author and artist John Ruskin. At a time when many believed that it was an individual's own fault if he were poor and that the poor were in some way to blame for their circumstances, Ruskin was one of the first to question the role of the economy in perpetuating the deprivations of the poor. In a series of powerful essays, *Unto This Last*, which appeared in the *Cornhill* magazine in 1860, Ruskin was so critical of capitalist economics that the magazine was forced to stop publication.

Ruskin argued for an ethical approach to economic transactions and pointed out that with wealth comes a moral obligation. A profit, he wrote, is legitimate only if it can be achieved without harming the greater good of society. His beliefs that every laborer should have a wage on which he can live, that all children are entitled to an education, and that land should be used to benefit everyone and not just the wealthy were considered subversive and outlandish.

Ruskin's political and economic thinking coincided with George and Richard's Quaker sensibilities. Their unshakeable faith meant that all issues shrank to nothing compared with the choice between "living for things of the spirit, or for things that perish." The idea of material success for its own sake was abhorrent. They were determined to use their growing business in a way that was compatible with "enlarging the riches of human experience."

Full of idealism, George and Richard began to discuss ways in which they might actually do something practical to test out factory reform. Did a factory have to be located in a slum? How could they raise men's ideals and help them improve their lot? How could they assist women and children break the cycle of poverty? In the late 1870s, the brothers began to nurture an idea. They could move the factory outside of Birmingham and create "a factory in a garden," where there was space, where the air was pure, and the sky hung a new shade of blue every day as though the world were born anew. It would be a model factory with "perfect friendliness among all." Through nature, through a garden city, they would lead their workers to the "celestial city." They would build this New Jerusalem in England's green and pleasant land.

Critics scoffed at the idea of altruism applied to a commercial enterprise. It was a "wild adventure" that highlighted the "rashness and folly" of the Cadbury brothers and would "end in disaster." Factories belonged in towns, and the very idea that fresh air could be relevant to a business venture revealed that the brothers were "no more than fanatics." The Cadburys' stated wish that they wanted staff to find work "less irksome by environing them with pleasant and wholesome sights, sounds and conditions" was derided. Whoever heard of "pleasant and wholesome sights" making money? Surely these men of God would soon be bankrupt.

The brothers did not listen to their critics. Each Sunday on their day off, Richard and George walked along the railway lines out from Birmingham, looking for the perfect new site. They knew these roads of iron were essential to their new venture. In barely a generation, more than 10,000 miles of track had crisscrossed the country, the roaring steam engines shrinking space. By the spring of 1878, they found what they were after, about four miles southwest of Birmingham, nestled between the villages of Stirchley, Kings Norton, and Selly Oak. An unspoiled fifteen-acre meadow set in the heart of a rural landscape.

From Stirchley Street Station, they approached the land down a quiet country lane, Oak Lane (now Bournville Lane). From this muddy track, they found the fields for sale bordered on the east by the Worcester and Birmingham Canal and a branch of the newly opened Midland Railway. To the north, flowing through a buttercup meadow, was a trout stream, which gave the site its name, Bournbrook. As

George and Richard viewed this country idyll in the full blossoming of spring, their ideas began to take tangible form. Ignoring their detractors, the brothers deemed the situation "unequalled." Their factory, they said, would be "replete with every adjunct requisite for carrying out a growing business." Here in this rural haven they would build a factory on the part of the land nearest to the station; it would be a factory that considered the needs of the workforce, rather than merely exploiting them.

On June 18, 1878, the Cadbury brothers bought the land at an auction. William Higgins, a crème tablet worker at Bridge Street, could remember the day he heard the "the incredible news" that they were moving to the country. "Hope sprang up in the hearts of everyone," he declared. Both brothers now had young families who were equally thrilled at the prospect. George eagerly brought his wife, Mary, and their young sons to the site in the works' horse-drawn van. Six-year-old Edward took boyish glee in the great quantities of mud and the mountainous piles of bricks. Family visits to the construction site made such an impression that years later he could still picture his father riding on horseback along the country lanes, their temporary rooms at a nearby farm, and his newborn brother, George Junior, who slept through the fun in his pram.

Richard's sons, Barrow and William, would later remember being taken to bare fields near Stirchley and instructed to "dig holes with our spades so that the subsoil could be inspected." Eleven-year-old William, who was far more excited to find a stream full of trout, proudly recalled that he broke the first ground for the beginning of the factory. Sixteen-year-old Barrow, who was studying mechanical drawing in Manchester, was keen to show that he could help his Uncle George with preliminary sketches for the designs: the roasting room, grinding mills, saw mills, engine rooms, the packing room, and chocolate room leading to the railway. As for grandfather John Cadbury, now in his eighties and looking not a little formidable in a black top hat and dark cloak, with Victorian-style mutton-chop whiskers completely white, he made his way slowly around the site with his walking stick. It was satisfying to see his two sons embarking on such a promising venture and his grandchildren playing in the fields.

George and Richard were determined not to allow costs to escalate and sink them into debt. They hired and managed their own building teams supported by a young local architect, George Gadd. A nearby Quaker firm, the Tangyes Brothers in Smethwick, offered practical help in the form of their foreman bricklayer. The Tangyes Brothers were also on hand to help with the engineering design. But no one could help with the weather. The first brick was laid in January 1879, and building started in earnest in March. But constant, drenching rain reduced the clay site to a dangerous quagmire of mud. "The horses that were moving the soil were half buried in clay," recorded the *Bournville Works* magazine. "Two or three of them broke their legs struggling to get out of it." The word went out that the brothers had come unstuck already. They would never finish on time. George, out-fitted in special long boots, would not be stopped by the rain. He supervised the works at first light and returned at nightfall after spending a full day at Bridge Street.

William Higgins was just one member of the Bridge Street staff who regularly trudged the four miles to watch the progress, whatever the weather. "So eager were the Bridge Street hands to get out here and our journeys so frequent," he said, "that we could almost tell how many bricks were laid weekly." It took 2 million bricks before the new "fairyland factory," as Richard's son Barrow called it, was close to completion. In just six months the brothers were able to close parts of the Bridge Street factory. They gave the female staff members a seven-week holiday while they transferred machinery by canal to the heart of the Bournbrook estate. Perhaps with a shrewd eye to fu-ture marketing, some bright spark suggested changing the name of the new site at the last minute from Bournbrook to Bournville, lend-ing it a French flavor when French chocolate was so highly admired.

By September, Richard escorted the first party of female staff to see the completed works. According to his daughter Helen, he bought train tickets from the center of Birmingham to Stirchley Street Sta-tion, "like a father of a family taking his children out for an excur-sion." As they drew near the station, everyone was "in a state of happy flutter and excitement," as Richard eagerly pointed out landmarks. The party stepped down from the train, momentarily halted by the enveloping silence of the country before taking their first glimpse of what their new life would be like.

They picked their way down the muddy country lane. Bournville was one storey high to avoid having to carry goods upstairs, Richard explained, and the property stretched over three acres. He and George had personally supervised the layout of the land around the factory. The coach house, stables, and smithy were already complete. Beyond the works, a large field was set aside for men's cricket and football. There was a garden for the women, complete with swings and seats and plans for shady pathways and "other contrivances for outdoor enjoyment." To the west, work was underway to build sixteen semidetached cottages for key members of the staff. The plots allocated for each one were spacious, with front and back gardens large enough for their owners to grow vegetables. Behind the houses, an orchard was being planted with 150 apple, plum, pear, and cherry trees. In the further fields, where the River Bourn widened naturally into a pool, the brothers had plans to create an open-air swimming bath for the men.

Stepping inside, the new chocolate works were unlike anything the women had seen before. Gone were the cramped conditions of Bridge Street, with its awkward passageways, dark corners, and steamed-up windows. The factory in the field was a revelation: a temple to space and light and order. There would be no more heavy lifting and carrying; it seemed invisible hands did half the work. A series of tramways were laid throughout to move goods effortlessly from room to room. It was lit mainly from skylights in the roof, although there were no windows in the southern wall to prevent the room from becoming too warm in the summer. With mounting excitement, the staff explored a series of airy, large rooms, the sound of their footsteps echoing in the cavernous space.

The roasting room was already in operation: a modern marvel where nine large cylinders driven by steam power rotated the beans over a coke fire. In the spacious milling room, a wonderfully scented creamy chocolate liquid emerged from heated granite millstones lining one side of the room. The packing room had "a most ingenious American appliance," which could weigh and fill 20,000 packets of Cocoa Essence a day. The box-making department, also mechanical, cut board into the required shape and glued the various parts together: Two machines could make 12,000 packets daily. The chocolate-making department turned out delectable little chocolate treats that proceeded in an orderly fashion on long conveyer belts to their appropriate box carrying a picture of a girl and her kitten.

Finally the wide-eyed staff entered what was called "the general girls room." Cathedral-like in its proportions, this vast auditorium of 240 square feet of pure white space was dedicated to packing the Fancy Boxes. Here the young ladies would be faced with nothing more tedious than guiding the scrumptious chocolate mouthfuls into their preselected boxes. Beyond the Fancy Box room were kitchens with the latest equipment designed to provide meals for the staff in minutes. Yet more thoughtfulness came in the form of warm changing rooms, should the weather prove inclement.

Richard and George had separate offices, their wood-panelled rooms joined by a private corridor. They planted a rose garden outside their offices, and beyond the gardens, the views opened onto a rural horizon. They were certain that they had made the right decision in building Bournville. Fired with renewed enthusiasm, they began promoting staff. After just five years, William Tallis, taken in as an orphan, was appointed works foreman, and his office was right next to Richard and George's. Although Tallis had almost no education, "he had natural abilities," observed one member of staff, "which enabled him to rise from the ranks and take the responsible position." The versatile Tallis could turn his hand to anything; one minute tackling an engineering problem, the next driving the works pair-horse van with goods to the station. He even delighted the owners' sons "by instructing us how to fish for the trout in Bournbrook stream," recalled Edward. Other members of staff who received promotions included seventeen-year-old Edward Thackray, who had been in the firm for just three years. Once promoted, Thackray learned from George how to purchase cocoa in the London auctions.

But for all the enthusiasm surrounding their country retreat, nature could be unkind to the new residents. The early autumn brought a plague of wasps despite concerted efforts to destroy all of their nests in the district. This was followed by a winter so bitterly cold and wet that it tested everyone's resolve and uncovered unwelcome anomalies in the factory's heating system; some areas were too hot while others were icy cold. One employee recalled his surprise to see "Mr Richard or Mr George go down on their knees crawling under the tables to see if the water pipes were hot enough." The brothers' fatherly interest, he added, "made a great impression on us." On wet days, George used to check with the forewomen in each department to make sure that all girls in their charge had changed into dry shoes. There was, however, an unexpected benefit from the icy weather. The two pools in the neighboring estate of Bournbrook Hall froze over completely. The Martin family who owned them permitted the Cadbury brothers and their staff to skate there. "Skating is associated in the minds of many with the first year here," recalled one worker.

The damp and the cold were not the only difficulties. Orders picked up before Christmas, and George and Richard "were at their wits end to know how to execute them," said chocolate worker Fanny Price. Eventually they decided there was no alternative but to add an early shift starting at six in the morning. Although George had negotiated special rates with the railway company for workers' fares to Stirchley Street Station, the company refused to provide an early train. Many staff on the early shift walked out from Birmingham across fields and muddy lanes in the dark—some rising as early as 4:00 AM to be sure to arrive at work on time.

As the critics had predicted, getting home was also a problem. At the time, the station was just an open platform with no shelter. Fanny Price recalled a unique system the brothers adopted to prevent the ladies from getting wet. The staff waited under a temporary shelter near the old station lodge. "Mr Richard used to blow whistle to intimate that the train was coming," she said, having waited in all weathers by the signal. For those unable to catch the last train, getting wet was the least of their worries. Crème room worker Bertha Fackrell remembered "rough times" that winter. The women walked through quagmires in the pitch dark "in twos and threes, arm in arm, groping our way along." There were no street lamps for much of the route to Birmingham. These difficulties "were remedied as soon as possible," Bertha said. A foreman with a lantern sometimes escorted the women home. Once the works' cottages were complete, the brothers set up impromptu sleeping arrangements with bedding and pillows for more than twenty girls. Rooms were also found in the surrounding villages. "We were all very happy," concluded Bertha, "for everything that thoughtful kindness could do for our comfort was done."

Despite his kindness, however, Richard occasionally had a hot temper, "which was a natural part of his energetic nature," said his daughter Helen. Although no one was "more alive than himself to this weakness," Helen insisted, flashes of anger could break through in testing times. In the early days of Bournville, her father took to wearing a jaunty little black cap. For some reason this became "a well known weather vane through all the works as to whether things were going right or not." If the cap was placed correctly on his head, "Everyone knew that things were going smoothly and well." But if the cap was hurriedly tucked under his arm, "It was a sure sign that something was brewing." Worst of all, said Helen, "was if it was being screwed and twisted in its owner's hands."

And there was plenty of cause for the cap to be wrung dry during the early days of Bournville. Apart from the expected teething troubles of installing new machinery and managing the transition, the sheer altruism of the two brothers could present problems. Since they managed their own building program, local slum builders had no chance to benefit from the large venture. Their plans to introduce a temperance zone around the works also cut out prospective pub owners. But what really fuelled the ire of Birmingham's slum landlords and publicans were the brothers' continued efforts to help people living in the inner-city slums through the Adult School. When George received a summons from a local policeman while on his way to the Adult School, many at Bournville believed the policeman was in league with local rack renters. George's offence was no more than to lead his horse on to an empty footpath because the frost made the road treacherous. In due course, the policeman was himself linked to serious crime and imprisoned, and it was easy to connect the two events.

George was keen to push through another huge gamble, which doubtless was the cause of much cap wringing. Although their adulterated cocoas were still making money, they cancelled some of their most popular lines, such as Homeopathic, Pearl, and Breakfast. They were handing their rivals a huge advantage. But George was clear: He wanted the Cadbury name to stand for quality. The debate about purity triggered by Cocoa Essence showed no signs of slowing. But by cancelling strong-selling lines, would he have enough orders to support his cavernous new factory? The skeptics saw it as another irresponsible step.

And there was still the issue of the factory itself. No amount of altruism and good intentions could get around the fact that there was nothing quite like Bournville in England and no evidence that it would work. Cynics and skeptics alike watched the bold experiment in quality, fresh air, and wholesome living, waiting for any sign of failure. Most thought it was only a matter of time.

BRISTOL, ENGLAND, 1870s

In Bristol, with Francis Fry and his brothers at the helm, Fry's business continued to prosper. They adopted a different approach to expansion and saw no need for the radical innovation of their Birmingham rivals. As they outgrew their sprawling premises in Union Street, rather than gamble on the huge investment of a brand new factory, they chose to expand piecemeal, acquiring outlying premises, often at some distance from the main factories in Union Street. Little by little, they acquired some twenty-four separate buildings of varying suitability, and chocolate goods in varying stages of manufacture were taken by horse-drawn vans from site to site through the busy, narrow streets of Bristol.

Francis Fry's team also saw no rush to find an answer to Cadbury's pure Cocoa Essence. Cadbury's invention had made it possible for the public to create a chocolate drink at home as easily as tea, but the Frys followed suit at a leisurely pace. Two years elapsed before they installed Van Houten presses. When they finally launched their pure new product, Fry's Cocoa Extract, they failed to see the need to promote it heavily. It was only when Cadbury's Cocoa Essence was outselling Fry's brands, which had been established over generations, that Fry's board began to ponder how they might seize the initiative in the adulteration debate. As the Cadburys were moving into Bournville and taking the bold step of eliminating their adulterated cocoas to focus their efforts on one superior brand, the Frys were still making almost fifty different types of cocoa, all of which had to be transported at least a mile to various premises during its manufacture.

Taking advantage of the docks at Bristol, Fry excelled at overseas expansion. There is evidence that Fry sent a traveller to Johannesburg in southern Africa as early as 1800. Fry's chocolate tins reached Queen Victoria's troops during the Crimean War during the mid-1800s. The Navy found that Fry's brands, without the benefit of the defatting machine, fitted their requirements perfectly. They were easy to transport, filling and nutritious, and worthy accompaniments to the ship's biscuit. Fry had long-established trading links between Bristol and Ireland. And the company pioneered sales in Britain's fast-growing empire.

In 1867 the British North America Act established Canada's role as a dominion within the British Empire. This same act also made provision for the Intercolonial Railway in Canada, which would make rail connections possible from the eastern port of Halifax on the Atlantic coast inland to the St. Lawrence River. From here goods could reach the vast interiors of the North American continent via the grand highway of the Great Lakes. This unknown territory was finally opening up. Francis Fry hired agents to investigate.

He learned that there was little in terms of chocolate production in Canada in the 1870s. Local, family-run confection businesses were producing penny candy in glass jars and earning barely $3 million a year between them. With Canadian grocers willing to try Fry's products, they began to ship goods from Bristol across the Atlantic. From Medicine Hat to Moose Jaw, Grand Falls to Niagara Falls, bright yellow tins of Fry's Breakfast Cocoa waved the flag for English manufactured chocolate goods. For British immigrants and loyalists, it brought great comfort during the bitter Canadian winters.

For the Fry management team leading this change, "the Fry spirit," built on centuries of Quaker values, remained all-important. Concern for their workers' welfare was paramount. Unlike Bournville, they had no space around the factories to provide recreation grounds, but their wages were generous compared to many local firms, and they organized choral and dramatic societies and clubs to provide games, libraries, and night-school teachers. Although Francis Fry continued his work for the community, his religious convictions took a more esoteric form compared with his Quaker counterparts in Birmingham. Gradually, "as the years rolled by and his business cares devolved on others," wrote his son Theodore, he dedicated himself to his consuming passion to understand different versions of the Bible. This interest went well beyond that of an antiquarian, observed Theodore, for the Bible was his father's "daily companion" in a "far higher sense." His belief in it "as the revealed will and love of God to man was bright and strong." Francis's long-nurtured dream was to understand the most faithful version of the actual "word" of God.

As Francis Fry's reputation as a biblical scholar spread, his correspondence mounted. He was in touch with an ever-expanding list of like-minded collectors. One day a copy of the *Codex Sinaiticus* arrived from the Russian czar, Emperor Alexander II. This fourth-century Greek manuscript, containing the earliest complete version of the New Testament, had been found at the Monastery of Saint Catherine on Mount Sinai and leaves were removed for publication during the 1840s and 50s. Francis Fry was "so gratified" to have such a precious tome to study that he thanked the czar with a complete set of all his biblical works.

Fry's efforts to trace early English translations of the Bible threw up some puzzling findings. His quest to track down the original "Great Bible" produced in 1539 by the archbishop of Canterbury, Thomas Cranmer, was thwarted by the fact that King Henry VIII had ordered 21,000 copies, one for every church in England. Despite his attempts to track down the master version, Francis Fry found "copies bearing the same date differed from each other in various parts," according to Theodore. He located 146 copies, and sometimes "as many as forty lay open on the table at one time," continued his son. No one "so critically examined them, or recorded his labours with such exactness." Watermarks and even "all such differences in spelling" were carefully recorded. In Matthew 10, line 38, "saying" could also be "sayige," "sayinge," "saying," "sayenge," and "sayig." In his forensic quest to find the true word of the Lord, Francis Fry's collection of 1,300 Bibles and testaments rapidly became one of the best in the world. It is perhaps hardly surprising, given where his energies were focused, that Francis Fry gave scant attention to the swiftly moving chocolate market.

Around the time that the Cadbury brothers moved to Bournville, both of Francis Fry's brothers died. In 1878, Francis retired and followed the custom of promoting to chairman the oldest son from the next generation—in this case, his nephew, Joseph Storrs Fry II. This Joseph was cut from the same cloth as his Uncle Francis. Shy and introverted, he did not marry and dedicated himself almost exclusively to the chocolate business and the Society of Friends.

As a child, Joseph Storrs Fry II had been mocked at school for his plain Quaker dress, an experience that did not appear to shake his adherence to the strict rules and values of the Society. Like his uncle, he was keen to keep Quaker tradition at the center of the business, and his daily routine was, in the words of a relative, "extraordinarily conservative." Rather than strike out in a bold new direction, he obligingly followed his uncle on many issues.

So the chocolate factory continued to operate in various sprawling buildings across town, irrespective of their suitability. The packing department moved to an old Baptist chapel. Numerous other departments jockeyed alongside each other for space. Although new products were produced, there were no notable innovations. The Bible study and hymn singing continued. Joseph Storrs Fry II was a keen champion of causes such as the Bristol City Mission and the campaign for the suppression of opium traffic. According to Fry company records, "his charitable gifts were almost numberless." Like his uncle, he was an enthusiastic follower of the British and Foreign Bible Society. And also like his uncle, he remained convinced there was no need for change.

YORK, ENGLAND, 1870s

While the House of Fry sailed blithely through the swiftly changing markets of the late-nineteenth century, and the Cadbury brothers embarked on a series of calculated risks, Joseph Rowntree in York struggled to keep his business afloat. In the 1870s his product list included all manner of delicious temptations, including Shilling Cocoa, Shield Chocolate, Chocolate Drops, the irresistible Half Penny Balls, and other more wholesome foodstuffs, such as Food for Infants and medicinal fruit salts. Yet there was nothing that had enraptured the northern palate.

Joseph Rowntree persisted in his stance against innovations such as advertising and marketing. This extended to keeping a watchful eye on shop owners who bought the right to rebrand Rowntree products. One such owner was Blanks, who relabelled Rowntree's Homeopathic Cocoa and took the liberty of adding a couple of words to the package that might actually prompt the customer to buy it. The luckless Blanks soon heard from his supplier. "It is *not* a pure ground cocoa," Joseph stormed. "It is *not* produced from the finest Trinidad Nuts. It is *not* the best for family use. In fact the whole thing is a sham, not very creditable to anyone concerned with it."

Joseph Rowntree wanted his consumers to benefit from his high trading standards, but he also wanted to bring benefits to his workers. He and and his brother Henry had a reputation as fair employers, but with the business struggling in the depression of the 1870s, good intentions were not enough. Although total sales rose from £7,383 per year in 1870 to £30,890 by 1879, the average net profit was as little as £372 a year. The years 1873 and 1876, when the company suffered losses, were particularly bad. No wonder that by the mid-1870s, Rowntree still saw himself as a Master Grocer first and cocoa manufacturer second.

As a plain Quaker, Joseph Rowntree appreciated thrift and frugality. Such parsimony without a clear vision might have driven the business into the ground, were it not for a curious visit that came out of the blue. In 1879 a French confectioner named Claude Gaget arrived in town and asked to see Rowntree. Gaget had worked for a French sweet firm, Campagnie Francaise of Paris, and adapted their recipes. He had created his own version of a new kind of sweet—a fruity, chewy pastille—that was popular in France but was not yet being made in England.

It is hard to imagine the middle-aged Joseph Rowntree, a Quaker who had proved most particularly set in his ways, with this eager young Frenchman tasting the pastilles. Perhaps it was the influence of Joseph's younger brother, Henry, that gave the Frenchman such a favorable reception. But as Joseph ruminated on this small, colorful fruity sweet, which was unlike anything he had tasted, curling his tongue appreciatively around the slowly released flavors, he caught a glimpse of deliverance. Here was a creation that might enable him to get one up on the French *and* his Quaker rivals.

Joseph was not a man to leap into anything suddenly. With a careful eye on the budget, he supported the development of the fruit pastille in a sober and responsible manner. Investment in a boiling pot was much cheaper than investment in Van Houten's machinery. There was room for a boiling pot or two in a corner of the factory, and money could be found for Gaget to hire an assistant. Joseph knew the French had a monopoly on pastilles and gums. If Gaget succeeded in creating a recipe that allowed him to mass-produce an expensive French speciality, he could launch a quality product at a low price. The new treat was honest and natural; just fruit and sugar. His faith in the fruity confection was boundless.

Yet after laboring over steaming cauldrons of fruit, Gaget delivered samples in 1880 that did not live up to their early promise. The texture was not right. The flavor was less than perfect. Joseph spurned sample after sample. The quest for an original breakthrough product remained as elusive as ever.

BOURNVILLE, BIRMINGHAM, ENGLAND

Meanwhile at Bournville, George and Richard found themselves in the fast lane. "Orders after a time came in so fast," observed chocolate maker Fanny Price, that the spacious new factory "at length became overcrowded." Any misgivings that the decision to remove adulterated lines might seriously harm sales were soon put to rest. The message that Cadbury stood for quality and produced pure cocoa in wholesome conditions distinguished the brand from the rest of the market and boosted sales. The brothers advertised for staff in the local villages of Kings Norton, Stirchley, Northfield, and Selly Oak. The number of employees jumped from 230 when they left Bridge Street to more than 300 within a year.

A comparison of Fry's and Cadbury's sales figures during this period show just how wrong the critics were about Bournville. In 1875, Fry's total sales were £236,075, while Cadbury's were much smaller at £70,396, and Rowntree's smaller still at £19,177. Five years later in 1880, Francis Fry saw his business grow to sales of £266,285. What he could not know was how fast Cadbury was catching up. That same year, Cadbury had sales figures of £117,505 and Rowntree of £44,017. In the twenty years since George and Richard had taken over from their father in 1861, they had turned a loss-making firm into one that was nearly half the size of their leading competitor.

The Cadbury brothers proved to be an unstoppable force. Richard's oldest son, Barrow, was impressed by the collaboration between them: "No two partners ever worked in more complete harmony than the two Cadbury brothers, Richard and George," he remarked. Material reward had not meant that the brothers abandoned their dedication to long hours and spartan self-denial. According to family records, it had long been their custom to make a small leg of mutton last for an entire week of meals: roast on Monday, minced by Wednesday, and "using the bones and any scrap end to furnish the meal on Friday." When their father, John, came to visit one day at Bournville, the mutton bones were bare. He delivered a gentle rebuke, pointing out that it was not acceptable fare for the young clerk who dined with them, thus ending not only "the tyranny of the leg of mutton" but also the tyranny of extreme frugality.

Four years after the move, a reporter from the *Midland Echo* made the trip out to see what the brothers had created. "In the midst of green fields, with the ripple of the brook-like Bourne on whose banks the kingfisher and the moor hen find a home, Bournville forms the central part of a natural picture as refreshing to the senses as is the cup of cocoa manufactured there," he enthused. The reporter was impressed with the creepers and shrubs "evidently glorying in the pure air" and the "well dressed happy looking girls trooping in at the door." He noted that each girl looks "neat and clean, as if they were out visiting, and great is their admiration for their employers." As for the Cadbury brothers themselves, "There is so little suggestive of the factory owner about them and so many implications of benevolence and kindly feeling that one becomes irresistibly impressed with the thought that money for themselves is the last thing on their minds!"

But business growth was indeed on their minds. News of the Swiss breakthroughs was starting to reach England, prompting George and Richard to create a research department to develop new lines. To take on the French, they hired a Parisian chocolatier, Frederick Kinchelman, known to the staff as "Frederick the Frenchman," to refine such delicacies as Nougat Dragées, Pâte Duchesse, and Avelines for the Fancy Box. They decided to open a shop in Paris, turning a blind eye to the expensive and exclusive address at 90 Faubourg Saint-Honoré that was far removed from their simple Quaker beginnings.

Richard and George began to think about expanding into the far-flung towns in the British Empire. The very first traveller to venture overseas was Simeon Hall, who had visited Dublin in 1873. Now, following Fry's lead, they worked through firms of exporters to set up sales further afield. In Canada, Edward Lusher, a local agent in Montreal, was hired to promote their goods. This was followed by a similar deal in Chile with Brace Laidlow & Co. A small sample of goods was selected to dispatch to Chile, the labels duly translated into Spanish. In early 1881, the brothers took their foreign ambitions a step further. The Frys were not yet in Australia, presenting them with an opportunity to break new ground. Instead of hiring local agents, they sent out one of their own staff. A solitary traveller, Thomas Elford Edwards, was dispatched to cover the whole of Australia and New Zealand. He was the firm's first permanent overseas representative. His mission: to find out whether the Australians had any interest in chocolate. In July 1881, a letter arrived at Bournville bearing an Australian stamp. It was from Edwards's office in Melbourne and gave details of his first order. For the brothers it was a triumph. The first tentative threads of a chocolate empire reaching to the other side of the world.

Before there was any clear understanding of "globalization," they recognized that their "new and handsome factory" stood at the threshold of something big. They wrote of an "extraordinary food revolution" that would transform Western lives where manufacturing would bring "internationality in food." For a family that just a few generations earlier had exemplified Napoleon's "nation of shop keepers," the Cadbury brothers stood at the brink of a much larger enterprise. "There is certainly untold pleasure in having to contend with overwhelming difficulties," wrote George. "And I sometimes pity those who have never had to go through it. Success is infinitely sweeter after struggle."

8

Money Seems to
Disappear Like Magic

PHILADELPHIA, PENNSYLVANIA

The success of Bournville was not lost on one impoverished entre-preneur from Pennsylvania: Milton Snavely Hershey. In 1879, the year that Richard and George Cadbury opened their "factory in a garden," things were not going well for twenty-two-year-old Her-shey, who was getting his first taste of failure.

The child of a broken marriage—a penniless father intoxicated by the pursuit of the American dream and a careworn mother who had long since tired of it—Milton straddled the gulf between his father's wild ambitions and his mother's strict Mennonite background by toiling at a business of his own. His shirt sleeves rolled high, his over-all stained, his shoes scuffed, he labored over scalding mixes and gas jets to create confections of boiled sugar from his proudly named Spring Garden Steam Confectionery Works in Philadelphia.

"Money seems to disappear like magic," his mother, Fanny Her-shey, reported to her wealthy brothers. She and her sister, Martha Snavely, dedicated themselves to Milton's business, working through the night wrapping the sweets, but after three hard years, Milton's candy shop was floundering.

The venture had started in 1876, after Milton took a trip to Phila-delphia with a few dollars sewn into his coat lining and a great deal of optimism. At first he had met with success, benefiting that year from the Philadelphia Centennial Exposition. But despite his fashionable cards promoting his "Pure Confections by Steam," there were three hundred confectioners in Philadelphia and competition was intense. Within a few years, Milton was forced into making humiliating appeals to his wealthy relatives on his mother's side. The Snavely uncles were inclined to help the young entrepreneur, but just as a real prospect of success came into view, so did Milton's estranged father, Henry Hershey.

Forgiving and full of foreboding in equal measure, Fanny stood back and let her husband rekindle his relationship with his son. Man and boy became friends at once. With spellbinding certainty, Henry, ever the dreamer, presented his latest moneymaking scheme to his son. Improbably it centered on cough drops displayed in elegant little cabinets. Milton put every cent he had into cough drops and borrowed more and then watched as Henry Hershey's scheme failed, spectacularly.

Milton ended up giving his father several hundred dollars before Henry disappeared in disgrace—to the silver mines of Colorado and another magical dream. Burdened with more debt, over the following months, Milton and his mother were drifting towards failure. The pretty sugary sweets he made himself looked so lovely in their rows of crystal jars, but he couldn't manage to sell enough to cover his costs.

On December 8, 1880, he begged his Snavely uncles for $600, explaining, "Otherwise I will not be able to pay my bills." His uncles obliged, only to receive another letter from their nephew on April 28, 1881: "I am in urgent need of $500." On December 3, Milton's Aunt Mattie wrote and asked for $400. This was followed a month later by a letter from Milton stating somewhat charmlessly, "I must have $300 which Aunt Mattie says you are to raise and send not later than the early part of next week." Milton Hershey pointed out that he had given his father $350. He expressed his regrets over helping his father, against his aunt's advice: "If only I had sent father on his way . . . as Aunt Mattie told me to," he said. The uncles once again paid up, but their goodwill was running out.

The humiliation of the appeals, the unrelenting hard work, and the sense of obligation to his father combined to put intolerable pressure on the young entrepreneur. As his Philadelphia candy shop spiraled into decline during 1881, Milton Hershey, too, went into decline. Before long, he had become seriously ill.

DERRY CHURCH NEAR LANCASTER, PENNSYLVANIA

Milton Hershey had grown up trying to reconcile the inherent contradictions between his mother and his father and between the Church and the hedonistic pursuit of wealth. His mother, Fanny, was the daughter of a bishop in the Reformed Mennonite Church, a faith like Quakerism that preached simplicity and plain living—although it differed in requiring a literal interpretation of the Bible. The doctrine of hard work and self-discipline seemed crystallized in the very air his mother breathed; those plain clothes she wore and that small, strong back that bore the weight her iron will imposed. Reward, she believed, would come after years of patient, honest work, and she never failed in her duty to toil on the path of righteousness and virtue. Sacrificing any kind of wild indulgent gamble to small, purposeful steps was the creed that had helped her own family prosper. Her brothers had built up a comfortable lifestyle through their prudent endeavors.

His mother's background reflected the wider world in which Milton Hershey grew up. Pennsylvania was Quaker country: plain, sensible, and wholesome. By 1870 there were 7,000 Quaker inhabitants. The state owed its very existence to a Quaker, William Penn, who founded the colony in 1682 following years of religious persecution for nonconformists in England and America.

During the seventeenth century, Quakers fleeing imprisonment in England had arrived at the ports of New England to face equally appalling treatment at the hands of Puritan leaders anxious to keep them out. In 1659 this fanaticism erupted into violence: Two Quakers who refused to leave, William Robinson and Marmaduke Stephenson, were marched to Boston Common and hanged. The following year, after two other brutal hangings, Charles II ordered the American authorities to stop religious persecution. Quakers were spared death, but just barely. There are reports of vicious punishment: ears sliced off, tongues pierced with hot irons, every brutality short of death.

The problem eased in 1682, when William Penn, the Quaker son of a distinguished English admiral, set off for America. When Admiral Penn died, the British government owed him £15,000, and his son, William, agreed to waive the debt in return for a vast slice of land in America. He was given 45,000 square miles of rugged wilderness stretching to the River Ohio to the west, Maryland to the south, and Lake Erie to the north. William Penn gave his name to the new colony of Pennsylvania and welcomed not just Quaker settlers but also persecuted minorities from across Europe, including the Mennonites. On one of his trips to Europe, Penn visited the Innesholden Alps—a German-speaking part of Switzerland—and persuaded the suffering Mennonites to come to the New World. Among them were Hershey's forebears.

Penn held out the promise of liberty to those living under the threat of persecution. His colony was founded on tolerance and religious freedom. The capital city, Philadelphia, the city of brotherly love, sat on the banks of the River Delaware and was a beacon for like-minded men. The Quaker leader George Fox came to visit, and by the time of his death in England in 1691, there were 50,000 Quakers across North America, many settled in Pennsylvania. John Cadbury's older brother Joel was among the many Quakers who put down roots in Philadelphia. Other groups in search of religious freedom also flourished in Pennsylvania, such as the Amish and Mennonite communities. Milton Hershey's great-grandfather, Isaac Hershey, established his Mennonite family in Dauphin County near Derry Church.

Three generations later, the young Milton Hershey came under Quaker influence. As a result of Henry Hershey's poor management, the family moved constantly, leaving their grandfather's homestead at Derry Church. At one stage, Milton and his family occupied a small farm at Nine Points, near Lancaster, where Milton was sent briefly to a Quaker school. The teacher reinforced the lessons taught by his mother, and he spent time improving his writing and learning to embrace discipline, sobriety, and hard work. But for the young Milton, many of the virtues encouraged by Quakers and Mennonites conflicted with a different and equally compelling message that he received from his father.

Although Henry Hershey had been brought up as a Mennonite, the iron discipline and severe self-denial that shaped his wife's character appear to have eluded him. He believed that there was no need for the laborious struggle that his wife advocated to claim a modest foothold on success. There were shortcuts, and he was determined to find them. But Henry's schemes were not blessed with good fortune. His marriage, floundering for so long on a series of disappointments that followed one wild venture after another, finally failed. The trigger seems to have been the death of Milton's adored baby sister, four-year-old Serena. His parents, coldly distanced and weighed down by grief, went their separate ways.

Henry Hershey could not give up his dreams. He needed them more than ever. Success, he told his son, came from exercising the imagination, from being bold, and from taking on the world. The bigger the risk and the more grandiose the idea, the more astronomical the reward. In Henry's view, "If you want to make money, you have got to do things in a big way." And there was plenty of evidence to support his position. The uneasy ghosts of the Civil War were gone, and America was busy making money, rushing headlong towards the promised Eldorado, with gold in the Klondike, Texas awash with oil, and the wheels of industry ceaselessly turning. It was the era of the dazzlingly wealthy—men like John D. Rockefeller and Andrew Carnegie, rich beyond imagining from oil and steel.

In the early 1880s, as Milton Hershey virtuously applied Quaker and Mennonite principles to his Philadelphia candy shop, the unprincipled John Rockefeller was holding the world in the palm of his hand. His oil kingdom was firmly rooted in refineries across the Northeast, the geysers of black gold serving as a visible contrast to his humble origins. Rockefeller had started out with nothing in Cleveland, Ohio, sixty miles west of Pennsylvania in the 1860s; twenty years later, he was well on his way to becoming the world's richest man. But his success had not happened without adventure and risk taking. This had not come about while Rockefeller applied Mennonite principles. Rockefeller was a true-grit American who had borrowed heavily to become the world's largest oil refiner in Cleveland. Brave moves and bold action led to the formation of Standard Oil in 1870; he made secret deals with railways and hounded the competition until it could be either bought or crushed.

Then there was Andrew Carnegie, the son of a Scottish weaver who came to Pennsylvania in 1848 on money borrowed to pay the fare. After changing the thread in a cotton mill for twelve hours a day, it did not take Carnegie long to find a few shortcuts. With what versatility had he moved from railroads to oil to steel mills in Pittsburgh making profit each time? Now, less than two hundred miles from Hershey's hometown of Lancaster, Carnegie's craggy steel works dominated the skyline of Pittsburgh. This steel provided the very bones of a new America, stretching across virgin territory—a newfound might forged in railroads, bridges, high-rise buildings, and industry. Carnegie, the industrial emperor, had the wealth of a small country. What young man could resist such entrepreneurial inspiration?

But life had dealt Milton Hershey a different hand. In 1881, at the still-struggling candy shop in Philadelphia, twenty-four-year-old Milton tried to tackle his growing losses, only to find himself physically wrecked. The harder he tried, the more ill he became. He had given six mercilessly hard years to the business, and with failure imminent, it was taking him down, too. With true determination, his mother, head covered with prayer cap and bonnet, did what she could. Early in 1882, however, her sister Mattie returned from a trip to see her brothers to say they could offer no more funds. By March, Milton Hershey had run out of money.

His Snavely cousins brought their farm wagon to pack up the shop and take Hershey home. Disgraced and in debt to his mother's family, Hershey wrestled with his options. He was torn between his father's self-confidence and his mother's conviction that reward came only through unremitting hard work. Once his health improved, he turned his back on his mother's puritan severity. Where had the Bible, virtue, and iron discipline got him? Milton opted for his father's approach to business and fixed his sights firmly on the West.

DENVER, COLORADO, AND CHICAGO, ILLINOIS

In the 1880s, while the Cadbury brothers at Bournville were finally reaping the rewards of twenty years of hard work, their future American rival was living hand to mouth in Colorado. By the time Milton Hershey reached Denver, he was hungry and desperate. When help from his father failed to materialize, he responded to a "Boy Wanted" sign and was shown into a room out the back. Inside were several dishevelled boys. Instinct told him to leave. But he was locked in. Fearing he had been tricked into slave labor, Hershey waited until the door was opened and he drew his gun and threatened to use it unless he was released. He was learning the hard way how to be tough.

During his travels west, it is likely he heard of an entrepreneur, Domenico Ghirardelli in San Francisco, who had recovered from bankruptcy by creating a business not too far removed from Hershey's line of trade. The vicissitudes of Ghirardelli's business sounded all too familiar. Ghirardelli arrived in California in 1849 during the Gold Rush. When the discovery of gold eluded him, and his business selling coffee and chocolate drinks to prospectors from a tent in the Sierra foothills proved equally lackluster, he went to San Francisco to open a coffee and confectionery shop. This got wiped out in the inferno of 1851. But the irrepressible Ghirardelli was soon back in business making a chocolate drink. He hit upon a low-tech process that enabled him to achieve modest success in defatting the cocoa bean and giving him the edge over his rivals. The chocolate liquor was hung in cloth, allowing the fatty butter to drip out while the cocoa solids were left behind. Although this approach did not deliver the purity of Van Houten's cocoa, Ghirardelli's drinking chocolate turned his fortunes around. In the early 1860s, he was importing just half a ton of cocoa beans per year; twenty years later, he needed almost two hundred tons. Ghirardelli's products were so popular they were selling around the Pacific, reaching to Japan and China.

For Milton Hershey, Ghirardelli's success on the West Coast echoed what he knew of the chocolate business on the East Coast. It was boom time—especially for New England's oldest firm, Walter Baker and Company.

The business was started by Walter Baker's grandfather, a Dr. James Baker, who rented a mill in Dorchester, Massachusetts, in 1765. Dr. Baker's partner, John Hannon, was an Irish immigrant with experience in making cocoa, and they soon outfitted the mill with kettles, pestles, and a large iron roaster. When the unfortunate Hannon perished at sea, the Baker family continued to expand the business. Their products mirrored their English counterparts: cocoa was mixed with starch, arrowroot, or sugar to mop up the fats, and they emphasized the medicinal value of several of their brands. Walter Baker, the third generation in the business, went to London and learned from market leaders such as Fry and the Taylor Brothers. In the 1840s, he used what he had learned and introduced a new line of chocolate sticks. "I learned to make them in London," Walter Baker wrote. "They are to be eaten raw or melted on the tongue to taste," and he pointed out that "they are much more suitable for children than candy or Sugar Plums." The firm's advertising also mirrored its English counterparts. In 1883 they introduced La Belle Chocolatière, a beautiful girl who decorated the lids of Baker's cocoas and chocolates in a range that had become known throughout New England.

Milton united with Henry Hershey, but they had no money to rent a mill or invest in expensive equipment. Their only asset was their broad experience. Henry had travelled widely and flirted with everything from painting to gold prospecting. His son's experience was much more focused. Milton's mother had enrolled him at the age of fifteen as an apprentice in an ice-cream parlor in his hometown of Lancaster, Pennsylvania. For four years, he learned how to transform large boiling pots of sugar and water into colorful temptations: lollipops, boiled candies, fruit drops, and a myriad of others. Six years of running his own business in Philadelphia had honed his skills; he had confidence in making all types of candy. Most recently he had taken a job at a sweetshop in Denver, where he refined his knowledge of caramels. Instead of adding paraffin to achieve the desired texture, his Denver employer had hit on a better recipe. "I put in fresh milk," he said. "They stay fresh for months and the milk makes them chewy too." Milton was impressed and took note of each step of the process.

The summer of 1882 found twenty-four-year-old Milton working in the stifling heat with his father on the shores of Lake Michigan. Chicago was a town hurrying towards the future; a population of five hundred people fifty years earlier had exploded to half a million. Meatpackers and livestock owners, railroad and factory workers—a lawless maelstrom hungry for nourishment and all potential candy eaters. The world, it seemed, was coming to Chicago. Here a sharp-eyed entrepreneur could glimpse the new America. A network of railroads was turning the city into a key junction between east and west as well as north and south, with steamboats sailing the Great Lakes to connect by canal to the Mississippi River. From their rented premises in State Street, the Hersheys were hungry for success. With Henry's imagination and Milton's experience, they planned to make caramels and cough drops.

Milton at last found there was just one drawback. It did not take him long to see what his mother had known all along. Henry was no team player or business partner. He was never there when he was needed and could be relied on for nothing. Before long, they decided to go their separate ways. For Milton Hershey, the lure of wealth and fortune remained maddeningly out of reach.

In the autumn of 1882, Hershey returned east to his mother and aunt in Lancaster, Pennsylvania. He told them he wanted to start again. This time he would take on the largest growth market of all: New York. And he wanted to do it properly. As his mother had tried to teach him, slow, incremental steps were needed to grow a business. He knew that now.

He paced Manhattan's grid of streets researching the competition. America's largest city had everything. The immigrants poured in from New York harbor, forming a ceaseless tide of humanity with hope on their faces and dust in their eyes. This was where the elusive dream started: on grimy streets, where wagons and horses mingled with dirt-poor Irish immigrants, New England Yankees, Germans and Scots from Pennsylvania, people from far and wide. The possibilities greeted you everywhere, blazoned across the billboards, and in advertisements and shop windows in a bewildering array of goods. There were new skyscrapers all of ten storeys high as well as run-down tenements, laundry strung between buildings soaking up the dirt. It was a wanting world looking hard for fulfilment.

In the fashionable districts of downtown Manhattan, Milton found there was stiff competition. Countless sweetshops in town already offered every kind of delight that could be whipped up from boiled sugar and water. Even novel forms of eating chocolate were on sale, such as chocolate drops, sticks, and bonbons. Undaunted, Hershey relied on his expertise in candy making to give him an advantage over his rivals. He leased a shop on Sixth Avenue between Forty-second and Forty-third Streets near the elevated railway and began laboring seven days a week in the kitchen basement. It was his second candy business, and this time it prospered. Feeling optimistic, he moved to larger premises on Forty-second Street, only to find he had made a critical mistake. He had accidentally overstayed at the original shop by a few days, and consequently the landlord sued him for a year's rent.

Faced with having to pay two rents, his mother and Aunt Mattie came to his aid once again. Always willing to provide free labor, they wrapped and packed, determined to win through. Yet just when it seemed that Milton Hershey might finally turn the corner, his father turned up.

Once again, the dashing Henry Hershey, full of seductive ideas and an unreasonable amount of self-confidence, urged his son to seize the moment. Winter was coming, flu was predicted, and New Yorkers would need cough drops. Despite all the puritan homilies and all the hard work, Milton found himself unable to resist a gamble. He borrowed $10,000 to purchase the necessary equipment. Once again, the son's success and the mother's peace of mind were hostage to the errant father's dream.

BOURNVILLE, BIRMINGHAM, ENGLAND

In 1882, the year that Hershey embarked on his venture in New York, in Birmingham, England, Richard Cadbury's oldest son, nineteen-year-old Barrow, was due to start full-time work at Bournville. His Uncle George suggested that he should first take a tour of the New World to investigate the chocolate market in North America. "It was one of Uncle George's generous and thoughtful propositions," Barrow wrote in his diary. He was to travel with William Tallis, the works foreman, and young Barrow appreciated his companionship and business insights. Richard Cadbury took them to Liverpool and saw them off on the beautiful steam-propelled White Star liner SS *Republic*. The ship had four masts, with full sails rigged on each one. "I remember this," says Barrow, because it was a stormy crossing and "in a strong gale one of the top sails burst with a loud explosion."

As part of their North American trip, William Tallis and Barrow Cadbury visited Canada. In chilly Montreal, where an ice railway had been laid two kilometers across the vast Saint Laurence River, they went to see the company's Canadian agent, Edward Lusher. Montreal was in pole position to benefit from a network of railways, lakes, and canals that were forging paths through great swathes of virgin territory. Travelling west, cities like Toronto were already within reach, and the Canadian Pacific Railway was inching its iron feet towards the vast snowy peaks of the Rockies. Going east, rail and shipping routes made connections to the booming Atlantic coastal towns of Canada and America. Wherever they ventured in this mighty landscape, they saw, cheekily stacked in shop windows, the bright yellow tins of Fry's Breakfast Cocoa.

Of all the cities on Barrow's tour, New York was the greatest wonder. Here Barrow Cadbury could see what Hershey had patiently researched. Sugar candy was everywhere; chocolate was not. No one in America had tapped the full potential of the little black bean. If Barrow passed Milton Hershey's dreary kitchen on Sixth Avenue, there was nothing yet to intimate a great confectionery rival in the making.

America, land of opportunities, lay in wait; a vast map studded with possibilities. Hershey saw it. He believed his God-given country was rich in potential, and he would prove it one day. But the saintly Barrow Cadbury, his horizons bounded by temperance movements and pacifist societies, picked his way through the brash American landscape, failing to spot the right opening.

9

Chocolate Empires

In the 1880s, it was the mysterious continent of Africa that held Europeans in thrall. Unmapped, unknown, a vast continent of possibilities could be glimpsed from forays inland from coastal settlements. The land with the largest desert on earth also had an immeasurable tropical rain forest along the Congo, wide open savannahs burning in a shimmering haze, and vibrant towns dotted along its eastern coast set against the enticing blue of the Indian Ocean. It was all the more vivid seen through the eyes of the great adventurers of the 1860s and 1870s, such as Dr. David Livingstone.

The British already controlled land along the coast of West Africa, including Gambia, Sierra Leone, and the Gold Coast. Now the empire builders of Britain saw a grand extension of Victoria's realm in a great swathe of land across the continent from the Cape of Good Hope in the south to Cairo in the north. But they faced new rivals. Recently formed European states wanted to compete with Britain, France, Spain, and Portugal to seize their own colonies and build their military and industrial might. Germany, formed in 1871, claimed land in southwest Africa. Belgium, created in 1831, eyed the great Congo Basin. Italy, founded in 1861, was maneuvering for Abyssinia. The scramble for Africa was so intense that just thirty years later, only Liberia and Abyssinia would be independent of the Europeans.

The expansion of European empires in the late nineteenth century was mirrored by changes in trade—and chocolate was no exception.

The exotic cacao tree that once thrived only in South and Central America reached the shores of Africa. Portuguese colonialists were the first to take the hardier variety, *Forestero*, from Brazil in 1824 to plant on the island of Sao Tome in the Gulf of Guinea. Spaced about three feet apart under the shade of banana or plantain trees, the cocoa trees flourished in the hot, humid climate to form a thick canopy. Cocoa eventually became the island's leading export, and *Forestero* spread to the neighboring island of Principe and made its way along the coast across the colonies of Portuguese Africa.

In Europe the price of beans began to fall. Ever greater quantities were shipped from Africa and South America to satisfy the rapacious demand of the West. Delicious concoctions, once available only to the wealthy, were reaching an expanding industrial workforce through Dutch firms, such as Van Houten, Peter, and Lindt in Switzerland, in addition to the French and British manufacturers. Imports of the cocoa bean rose fast. In Britain, demand soared from just over 1,000 tons a year in 1850 to almost 5,000 tons by 1880. And Britain's chocolate dynasties followed the trail of the colonial empire builders as immense global horizons opened up.

George and Richard's new factory at Bournville was well placed to benefit spectacularly from the boom in global infrastructure. The British passion for railways would lead to continents conquered as tracks of iron and steel hurried to reach profitable new markets. The railway at Bournville became double track and was part of the mainline into Birmingham, linking their chocolate works to all British ports. New waterways joined the canal route at Bournville, connecting it to both the Liverpool docks and the Bristol Channel, where ever larger steamships sailed around the world. By 1880, Britain was linked to her colonies by almost 100,000 miles of cable spun under the world's oceans. Telegraph messages could be relayed across the world overnight. Cadbury—like Fry—had firmly established its national reach and began to explore international links to the furthest reaches of the British Empire.

The Cadbury brothers' exploration of Africa began with a single traveller, Harry Gear. Gear had been pioneering sales in New York but in 1886 set sail for Cape Town. He soon wrote back asking for help, which arrived in due course in the form of a clerk from Scotland, R. B. Brown, who answered the call to adventure. Brown's ambition was considerable, and he requested the whole of southern Africa as his "patch." He must have been a singular sight on his pony, traversing wide tracts of land, his stock of cocoa and chocolate wares like nothing recognizable in Africa, constantly fingered in a meltingly hot sun. Blazing a trail through thousands of miles of bush, he went where no confectionery salesman had ever been seen before, forging a route from the cape to Northern Rhodesia, Portuguese East Africa to Southwest Africa, and encompassing Madagascar on the way.

The Frys also sent travellers to the South African coast. Their literature shows they found the dangers of travel in Africa "immense" and were stunned by the sheer scale of the unexplored interiors. Nonetheless, "the Dark Continent," they wrote, was beginning to open up "to the enlightening influences of trade." Their best markets were in the towns that sprung up around the South African diamond and gold mines. Fry found that the boys working in the heat of the gold mines more than 9,000 feet underground would start to shiver with cold once they climbed above ground. And Fry had a remedy for those chills: cocoa. Demand rose, and they established branches of the company in Cape Town and Johannesburg.

Meanwhile Cadbury's overseas travellers were also making headway in Australia. Their first Australian traveller, Thomas Edwards, informed the Richard and George that there was so much interest in their products that he required assistance. He was joined by William Cooper, a personal friend of George Cadbury. Their goal was wildly ambitious. The two travellers took a map and divided the continent between them. Edwards would promote Cadbury's goods in South and West Australia, Tasmania, and New Zealand from his Melbourne office, while Cooper tackled Sydney, New South Wales, and Queensland.

William Cooper launched his sales efforts from a cramped apartment in a run-down part of Sydney. "The houses or hovels are perched higgledy-piggledy on the rocks," he wrote to his Birmingham colleagues, adding that from his window he had a splendid view of "goats wandering about at will, chewing off the posters as high as they could reach." It was an inauspicious start, but Cooper had a boyish sense of adventure and asked his brother to join him. Initial sales for the continent were little more than for a single small English town, but they grew exponentially.

Fry's overseas department followed Cadbury into South Australia. There they promoted their products across the country region in an original way, taking advantage of local sensibilities. "Please shut the Gate and Drink Fry's cocoa" was the printed slogan they pinned to farm gates. Fry also ventured to India, where they faced difficulties arising from the huge variations in temperature from tropical regions in the south to much colder regions in the north. The same problem greeted Fry's traveller in South America. Their cocoa drink proved popular in Bolivia at La Paz at an altitude of 12,000 feet, but in the humid lowland plains, they needed to devise sealed packages to keep the product fresh.

In the race to meet the global challenge, George and Richard Cadbury set up an export department in 1888 with a modest staff of six. Travellers spread to far-flung corners of the globe. That year, their Australian traveller, William Cooper, enlarged his territory and introduced the Indian citizens of Ceylon, Calcutta, and Karachi to the homely English fireside drink. His success encouraged the firm to assign a permanent traveller to the region, and they hired J. E. Davis to cover India, Burma, and Ceylon. Davis worked ceaselessly, in spite of illness, to bring the English drink to countries as strange and exotic as the Arabian Nights.

But Davis was outdone. Harold Waite from Birmingham was hard to beat. With magnificent determination and belief in his product, he won customers for Cadbury on the grand scale as he trekked by train and boat and on horseback through the West Indies and South America before tackling the Middle East, and then striking out east to Bangkok and Java. Unbelievably all those countries that the Victorians of Birmingham thought of as bewitchingly mysterious were hungry for a taste of English chocolate.

It was small wonder that the staff at Bournville looked forward to the annual travellers party, held just before Christmas each year.

The travellers brought back colorful tales of the great global odyssey: travelling mindless distances over fiery deserts and crossing alien continents carrying with ant-like patience and determination their knowledge of chocolates and of self-indulgent European sophistication. Demand for English cocoa and chocolate was so great that Richard and George Cadbury's fast-growing export department soon grew to a travelling staff of fifty.

At the center of all this activity, Bournville defied its critics. Sales more than quadrupled in the 1880s, rising from £117,505 in 1880 to £515,371 in 1890. Richard and George seemed unlikely figureheads at the helm of this fledgling global enterprise. The manager of the general office, H. E. Johnson, affectionately remembered "Mr George with a row of small tins on a counter in front of him, the tins filled with roasted beans just brought in from the factory, and Mr George with unerring skill testing them and pronouncing judgment." Sometimes during these tests of quality, Richard would join him, and they sat together, happily absorbed in checking out the batches. "They consulted each other so much that no definite line seems to have existed," continued Johnson. The two brothers "were the centre round which everything moved. It was a kindly duocracy and those who served under it . . . have nothing but happy recollections of the early days of Bournville."

These eccentric philanthropists, who worked for the Lord and for whom abstinence and self-denial was a way of life, showed surprising flair in devising ever more enticing forms of chocolate indulgence. Apart from their Cocoa Essence, their Fancy Boxes took increasingly luxurious forms. They were styled as a myriad of fashionable accessories: satin-lined jewelry boxes with elegant fastenings and locks, handkerchief cases or glove boxes, little cabinets to hold photographs or pens and other essentials. Each one was a work of art, with embroidered fabrics, painted illustrations, and lace trims.

The rewards of running a growing business empire, however, presented fresh concerns for George and Richard that were increasingly in conflict with Quaker values. A Quaker business was meant to succeed, but to succeed quite so spectacularly was something they had not envisaged. Creating personal wealth on an industrial scale was a problem. Did it not say in the Bible, "It is harder for a rich man to enter the kingdom of heaven than a poor one to go through the eye of a needle?" The turning wheels of industry at Bournville were spinning a small fortune for their owners, but the Society of Friends' code of conduct had been fashioned in an era when manufacturing on such a vast scale could not be foreseen. The austerity and self-denial of the Quaker fit in with a world where bounty for most people was still measured in terms of a good harvest.

Banking families, such as the Gurneys and Barclays, gradually drifted away from the Society of Friends. They had come a long way from the days when Robert Barclay was so inspired by George Fox that he wrote a defense of Quakerism, *An Apology for the True Christian Divinity*, published in Latin in 1676. When it was translated into English, it was acclaimed as "one of the most impressive theological writings of the century." Several generations later, the rise of mass-market consumerism brought unimaginable wealth to his descendants. It proved hard to reconcile the plain living of Quaker forebears with the potential for enormous wealth. Successive generations left the Quaker movement, a path that Richard and George did not feel they could follow.

Apart from the issue raised by personal wealth creation, the Cadbury brothers faced another challenge as staff numbers continued to expand. The Quaker creed holds that everyone is equal: The "inner light" shines in everyone. But how could the master and the worker enjoy the same close friendships that they had shared in the early days of Bridge Street, when leisurely afternoons were given over to companionship. By the late 1880s, the firm had nearly 1,000 staff. The sheer size of the business set the management apart and worked against the formation of close ties between everyone. So how did a Quaker firm acknowledge the inner light in each individual?

One solution to this had come from Joseph Storrs Fry II, who held a meeting for all 2,000 staff members each morning. In an exchange of letters with George Cadbury, Joseph offered advice on the content and style of the service, the size of the hall, how to ventilate it, and the need for separate entrances for men and women. George and

Richard found that the daily discussions they used to have with staff at Bridge Street evolved quite naturally into a service for their now larger staff. One visitor, Dean Kitchen, was much moved. He described a women's service filled with "a vast multitude all dressed in pure white and ready for a day's active service." For him the "short reading, kind words and simple prayer preceded by a hymn . . . was a revelation of religious purity and simplicity at full force." The service might set the tone for the day, but was this enough?

George and Richard's father, a plain Quaker to the last, found Quaker beliefs so intrinsic that even when he was old and in pain, he refused to exchange his hard, straight-backed wooden chair for one that was more comfortable. Reconciled to the physical pain of his illness, John submitted humbly to God's will. There would be no concession to personal comfort, whatever his need. He also insisted that his daughter, Maria, no longer dedicate her life to his well-being. Although it was too late for her to have children, she married in 1881 and left home. John meanwhile lived quietly near his thriving family, a gentle old man who sat bolt upright on a hard wooden seat. He was occasionally seen at Bournville with his stick, noting his sons' progress with pleasure, while his life remained a living testament to plain Quakerism and its insistence on the "life of the spirit."

In York, Joseph Rowntree was not vexed by the problem of reconciling personal wealth with Quaker ideals. His business was still struggling.

The Frenchman Claude Gaget toiled over boiling cauldrons of fruit in the quest for the perfect fruit pastille. Joseph and his younger brother, Henry, dedicated precious resources to finding just the right formula. Anxious words were exchanged as early efforts were spurned. But by 1881, they believed they had cracked it: Gaget's recipe was luxuriously chewy and fruity. Advertising was unnecessary, Joseph insisted: Here was an honest product that he planned to sell at a fair price. How could it not be a huge success?

But the first launch of Crystallized Gum Pastilles in 1881 did not bring about an immediate change in the Rowntrees' fortune. Although demand rose steadily, the costs kept pace. The Rowntree brothers had to order more boiling pots to support production, and over two years, the number of staff at the ramshackle factory at Tanner's Moat doubled, reaching two hundred. If they dared to entertain thoughts that they were, at long last, turning the corner, they were sadly mistaken.

The year 1883 was a difficult one for the Rowntree family. In May, Henry died of complications from appendicitis. He and Joseph had operated the business together for fifteen years, and Henry's cheerful presence had always balanced Joseph's seriousness. Now Joseph was alone with his worries at the helm of a business that had grown but continued to struggle.

When Henry Rowntree died, he was in debt to the family firm. His widow and three children needed some kind of modest support, and there was still an outstanding £10,000 owing in overdrafts and mortgages on the factory. Although sales jumped in the 1880s after the launch of the pastilles, Joseph fought to control costs. By 1883, the neat columns of red figures in his account ledger told an unbelievable story. Sales reached a record £55,547, but the company still lost £329. Worse, Joseph knew that the business was unstable. Sales for his cocoa, which he knew was no match for Cadbury's Cocoa Essence and Dutch pure cocoa, could plummet at any time. Despite years of unforgiving hard work, the future was insecure.

Joseph Rowntree had good reason to fear that his cocoa business could vanish altogether if he failed to develop a pure cocoa of his own. His first effort, which he called Elect Cocoa, debuted without advertising in 1880. It was not a success and was soon removed from sale. Fry had also launched a pure cocoa that failed. In 1883, however, Fry relaunched their pure cocoa, and this time they made sure to get their message across. Fry's Pure Concentrated Cocoa won the backing of the *Lancet* and other medical journals and was soon selling well. Joseph Rowntree, watching from York, could see that the market for pure cocoa was getting more crowded by the day and he had nothing to contribute.

In 1885 Joseph Rowntree embarked on a tour of Europe in an urgent quest to understand the Dutch process. Rising sales from his pastilles enabled him to invest in a Van Houten press, but it was still not clear how to create a superior pure cocoa. In May, Joseph arrived in Cologne, Germany, to visit Stollwerck Brothers to buy new equipment. Soon after, he was in Amsterdam, where things looked more hopeful. He met a Dutchman, Cornelius Hollander, who assured him that he had a process that could match the quality of Van Houten's cocoas. The Dutchman was convincing and persuasive. Joseph could not resist the promised gem of knowledge that could turn his company around. Deciding to take a risk, he agreed to pay Hollander £5 a week for six years, and Hollander promised "to communicate the secret of the Van Houten manufacture of cocoa and make cocoa powder for the Rowntrees."

Five pounds per week was a handsome payment, and Joseph Rowntree did not want the rest of his staff to know how much he was paying Hollander. So when Hollander arrived in York and insisted on working in absolute secrecy, Rowntree heartily agreed. At Hollander's insistence, his research room in North Street was carefully padlocked when he left each night.

Weeks turned to months as Joseph Rowntree was obliged to watch and wait. His slippery Dutchman failed to deliver: no satisfactory recipe for pure cocoa emerged from Hollander's locked room, and his behavior became increasingly strange. He guarded his workroom, overcharged for materials, burned his mixtures, and exhausted everyone who dealt with him with endless haggling.

Joseph Rowntree's patience ran dry. An indignant Hollander found himself locked out of his workroom one day. Rowntree's staff had broken in and and finally uncovered his secret. Hollander knew next to nothing. Worse, with the help of the police, Rowntree's staff entered Hollander's house and removed numerous objects that had been stolen or copied from them, including "boiling glasses, drawings of hydraulic presses, drawings of the grinding mill, cocoa breaking machinery, a cocoa roasting machine," and more.

It was not until 1887 that Joseph Rowntree relaunched a pure and new Cocoa Elect. By now, four tons of pastilles left Tanner's Moat each week, and demand showed no signs of flagging. When Joseph did his annual accounts, at last he could see that sales, at £96,916, had almost doubled since he launched his gums and pastilles. After deducting costs, his profits were also rising—although at £1,600, they seemed a poor return for the huge volume of output. Had they turned the corner? It was hard to tell. There were steps he could take to help streamline the business, but at least some of them stood in opposition to his Quaker principles.

After Henry's death, Joseph was joined in the business by his sons. John Wilhelm, the oldest, saw the fragile state of the business and was outspoken in his views. He pushed for change, insisting that certain aspects of Quaker thinking were holding the business back: "Quaker caution and love of detail run to seed." His father was persuaded, and one year after John Wilhelm joined the company, advertisements for Rowntree's products began to appear for the first time in popular magazines such as *Tit-bits* and *Answers*. And as he worked his way around the firm's various departments, John Wilhelm proved to be a natural deputy to his father. In 1888, he was joined by his younger brother, Benjamin Seebohm. Benjamin had read chemistry at Owen College in Manchester and created a laboratory to experiment with new product lines.

Joseph's attitudes toward running the business softened under the persuasive influence of his sons. He began to see modernization through fresh eyes and this gave urgency to the need for change. It became clear that the business was also being held back by the inefficiency of their premises at Tanner's Moat. The ragtag factory with its outdated machinery and many floors was a far cry from the gleaming, smooth operation at Bournville.

At first, Joseph Rowntree prevaricated about borrowing money to move to a larger site. This was not Quaker philosophy as he interpreted it. Make do and mend. Thrift. This he understood. And ramping up the business created another conflict for him. Making money on an industrial scale held no appeal. He did not "desire great wealth," he said, "either for myself or for my children." Worse, it could damage his children, prompting them to self-indulgence and greed. There was, however, one major consideration in favor of moving the business. He shared the Cadbury brothers' view that it would be easier to improve conditions for his fast-growing staff at a site out of town.

Joseph Rowntree heard there were twenty-nine acres for sale on the outskirts of York. With the city walls and York Minster Cathedral behind him, he followed the path for twenty minutes out of town, past rows of humble terraces, along Clarence Street, and into Haxby Road. He crossed a stream and on the left he found the site. The potential was immediately clear. In these spacious grounds, he could build the ideal chocolate factory, where there was room to grow. He could have a porter's lodge on Haxby Road, stables would be needed, and he envisioned tennis courts, a bowling green, parkland, and lawns. With a special line built to the site by the northeastern railway, the possibilities seemed endless.

It was a bold move that would require painstaking attention to detail. But Joseph Rowntree now recognized that bold moves and investment were needed to stay ahead. At last they could match the progress of Bournville. After a long, hard struggle, Joseph Rowntree and his sons were going to join the chocolate aristocracy. They were going to make pastilles, cocoa, and chocolate for England.

While Joseph Rowntree had his eye on Bournville as a way forward, the Frys continued to conduct their business as they had always done. Joseph Storrs Fry II felt the company's success was due to "patience, prudence, honesty and hard work." This guiding philosophy had served the family well for two hundred years and would carry them forward into the future. In 1885 Fry sold £404,189 of chocolate and cocoa. By 1890 this figure nearly doubled to a staggering £761,969, and in five more years, they were approaching a million pounds in sales. They remained the undisputed Quaker chocolate giant.

It is hardly surprising then that Joseph Storrs Fry II and others in Fry's management did not "take readily to new fangled ways," according to the firm's *Bicentenary Issue*. The management believed there was no need to discard old methods that were so spectacularly successful unless "thoroughly assured that they had something better to put into their place." Joseph Storrs Fry II was doing well in areas such as overseas sales, but these were aspects of the business in which his forebears had already taken a lead. The innovative streak and initiative that had prompted his great-grandfather to create the business in the first place and that drove his grandfather to pioneer the use of steam technology in cocoa production was missing.

Furthermore, in his desire to promote a Quakerly concern for all that was honest and true, gradually his advertising budget was slipping behind that of Cadbury or Rowntree as a proportion of his sales figures. Fry favored the gentler promotion of trade fairs rather than bombarding the consumer with advertising campaigns. The efficiency of their production was also slipping behind the competition as the sprawling citadel around Union Street continued to spill out into any spare buildings regardless of their suitability.

For Joseph Storrs Fry II, the welfare of his workers remained a priority. This extended to such thoughtful touches as giving each girl who left to get married a copy of Mrs. Beeton's *Book of Household Management*. He appreciated simple pleasures, such as the firm's annual outing. Because the staff had few opportunities to travel around the countryside, he arranged for an excursion train each year. Long before it was due to depart at 6:00 AM, "The platform would be crammed with Fry employees all dressed up in their best," many with flowers in their coats, anxious to set out on their journey to "furrin parts," according to one member of staff. As their numbers swelled, literally thousands of staff descended on seaside resorts such as Weymouth, "laying siege to all the restaurants," and almost reducing the town "to a state of famine."

Little by little, almost imperceptibly, the paternalism began to seem quaint, the religious values otherworldly, and the success of the business, a miracle. Dressed in sober colors as a plain Quaker, his black suit and waistcoat immaculate, a neat bow tie at his chin, Joseph Storrs Fry II's style and manner formed an increasingly striking contrast with those around him. Gradually, the head of the giant chocolate company, looking a little more tired and a little more grey with each passing year, appeared to belong in another world that was being left behind.

The success at Bournville in the late 1880s was marred by a deeply personal loss for George Cadbury. On March 23, 1887, thirty-eight-year-old Mary gave birth to her sixth child, a baby boy who died a few hours later. About a month later, the family was on holiday in Dawlish in Devon. George organized an outing for the children, leaving Mary behind to rest. He soon received a telegram saying that Mary had been taken seriously ill.

The family was staying at a boarding house in Dawlish. The place was homely but it was not home. Mary did not have her familiar doctor. She made light of her illness, as was her custom, while a fever, almost unnoticed, took deathly hold. To George's alarm, he found his wife's condition had deteriorated beyond remedy. The doctor informed him there was nothing he could do. They must both prepare for the end, for that long separation in the quiet unfamiliar room while the fever marked out those final hours on Mary's face.

"She was most patient during her illness," George told the children later. "She seemed willing to leave all in her Father's hands." After twenty-four hours, "Her countenance was calm and peaceful as she passed into the presence of her King." George and Mary had been married for fifteen years. Richard's eldest daughter, Jessie, moved in to help care for the five motherless children. In spite of her help, the loss of both wife and mother made for a somber household.

As the months passed, a distraught George turned to a friend, Elizabeth Taylor, confiding the terrible sense of loss that he and "my precious little ones have sustained." Elizabeth, or "Elsie" as she was called by her family, had known George for over ten years, when they had met by chance while she was visiting her uncle and aunt, George and Caroline Barrow, in Birmingham. Inevitably it was Quaker interests that had drawn them together. George had been organizing a temperance meeting and called upon the Barrows and was pleased to discover that they were hosting a young visitor, Elsie, who offered to help out by making a speech at the meeting.

Over the following years, George and Elsie met occasionally through the Barrows. She was inspired by his discussions of such thinkers as Ruskin and his practical vision of how social problems could be solved. He was impressed to find a forceful woman who was as passionate about Quaker values as himself. She taught a class of forty boys from the poor districts of south London on Sundays in addition to organizing choirs and Bible lessons. Although she was in her twenties, she pursued her education rather than rush into marriage, and took over the role of governess to her younger brothers and sisters. Elsie was thirty when her father asked George to visit their home in London in the spring of 1888.

A whirlwind courtship followed. Elsie, with her even features, intelligent expression, and high forehead, may not have been pretty but was most certainly handsome. More important to George, she had a strength of purpose, an abundance of energy, and shared his passion for social reform. He felt confident that in this unusual and attractive woman he could build "a life in the kingdom of the spirit." They married at a Quaker meeting in Peckham in June 1888. "The bride," said the *Ladies Pictorial*, "wore a gown of ivory satin trimmed with brocaded velvet, and a tulle bonnet with orange blossom and a veil. Her ornaments were a gold bracelet and a diamond and gold bracelet and brooch, the gifts of the bridegroom."

It was soon clear that George had found a true soul mate. As soon as they returned from their honeymoon, in a clear signal of her intentions, she joined her husband in the Adult School in Severn Street. In the hopeful, anxious faces of the wives of George's students who had come in to meet her, she could see her duty. The women asked if she could teach them, and Elsie happily agreed.

With her considerable experience teaching children, Elsie made a good stepmother to George's children. In March 1889, they welcomed a child of their own, Laurence. He was born just in time to be held by his grandfather, John Cadbury, who died at the age of eighty-eight six weeks later. Another son, Norman, was born in 1890, followed in quick succession by Dolly in 1892, Egbert in 1893, and Molly in 1894. By now, George's oldest son by his first marriage, twenty-year-old Edward had joined his father at Bournville and was working his way up from the factory floor. Edward's cousins, Barrow and William, had already gained experience in the packing room, the chocolate room, the grinding room, and the hot room—before the days of ventilation. To qualify for advancement, it was made clear to the younger generation that they had to understand the company "in spirit" as well as industrial and financial efficiency.

In 1894, George Cadbury's rapidly expanding household moved into a much larger home a couple of miles from Bournville. It was approached by carriage from Bristol Road, where a lodge-house marked the entrance to a drive over a quarter-mile long. Stately cedars and oaks bordered the driveway, affording glimpses of a grand house beyond. To the left was a large lake with an island, and to the right, sitting on a gentle rise in the land, the rambling Victorian manor house came into view. Nestled around the house were a series of gardens bordered by brick walls or herbaceous borders, including a dairy and George's rose garden. The household and grounds staff numbered thirty, the women neatly turned out in starched white pinafores and caps. This was not the home of a plain Quaker but of a successful Victorian industrialist. The former grocer's son—known to his friends as "the practical mystic"—took his place at the center of his own chocolate empire.

Among the Society of Friends, there were purists who doubted that such an imposing manor, which went well beyond the simple lifestyle embraced by his forebears, could be reconciled with Quakerism. How did such Victorian luxury fit with the plain black coats, the frugality, and puritanical beliefs of the movement's seventeenth-century founders? The Cadburys did not adhere rigidly to the rules of their Quaker forefathers but nor could they abandon their faith altogether like some wealthy Quaker industrialists. They found a third way through the ever-widening gulf between the demands of their faith and the secular world. They belonged to a growing breed of successful Quakers who maintained their faith but did not turn their back on material prosperity.

For those in the Quaker community who considered the Cad-burys too worldly, there was a surprise in store. In 1895 George was poised to use his wealth to pursue his ideal of building a utopia. It was the culmination of a family dream first discussed by his father and Uncle Benjamin nearly fifty years earlier. George's aim was to turn his garden factory into a garden city.

Worried that his goal might be thwarted if speculators and slum builders got hold of the land surrounding his factory, George had been discreetly using his income to buy parcels of land around the chocolate works. In 1893 he bought fields to the north of the choco-late works and then he purchased the imposing Bournbrook Hall, a 118-acre estate adjoining Bournville to the west. He was now ready to embark on the first stage of his ambitious plan.

Initially he could only afford to build 142 homes around the chocolate factory. But it was a start. He was convinced from his work at the Adult School that if slum dwellers were provided with homes that gave them a sense of dignity, they would thrive and their health would improve. The key to his scheme was land: Each home should have enough land for a family to cultivate a garden and grow food. This, he believed, would improve their quality of life and lead to a better diet. "About a sixth of an acre is as much as a man work-ing in a factory can cultivate in his leisure time," he reasoned. Con-sequently, his village was designed with no more than six or seven houses to an acre.

Poring over a map of the fields—Yellow Meadow, Far Hall Meadow, Barn Close, Fox Hill—George began to sketch out his plans. He appointed William Harvey, a young local architect to help him. At the heart of the model village would be a green, graced with trees, winding paths, and rose beds. The homes would be nestled around the village green, each one individually designed to avoid ugly uniformity and set back from wide, tree-lined carriageways. Harvey was strongly influenced by the Arts and Crafts movement, which was inspired by John Ruskin and others to promote crafts-manship in art and architecture. Harvey's houses had a cozy English cottage feel, with stepped gables, timber porches, and Venetian windows over canted bays. Their spacious gardens were 140 feet long at the back and were planted with several fruit trees to give a vista of blossoming trees in the spring. More than 10 percent of the land was set aside for open spaces, including parks, lawns, tennis courts, and playgrounds. On hand to help was the Gardeners Department at Bournville, which could provide support to those aspiring owners who had never grown anything before.

The model village served to complement changes at the rapidly expanding factory. In 1895 George and Richard turned land adjacent to the chocolate works into a men's recreation ground with a lodge. Soon plans were underway to build a cricket pavilion. On the other side of Bournville Lane, twenty-three acres around Bournbrook Hall were turned into women's grounds. The Martin's pool, where the brothers and staff had skated in the early years, was turned into a lawn surrounded by shady pathways. A section was laid out for croquet, swings, and other games. Plans were made for a swimming pool and an ornamental pond. George's grand scheme was meant to demonstrate that rather than using land to benefit private individuals, land reform could benefit the whole community.

Bournville village, however, was not a charity. Houses were available at a price of up to £250. Loans were available at low rates; 2½ percent if borrowing less than half the value of the home, 3 percent for a larger loan. These loans were lower than the average rent and enabled an applicant to own his house outright after twelve years. In this way, the would-be homeowner was not only encouraged to save but could also aspire to a better lifestyle and more secure future for himself and his family.

George Cadbury was not the first to try creating a model city. In 1853, a pioneering industrialist in the Yorkshire wool industry, Titus Salt, had constructed a model village for his millworkers. In 1888, the leading soap manufacturer, William Lever, created Port Sunlight on fifty-six acres of marshy land on the banks of the River Mersey near Liverpool. Both schemes were designed to benefit the workers. George's plan, however, went further in that he hoped to provide housing for Bournville staff and a broad, social mix of people drawn from all walks of life. He wanted his model community to become a template to raise living standards of the poor elsewhere in England. Any investor, he believed, could operate such a scheme without losing money, something he hoped to demonstrate by extending his model village using revenue from the estate. As building got underway in 1895, the homes proved so popular that George was soon negotiating for additional land.

But the utopia could not survive without funds. The Cadbury brothers faced growing competition from abroad. The next challenge came from left field, from their old rival, the Dutch firm of Van Houten, which had come up with a technical breakthrough that could threaten the success of their chocolate empire.

10

I'll Stake
Everything on Chocolate!

WEESP, HOLLAND

At his factory in Weesp, Holland, Coenraad van Houten, who sold George Cadbury his first cocoa press, was sitting on top of another breakthrough that had the potential to radically transform the cocoa business once again.

Van Houten wanted to improve the quality of drinking cocoa. He took a scientific approach to the problem, systematically testing out different ideas. It was known that the Aztecs added wood ash to their preparations to counter the stringent acidity of cacao. Working on the same principle, Van Houten experimented with adding alkalis, such as potassium or sodium carbonate, during processing. The result took him by surprise.

When Van Houten added alkaline salts before roasting the bean, he found the cocoa tasted less bitter. But to his delight, there were other unexpected benefits in the texture and flavor of the drink. Although the alkalized cocoa was not completely soluble in milk or water, it was more miscible than any other cocoa product, blending more evenly in solution and becoming easier to swallow. Better still, the alkali enhanced the rich cocoa taste. The cocoa powder was darker, strongly aromatic, and altogether smoother and more chocolatey. When he released samples of his new drink to the public, they loved it. He began selling the product in the 1860s and gradually word spread. No one knew the exact secret, but the process earned the nickname "Dutching."

By the late 1880s, Cadbury's travellers were troubled by the growing presence of Dutch cocoa. Wherever they went, the smiling face of the glamorous model on the packaging of Van Houten's cocoa greeted them, proclaiming this was "best and goes furthest." What is more, this seemed to be achieved effortlessly. Grocers stocked Dutch cocoa simply because the public asked for it, and for the Cadbury brothers, this could spell catastrophe. Their winning streak could be in jeopardy. Although sales of their Cocoa Essence were still growing as more people consumed cocoa, there was strong evidence to suggest that their best-selling product was achieving a smaller slice of a burgeoning market. By the early 1890s, their market share was clearly in decline.

Richard and George were caught in a dilemma. They had staked their reputation, even their name, on purity. So how could they possibly start adding chemicals like alkaline salts? It would make nonsense of all their earlier claims.

Worse still, Van Houten's flyers showed that a distinguished group of British scientists agreed that their cocoa drink was superior to anything else. Professor Attfield of the Pharmaceutical Society of Great Britain, Dr. Theophilus Redwood, emeritus professor of chemistry and pharmacy, and Dr. John Muter, former president of the Society of Public Analysts, tested Dutch cocoa, and they sang its praises: "The alkaline salt as introduced by the Van Houten preparation, not only does not spoil but very greatly improves the cocoa both in its sensible and nourishing properties." The eminent panel applauded Van Houten's ingenuity and scientific approach, adding, "Van Houten's cocoa merits the term 'soluble' more fairly than any other cocoa."

George Cadbury, true to character, went on the offensive. Convinced that purity stood for quality, he set out to prove that alkaline salts were risky contaminants. The public must be warned that Dutch cocoa was not pure and had added chemicals. Once they knew, surely they would win back consumers. The first step was to use the Cadbury packaging to communicate their views. An explicit warning appeared beneath the sweetly smiling Cadbury girl assuring the public that while their cocoa is pure, "Among the Cocoas that do not answer to this description are those of foreign make, notably the Dutch, in which alkalis and other injurious colouring matter are introduced." Richard and George soon found experts of their own willing to fight on their side of the battle, including the ever-obliging medical profession.

The *Birmingham Medical Review* of October 1890 was in no doubt where they stood. "Quite apart from any question as to the *injury* resulting to the human system from taking these [alkaline] salts," they stormed, "it would only be right that the medical profession should resolutely discountenance the use of any and all secret preparations." Scientists writing in *Peterson's* magazine in 1891 went so far as to spec-ify what injury alkalis might cause: "They dissolve animal textures . . . and excite catarrh of the stomach and intestines." Dr. A. J. H. Crespi went further, arguing that foreign cocoas with alkaline salts were quite simply "dangerous and objectionable." Even on the continent—though not in Holland—Dutch cocoa was given the thumbs down. One anonymous German expert declared that Dutch alkaline cocoa is "in the highest degree destructive," damaging "the essential constitu-ents of cocoa." In short, he fumed, the Dutch method is "perfectly bar-barous." Cadbury's efforts soon made Dutch cocoa look like something Machiavelli might administer to a sworn enemy.

But nothing could entice the British public away from its favorite new chocolate drink. Sales for the more soluble Dutch cocoa soared, reaching 50 percent of the British market in the 1890s. George and Richard had to accept that purity was less of an issue than in the past, when people had to worry about manufacturers adding red lead and brick dust to their cocoa. Consumers were now confident that their cocoa would not harm them, and they wanted a more enjoyable drink. The Cadburys had nothing to match what the Dutch offered.

And then the travellers arrived with more bad news. It came in the form of Swiss chocolate.

VEVEY, SWITZERLAND

It had not been easy for Daniel Peter. After the initial excitement of discovering his revolutionary milk chocolate drink in 1875, it took almost twenty years to make headway scaling up his chocolate enterprise. His efforts to turn milk chocolate into a bar for eating were equally troubled. A key stumbling block was funding. In the 1870s he paid several visits to England, where he confirmed that there was a hearty appetite for his creamy, milk chocolate drink. It was unique, unlike anything else on the market, and very popular. The English could not get enough of it. But Peter struggled to convince potential backers in Switzerland of his business proposition. His manufacturing process was fraught with pitfalls that steely-eyed Swiss financiers could spot a mile away.

It was hard to create a standardized milk-based product for export in bulk. Milk was a tricky commodity to deal with. Thundery summer weather could turn it sour. Large quantities of milk often went bad before it could be processed. The quality of the milk could vary from farm to farm and season to season. Attempts to manufacture a milk chocolate bar presented other problems. Early efforts were dry and crumbly, and all too often the milk went bad, making the bar rancid. Convinced he had a great product, Peter searched long and hard for a financial backer but without success. Henri Nestlé had retired, but the new directors of Nestlé would not support Peter. Nor did he partner with Anglo Swiss, the firm that produced condensed milk. Peter found himself utterly shut out by Swiss bankers who dismissed his product and its ingredients as too risky.

He soldiered on, and after years of low-budget experiments, he finally mastered a technical process in 1886 that produced a temptingly soft and creamy milk chocolate bar. It was launched as Gala Peter and received immediate acclaim. When demand far exceeded supply, bankers finally began to pay attention. Everything came together for Peter in the early 1890s, when two Swiss businessmen, Albert Cuenod and L. Rapin, and a banker, Gabriel Montet, invested enough for him to create a new company, Société des Chocolats au Lait Peter, and scale up production.

"I think I can say with a pretty high degree of certainty that the majority, if not all, of the Swiss chocolate makers, have tried to copy me," Peter proudly told his new board. "All have had to give up!" The only product still in the running was a treacly milk chocolate paste, manufactured by the Anglo Swiss Condensed Milk Company, that was no match for the quality of Peter's goods.

With resources now dedicated to ramping up production and advertising, orders rushed in from across Europe. In the first six months of trading in 1895, Peter's sales doubled to ten tons of chocolate. The business was such a success that he and his team decided to recapitalize the company at a million Swiss francs, and they opened a second factory, which doubled their production capacity. The milk chocolate that had been a novelty luxury fifteen years earlier was becoming widely available, and no export market had a sweeter tooth than Britain.

British grocers took to Swiss chocolate as they had taken to Dutch cocoa: They could not get enough of it. But the English Quaker chocolate makers could not fathom how the product was made. It was a conjuring trick; no clues given. Those who had wrestled long to make this particular "food of the Gods" had no intention of disclosing the recipe.

BERNE, SWITZERLAND

Daniel Peter was not the only Swiss chocolatier whose secret was becoming legendary. When Rodolphe Lindt built his unique conching plant at his factory in Berne, he had ensured that only a few of his workers had the key to the door. As the years passed with no one able to top the quality of his chocolate, the mystique and intrigue surrounding his special process caught the public's imagination. A German magazine, *Gordian*, published an article in 1899 inviting readers to guess Rodolphe Lindt's special recipe. The magazine was inundated with letters. Did Lindt have a new type of grinding machine to crush his beans to a finer texture? Did he beat his chocolate mixture for longer? Could it be the addition of essential oils like peppermint? No one had the answer. *Gordian's* editorial team pronounced their verdict: Lindt's secret would never be known.

But Rodolphe Lindt, the gentleman entrepreneur, was in a selling mood. His business partnership with another Berne confectioner, Jean Tobler, had fallen through. Lindt, now almost fifty, was approached with other offers. The Stollwercks in Germany offered as much as 3 million marks. But in 1899, Lindt opened the door of his conching plant to another Swiss manufacturer: Johann Rudolf Sprüngli of Zurich. Sprüngli had made a canny offer. Lindt would receive 1.5 million Swiss francs—a small fortune worth roughly 100 million Swiss francs today—and be a director in their new joint venture.

Johann Rudolf Sprüngli, described in company literature as a shy man, was anything but reticent when it came to business decisions. Shortly after inheriting his share of the Sprüngli chocolate business from his father, he initiated a rapid expansion program that culminated in his moving the family firm from cramped headquarters in the old town of Zurich to a new, modern factory on the shores of Lake Zurich by the railway at Kilchberg. The following year he joined forces with Lindt. Their new company, Chocoladefabriken Lindt and Sprüngli, was a force to be reckoned with. For Rodolphe Lindt, it was a far cry from his inauspicious start in fire-damaged buildings in Berne. Together they were about to scale up the production of some of the most acclaimed chocolate in the world.

YORK, BRISTOL, AND BIRMINGHAM, ENGLAND

In Britain during the 1890s, cocoa changed from being a product that only a few could afford to a product that was on every household shopping list. Cocoa consumption more than doubled over the decade, from 20 million to 43 million pounds. But it was the continental chocolatiers with the miracle of chocolate fondant and milk chocolate that were poised to collect.

The Quaker firms had established a clear lead over their English rivals. The Taylor Brothers and Dunn and Hewitt of London watched as their profits slid. There were newcomers, especially in confectionery. John Mackintosh of Halifax launched his toffee and confectionery business with a £50 loan, and it was worth £15,000 ten years later. Terry of York prospered at its Clementhorpe works on the River Ouse, producing a considerable range of chocolates and sweets alongside the company's traditional candied fruits and peels. But during the 1890s, Fry, Cadbury, and Rowntree were the dominant players in cocoa and chocolate.

By 1895, Fry had sales of £932,292. Cadbury was close behind with sales of £706,191, and now there was heady talk: How long before they caught up with Fry or even overtook them? Both firms were among Britain's largest employers: Cadbury with 2,600, and Fry with over 4,000. After a prolonged struggle, Rowntree was at last making headway. Their sales of £190,328 in 1895 had more than tripled over ten years, and they were narrowing the gap between them and the two leading Quaker chocolate firms. The prodigious appetite for pastilles continued to grow and was complemented by the successful launch in 1893 of Rowntree's clear fruit gums. But Joseph Rowntree knew his Cocoa Elect was struggling next to established brands of pure cocoa, and he had a huge investment underway in Haxby Road. As he made the transition from a family firm into a large-scale manufacturer, his personal notes reveal he watched the foreign competition anxiously.

To take on the Europeans, Joseph Rowntree took the unusual step of approaching Joseph Storrs Fry II and the Cadbury brothers to discuss some form of collaboration. The English Quaker firms had much in common and were soon discussing policy on a number of issues. For example, at the time, shopkeepers could charge what they liked for a product, sometimes overpricing chocolate to increase their profits or underpricing to undercut a competitor. The Quaker firms wanted shops across the country to sell at the price that was printed on the label: Six pence on the packet meant shopkeepers had to sell at six pence. By uniting on such issues, the Quaker firms aimed to guarantee that distributors received good margins but that they could not go above them to the detriment of their companies' chocolate sales.

Their informal discussions on discounts and shop displays during 1895 ensured that a price war or a margin war did not break out between the English Quaker firms. In discussing pricing and advertising strategies, they hoped to fend off the European giants. But Dutch and Swiss sales were strong, and the fast-growing Nestlé Company was waiting in the wings: The battle lines were being drawn for Europe's Chocolate War, with the unsuspecting British consumer the prize. The winners in this financial jeopardy would be those who could devise the most irresistible chocolate mouthfuls to woo and win the English palate. As the European chocolate firms lined up to do battle to produce ever more luscious concoctions of chocolate and cream, a newcomer appeared on a different continent with a plan for a chocolate enterprise that could dwarf the contest in Europe.

CHICAGO, ILLINOIS

In 1893, Chicago was host to a great exhibition: The Columbian Exposition. Twenty-seven million visitors showed up to view the most exciting inventions of the industrial world: engine-powered vehicles, electric lights, telephones, brand new household creations of every description. Among the crowds, one man kept returning to the machinery building: Milton Snavely Hershey.

There was one stall in particular that caught his eye. A German manufacturer, J. M. Lehmann of Dresden, displayed his latest designs for making chocolate. Lehmann had a long-standing reputation for the quality of his machinery. In fact, it was his firm that provided the engineering know-how that helped Van Houten develop his first cocoa press. Now Lehmann unveiled something that intrigued Hershey: a chocolate factory in miniature. The raw beans were roasted and then crushed by granite rollers, producing an aromatic stream of chocolate liquor. Sugar, cocoa butter, and flavorings were added before the mix was set in molds. Hershey was mesmerized, taking in every step of the process. After pondering this deeply for some time, he then turned to his cousin, Frank Snavely: "Frank," he declared, "I'm going to make chocolate!"

Hershey knew that American cocoa imports, although modest compared to Europe, were rising fast. Europeans were consuming 100 million pounds of chocolate per year—while Americans only consumed 25 million pounds—an amount that had almost tripled in ten years. Yet in just a generation, with immigration and rapid pace of progress, America was becoming the greatest industrial power in the world—outproducing Germany, France, and Britain combined. America's vast mass market would surely wake up and smell the chocolate.

Hershey was a gambling man, and by the 1890s, he felt he was on a winning streak. After fourteen years of ceaseless labor, two failed businesses, and a lawsuit, things were finally going his way.

He had come a long way from the turmoil of 1886 in New York. After borrowing $10,000 to help fund the sale of the cough drops his father so believed in, he found he was unable to repay the loan. Every day as he had labored in his basement enterprise by the elevated railway, the gulf between what he could make in profit and his escalating debt widened. According to one sad tale in the Hershey archives, in a last determined bid to raise the money, Milton hired a horse and wagon. With the cart brimming over with sweets and cough drops, Hershey went out in search of new customers. When he entered a sweetshop, a gang of youths looking for some fun put firecrackers under the wagon. Milton emerged from the shop to see his terrified horse bolting up the street, the wildly veering wagon scattering its precious load in all directions. Stripped of hope that he would meet the deadline to make a partial payment on his $10,000 loan, he sold everything and went home to Pennsylvania.

This second failure proved decisive. His determination to succeed channelled steely grooves through his personality. He had learned so much, why work for someone else when he could try again? Unfortunately he found his own resolve was equally matched by that of his mother's family. No more money was forthcoming. The charming youth who had carried all their hopes of fifteen years ago had been transformed into the twenty-nine-year-old man, greying prematurely, who was a bitter disappointment. Money was not available. Not so much as a penny.

In 1886, with no capital available, it was back to basics for Milton Hershey. He believed in his new recipe for caramels. It bore a remarkable similarity to the recipe he had learned in Denver, Colorado, using milk instead of paraffin to create the creamy chew. No one on the East Coast was making a caramel quite like it. Hershey started once more, peddling his sweet dream from a pushcart around the streets of Lancaster, Pennsylvania.

This time, people came back for more. He couldn't make them fast enough. The sales made it possible for him to rent workspace in a warehouse. He had to share it with noisy neighbors—a carriage works and a piano manufacturer among others. But he had room for his kettles and sugar stores. Once again his mother and his Aunt Mattie came to help with wrapping the sweets. As word spread, in a stroke of extraordinary luck, a British traveller passing through town in 1887 placed a big order for caramels to ship to England. Hershey duly set off to the banks in Lancaster to secure a loan to buy equipment to fulfill the deadline. No one would back him.

Hershey's luck finally turned when Frank Brenneman, the cashier at Lancaster National Bank, agreed to loan him $700. But it turned again when he failed to repay the money within the agreed-upon ninety days. Worse still, he required an extra $1,000 to meet the English delivery. The records show that Brenneman, knowing full well that his superiors at the bank would turn down the request, authorized the additional funds personally. Unknown to the bank, Hershey now owed them $1,700 and some sort of payment was soon due, if another slide down the ladder on Hershey's life was to be avoided. The familiar sickening situation had caught up with him again. He awaited his fate in the warehouse. Into the gloom, a letter from England arrived. Expecting more bad news—the ship had sunk, the caramel was inedible—he opened the letter to find a check for £500.

He was still in business. It was a turning point. The sun had begun to shine on Milton Hershey.

From that point on, Hershey's Lancaster Caramel Company started to reach out to the fast-growing industrial cities of the East Coast. Somehow his family managed to keep his father, Henry Hershey, at bay before he could spoil it. Milton Hershey was soon in a position to open what he loved to call his "western branch" in Chicago, followed by another branch in Pennsylvania at Reading and a shop on Canal Street in New York City. By the early 1890s, he was employing some 1,000 staff. The surge in immigration, the explosion in consumer demand, and skillful use of new types of machinery: it all helped his business grow at an astonishing rate. "Milton Hershey has made a complete success of his life so far," declared *The Portrait and Biographical Record of Lancaster County* in 1894. Noting that his company did over a million dollars of business a year with exports to Europe, Asia, and Australia, they concluded, "No man stands higher in business and social circles in the city of Lancaster than this man, who has been crowned with success." It was quite a turnaround.

When Milton Hershey travelled to the Chicago exhibition in 1893, he was a man of substance with money to spend. A man who no longer lived from hand to mouth but had a grand brick house in his hometown of Lancaster filled with soft furnishings, fine art, and other luxuries he had been denied as a child. On his last day there, he bought Lehmann's entire display: the chocolate factory in miniature.

In 1894, when George Cadbury was moving into his manor house, Lehmann's chocolate machine was hidden unobtrusively inside the factory of the Lancaster Caramel Company, and it started to produce Hershey's own chocolate. The first attempts were not auspicious. They were coarse and dry compared to the Swiss milk chocolate. But Hershey was a great experimenter, and he began to test out different ideas: chocolate wrapped around caramel, chocolate cigars with exotic sounding names like Hero of Manila and fancy chocolates with imposing French titles such as Le Roi de Chocolat.

Hershey took frequent research trips to check out the competition. In New York in 1896, he met Catherine Sweeney, the young daughter of Irish immigrants who worked as a clerk in a candy store in Jamestown. The beautiful "Kitty" proved to be an irresistible and charming confection, and Hershey's trips to New York took on a new urgency. Wide differences in their ages and backgrounds and his mother's disapproval counted for nothing. The pretty Irish immigrant became Mrs. Milton Hershey in no time at all and moved into her husband's house in Lancaster in 1898.

But Kitty was no Quaker wife. Unlike George's wife, Elsie, with her air of sobriety and plain clothes buttoned to the neck, Kitty had a sensational wardrobe crammed with the latest fashions. While Elsie was applauded in Birmingham for her generous charitable works, Kitty was learning how to spend Milton's money for him, and her flirtatious style attracted comment. At least one Lancaster resident confided to being so taken by her beauty that she could not resist spying outside her house, hoping for a glimpse of the woman who provided such an exotic contrast to the closed, religious community.

Hershey indulged Kitty's desire to travel with long trips to Europe. Hershey had a purpose to these visits. While she enjoyed the shopping, Hershey went to see the British and continental chocolate manufacturers. He had heard about the chocolate works at Bournville, both through his burgeoning export trade and from admiring reports in fashionable American magazines such as *Cosmopolitan New York*.

Annie Diggs, a reporter for *Cosmopolitan New York*, took a tour of Bournville in 1903 and could see for herself the results of William Harvey's designs. "The very streets of Bournville laugh in the face of crude conventionalism," she declared. "The monotony of capitalistic housing . . . with rows of all-alike houses is prohibited." In its place were tree-lined walkways set out in curves and angles "that follow the natural undulation of the land in all its native beauty." She applauded the commercial basis of the village. "Even the lowest priced of the cottages affords . . . attractive interior features, alluring gardens and environment soul-satisfying to refined tastes—and all this at less cost than one clammy blackened room in a fever haunted city court where human creatures herd from birth to death." She even praised the gardening: "Why it is the very joy of life among the villagers! . . . The men not being overworked in the factory go straight to their gardens with keen delight." She caught sight of "gloriously happy youngsters . . . skipping after their fathers . . . with spade and barrow to work their allotments after factory hours."

At the chocolate works, Diggs was impressed by the efforts to improve the health of the employees and described the recreation grounds "with charming woodland haunts." She found the Quaker owner a passionate advocate for his scheme: "We must destroy the slums of England or England will be destroyed by the slums," said George Cadbury. "We must give English children a chance to grow. We must not house our workers in a vile environment and expect their lives to be clean and blameless. We must do justice in the land." For Annie Diggs, Bournville "was a good dream come true" that "invites duplication throughout England." Indeed, she concluded, why stop there? "Why not the United States as well?"

For Hershey it was a revelation—a model for the perfect business empire. While travelling to Europe with Kitty, he almost certainly had a chance to visit Bournville to see for himself what Quaker philanthropy could achieve. From his carriage, Hershey took in the neatly cultivated gardens and village green bordered by friendly clusters of houses. He travelled the shady streets, each one named after trees that added to the feel of a country haven: Willow Road, Oak Tree Lane, Hay Green Lane, Selly Oak Road, Holly Grove. Hershey saw it as some kind of improbable utopia as he watched the modern lights wink on in the village at dusk. What a thing to create: a little world set apart from the festering city. Hershey had never seen anything like it. This money-making idyll was the perfect community in miniature, an entire template for the rest of society. He was inspired.

And there was more to inspire him on his trip through Europe: milk chocolate. Through the Lehmann brothers, he was introduced to Swiss chocolate manufacturers. Hershey's chocolate experiments at his Lancaster Caramel Company had shown him that it was not easy to make a chocolate bar. He wanted to know how the Swiss created their superior milk chocolate. There are unconfirmed reports that while in Europe, Hershey attempted a little industrial espionage, although he remained silent on this issue. Some claim that he was hired in Swiss chocolate factories without revealing his interest. Other sources imply that he lured staff away from chocolate firms by promising them better deals if they joined his enterprise.

Whatever the truth, by 1899, the King of Caramel had made a radical decision. He would sell his caramel company. "Caramels are just a fad," he reasoned, convinced his sales had peaked. "But chocolate is a food as well as a confection. I'll stake everything on chocolate!" After prolonged negotiations, in August 1900, he finally received a check for $1 million for his Lancaster Caramel Company. Basking in his newfound status, the former pushcart vendor to whom no one would lend money was now a millionaire occasionally to be seen cruising around in the first "horseless carriage" on the streets of Lancaster.

Milton Hershey had a new dream: He would build a factory in a cornfield and open the Hershey Chocolate Company, the largest chocolate works in the world. He too would create a model town around his chocolate works. And he would build this American Bournville where he started out as a child in Pennsylvania's Dauphin County near Derry Church.

There was, however, just one obstacle. He had the expertise to build a business and the resources to create his chocolate town.

But a key ingredient was missing.

He did not have the recipe for Swiss milk chocolate.

PART III

11

Great Wealth Is
Not to Be Desired

Richard Cadbury was a passionate supporter of the Egypt Exploration Fund, formed in the late nineteenth century to conduct
excavations on sites in the Nile Delta that "had rarely been visited
by travellers." In January 1897, he embarked on a tour with his family to see these hidden treasures, an experience of "unclouded happiness," recalled Richard's daughter, Helen. After touring Egypt, the
Quaker party made their way to Palestine, with Bibles in hand as a
guide. They wanted to retrace the steps of biblical heroes such as
Joseph and Moses, seeing what they saw, feeling what they felt.
When their carriage drove through the Jaffa Gate into Jerusalem,
"We were all quiet," wrote Richard's wife, Emma. "It seemed so
strange and wonderful to be in the city of which from babyhood we
had heard and read and sung." The trip was so inspiring that Richard
was soon planning their return.

On February 2, 1899, he and his family set sail once again for
Cairo. "I wish you could all see father," Emma wrote home. "He is
most enthusiastic, taking rubbings and drawings wherever he can."
The family could not resist visiting the Pyramids, and they rode on
camels to see the Sphinx. Someone took a photograph: a moment
frozen in time. It shows a happy group of Europeans laughing in the
sunshine—the women in prim, high-necked blouses, long skirts, and
boaters; the men dressed like country squires; except for Richard.

Happy, sunburned, he had turned native and looked in his long, flowing robes as though he would never return to the land of grey skies.

Shortly after a trip up the Nile, sixty-four-year-old Richard felt unwell. The doctor dismissed it as nothing of consequence; an ordinary case of "Nile throat." Richard did not fuss. He was eager to see Jerusalem again and pressed on with the tour. By the time he arrived, after a two-day carriage ride from Jaffa during which he was unable to eat or drink, he was clearly more seriously ill.

Richard's decline was terrifyingly rapid. He grew weak and frail, and within three days, he was slipping in and out of consciousness. Emma saw his eyes open and "brighten with a joyous surprise . . . as he . . . gazed upon some glorious sight that was hidden from her." In that moment she felt a frightening certainty "that he could never come back to earth again." During the night of March 21, before she could summon the children, Emma watched her husband die as quickly and quietly as a candle being blown out.

At Bournville, George had no idea his brother was ill, and it was a shock when the telegram arrived from Egypt. He had only just received Richard's happy letter from Abu Simbel: "The sun had set when we anchored . . . so that we could only see in the shadow of the rocks a faint outline of the mammoth statues that guarded the celebrated temple of Rameses the Great." It was a terrible loss. As brothers and partners, their lives had been bound together. The early days at Bridge Street were still vivid, and George's mind was alive with images of everything they had shared. Almost as one mind they had conjured up the dream of a utopia and by sheer determination made it work. It was hard to believe that forty years had elapsed. Hard to believe that the brother who in robust health just weeks earlier had walked with him around newly completed almshouses that he had donated to Bournville would never again be seen around the village. His body lay on a cold slab in the cemetery at Lodge Hill.

Over the spring and summer of 1899, the family catastrophe prompted a complete reorganization of the chocolate factory. The Cadbury brothers had already agreed that in the event that either of them died, the firm would be reorganized as a private limited company, handing opportunities down to the next generation. Accordingly, Richard and George's oldest sons found themselves joint man-aging directors of the vast enterprise. For the four Cadbury cousins, it was a complicated inheritance.

Richard's oldest son, thirty-seven-year-old Barrow, had a decidedly nonmaterialistic streak that sat incongruously with the directorship of a large chocolate firm. He was intensely committed to the Society of Friends and promoted its ideals such as peace and the unity of churches. With his eye for detail, he was scrupulous in the manage-ment of Bournville's cashiers department. He also delighted in intro-ducing new technology: adding machines that could print on paper tape, typewriters for the office, and telephones that could be installed through the recently formed National Telephone Company. Barrow's brother, thirty-two-year-old William, favored the outdoor life like his father. He already had ten years' experience at Bournville running the engineering department and introducing machinery to keep pace with new product lines. Now he took responsibility for sales and was involved in sourcing cocoa for the firm.

Their two cousins, George's oldest sons, had less experience in the family factory. Twenty-three-year-old Edward, a shy man known for his business acumen, was appointed to lead the fast-growing ex-port department, and he hastily made plans to check on sales teams across the world. His twenty-one-year-old brother, George Jr., who had a passion for science, found himself on the front line of arguably the most nerve-wracking assignment of all: creating new brands with which to challenge the Dutch and the Swiss.

For George Jr., it had been a "shattering blow" when his father had sternly ordered him to leave his science studies at London Uni-versity two years earlier to join the family business. Impatient and mischievous—as a child, he rowed the maids to the island in the lake at the manor and left them there—now the burdensome role of joint managing director sat heavily on young shoulders. To his father, the culture of secondary education was unimportant compared to "the culture of the soul and earning a livelihood." His son should apply his scientific skills to the needs of their new chemistry department.

The Cadbury team had struggled for ten years to find a formula that could beat the Swiss milk chocolate. Nothing seemed right.

Their first attempt, made with milk powder, was not launched until 1897 and was struggling to secure a foothold in the shops. Grocers preferred to stock Swiss chocolate because the public asked for it. Whatever combination of ingredients George Jr. and his team tried in the laboratory, their milk chocolate remained stubbornly coarse, dry, and unsaleable. Rumors were rife that both Rowntree and Fry were preparing to launch a milk chocolate brand.

George Jr. knew he had a young rival at Rowntree in Haxby Road in York. Like George Cadbury, Joseph Rowntree had turned his chocolate works into a limited liability company and passed the baton to the younger generation. His second son, twenty-eight-year-old Seebohm Rowntree, was running their research laboratory. He too had been tasked with developing products to rival the Swiss. For George Jr., there was no knowing what Rowntree might come up with. Joseph Rowntree's nephew, Arnold, had already proved himself in areas where his uncle had been sadly lacking. What Joseph thought of as Arnold's advertising "stunts" had served as a wakeup call. First there was the motorcar—at a time when such a thing was a novelty—with a gigantic tin of Rowntree's Elect Cocoa attached, which rattled disconcertingly and demanded attention as it was paraded through towns. Then there was the Oxford and Cambridge boat race of 1897. Arnold had the temerity to cover a barge with posters for Elect Cocoa and sail it right through the course. It was nothing his uncle would have done, but it was yielding results. Sales of Elect Cocoa were taking off. As for the Frys, it was anyone's guess what they might conjure up next.

After a short apprenticeship at chocolate factories on the continent, records show that George Jr. secured an invitation to tour Peter's plant in Vevey, Switzerland. This prompted him to set up a specialist milk condensing plant at Bournville to investigate the best ways to evaporate milk in bulk without spoiling it. On outings every weekend in his shiny new Lanchester car—the modern one with the roof—George Jr. could see the dispiriting results of Cadbury's first milk chocolate bar only too plainly in the shops. It was a disaster. The Swiss were winning hands down. They sold thirty tons of milk chocolate a week in Britain, where Cadbury could not manage one ton. It was a shattering defeat. But what George Jr. came up with next would transform the fortunes of the company.

In Bournville, George Cadbury Sr., still chairman of the company, was able to step back from the day-to-day operation of the business. He was keen to use his time to expand his philanthropic interests. This was something he had discussed with his wife, and they had many plans.

Elsie had proved to be the perfect wife for George, capable, warm-hearted, and totally committed to Quaker principles. The manor re-sounded with the exuberant sounds of their growing family; by 1899 there were ten children from George's first and second marriages. Portraits of the time capture the strength of the Victorian family. George, bearded and smiling beneath his top hat, has Elsie seated at his side. The teenagers are grouped behind them, the babies sit on their laps, and the younger children are arranged at their feet. The girls are good-looking with flowing hair, long skirts, and frilly white blouses. Even the young boys are dressed to copy their father in smart dark suits and ties. It is a portrait of success but not merely material success. Both parents believed that children must have a firm foundation from which to explore the world.

Despite the formality of the family pictures, Elsie was not one for stuffy restrictions. The children were left with their governesses during the day while Elsie went on rounds of public engagements. When she returned one day to find that her daughters Dolly and Molly had been sent to their rooms for the most unladylike act of climbing on the roof, she summoned them at once. She told them that all children should learn to take risks, without which they will have no chance to learn. As an ardent Quaker, Elsie was committed to good works, nothing if not zealous, even putting her holiday in jeopardy. It was not uncommon for George Sr., who liked to arrive thirty minutes early for a train, to go on ahead with the children in the pony and trap. Elsie, working for the poor until the last minute, would dash up as the whistle blew. "My recreation begins the moment I drop into a comfortable railway carriage," she told a friend, "having counted my family to see that none is missing." On Sundays she played the organ installed in the oak room on the ground floor as the family gathered to sing hymns. George doted on her, and if they were apart, they wrote sometimes twice a day. "What a thing it is to be ruled by one's wife," he said.

Each year they threw open the grounds of the manor house for a party attended by children from some of the roughest districts of Birmingham. They built a large hall known as The Barn in the park to provide tea and refreshments for up to seven hundred children. George Sr., with his love of nature, believed strongly that every child should have access to playing outside in clean air. Games were organized in the open fields, but the star attraction was the open-air baths. More than fifty children could bathe at any one time, and for the young visitors, most of whom had no access to a bath, it was thrilling. The sun on their backs, the sparkling water always inviting, the boys from the inner cities had no desire to leave and would stay in all day, until they were blue and shivering and cleaner than they had been in years.

The parties at the Barn were just an informal beginning. George and Elsie had both witnessed the critical problems of urban industrial living: housing shortages, inner-city crowding, poverty, and the social problems that come with deprivation. George wanted to take a scientific approach to tackling these problems. He aimed to use Bournville as a testing ground for reform. As a Quaker, the business was not just to benefit the owners and the workers but also the local community and society at large.

Before George Cadbury could implement his plans, an outbreak of war raised difficult questions for how a man should best use his wealth. On October 11, 1899, an ill-equipped army of 35,000 Boers prepared to take on the British Empire. The Boers, a group of farmers of Dutch descent, had settled in the Orange Free State and the Transvaal in southern Africa, territories that were rich in mineral wealth. But there were many who agreed with the British mining magnate Cecil Rhodes that the British Empire should command a sweep of land from "the Cape to Cairo."

George and Elsie were shocked at the way the national press fuelled the appetite for war. The brash new *Daily Mail*, under such rousing headers as "For Empire and Liberty," glorified British prospects. "Brain for brain, body for body," the paper assured its 750,000 readers, "the English speaking people are much more than a match for the Dutchman" despite "the trickery and cunning of men from the Low countries." Patriotic crowds gathered in throngs to give an ovation to those stalwarts departing for the Cape, "equal to any that even victorious troops have ever been accorded on returning from a campaign." In Waterloo station, soldiers departed to the triumphant crash of brass and cavalry bands. "All semblance of military order disappeared. The police were swept aside and men were borne, in many cases, shoulder high. . . . Even total strangers, carried away with enthusiasm broke into the ranks and insisted on carrying rifles and kitbags."

George Cadbury was approached by a rising star of the Liberal Party, the radical Welshman David Lloyd George. He was opposed to the war and knew that George Cadbury shared his views. Lloyd George had a challenging proposal. The national press was speaking almost in one voice in favor of war and fuelling the jingoistic fervor of the public. Lloyd George was keen to ensure that the public heard alternative views. Very few papers dared to take on the establishment, challenge the policy on war, and probe the interests of the mine owners. The *Manchester Guardian* in the north and London's *Morning Leader* in the south were the only papers consistently opposed to war. Lloyd George had a special interest in the *Daily News*. This once-radical paper had been founded by Charles Dickens in 1834 and had championed liberal reforms and social issues; now it was taking an editorial line that sanctioned the war. He asked George to join a syndicate to buy the paper.

George Cadbury was sympathetic to Lloyd George's view. He believed that British diamond speculators and mine owners in southern Africa like Cecil Rhodes wanted to suppress the Boer government in the Transvaal to keep control of the mines for themselves. He abhorred the greed and imperialism masquerading as a just cause and like Lloyd George believed that the cost of the war was delaying social reforms at home. But he hesitated. The ownership of a national newspaper would be a completely new venture. He had avoided a prominent role in politics when he turned down an invitation from William Gladstone in 1892 to stand as an MP. George wrestled with the decision. What was the best way to use his wealth to benefit society at large? Should he seek to influence and educate public opinion and present issues honestly through a national newspaper? Or should he develop his template at Bournville?

He told Lloyd George that he was reluctant to take on the *Daily News*, but he could make a small contribution. He paid for an early train to take copies of the *Morning Leader* each day to key towns between London and Sheffield so the public would be exposed to an alternative view. George's greatest priority was his plan for Bournville. Ever mindful of the corrosive effects that great wealth can have on the soul, his first step, on which he had his wife's complete support, was to partially disinherit his children.

There is a family picture that marks the day, December 14, 1900, when George Cadbury gave away his wealth. The Quaker parish he first established with 142 homes clustered around the chocolate works had blossomed into an idyllic English village with 370 cottages and 500 acres of land. Now he wanted to give it away to create the Bournville Village Trust. A large and solemn group had gathered in front of the Friends Meeting House on the village green to hear what he had to say.

"I am not rich as an American millionaire would count riches," George declared. "My gift is in the bulk of my property outside of the business. . . . I have seriously considered how far a man is justified in giving away the heritage of his children and have come to the conclusion that my children will be all the better for being deprived of this money. Great wealth is not to be desired and in my experience it is more of a curse than a blessing to the families that possess it."

He explained that six of his ten children were of an age to understand how this action affected them, "and they all entirely approve."

Provision was made for "an insurance of a modest competence" for each child. Beyond this, it was up to them. Judging by the sober faces of the large family around him, the enormity of the decision and his high expectations of them were all too plain.

George Cadbury was the first English chocolate entrepreneur to create a trust, and his hopes for what it would accomplish are clear from the deeds. The aim of the Bournville Trust was for "the amelioration of the conditions of the working class and labouring population," with a special emphasis on improving their quality of life with "improved dwellings with gardens and open spaces to be enjoyed therewith." The homes were meant to be inhabited by a cross section of society and this was reflected in the price or the rent. At the time of the gift, 143 houses had already been sold to tenants on 999-year leases—some for as little as £150. The remaining 227 homes were let on varying rentals depending on the size of the house. All houses had a garden that was sufficiently large to grow a significant amount of food. Each plot could produce around two shillings' worth of fruit and vegetables per week—worth roughly £375 a year today—increasing the value of the home to the tenant still further.

George wanted the village to grow while maintaining its quality. Once repairs and maintenance were carried out, the trustees were to use any extra rental income to buy land and build more homes, applying the same generous ratios of parkland and gardens to buildings. He wanted to prove that the scheme was economically viable so that other philanthropists or investors could see its benefits and follow suit. If investors could make a return on quality housing for tenants of varying backgrounds without resorting to building a slum, they might be inspired to copy it. In this way Bournville could influence society at large.

The experiment at Bournville was part of a wider debate concerning the problems of inner cities. In 1898 a parliamentary shorthand writer, Ebenezer Howard, had published *Tomorrow: A Peaceful Path to Real Reform*, which set out a grand scheme for a revolution in town planning. Howard was concerned by the waves of people moving from the country into the towns; London had almost doubled in size between 1870 and 1900 from a population of 3.9 million to 6.6

million. This brought all the familiar problems of urban poverty. Howard believed the solution lay in a futuristic scheme in which "Town and country *must be married*." He toured Bournville and believed the garden city idea could be developed to provide an entire social and economic system with the potential to tackle key problems of Victorian capitalism.

Howard's idealistic scheme saw large areas of land converted to clusters of garden cities. Each garden city of approximately 32,000 people would be geometrically arranged around green belts separating it from the next garden city. Unlike Bournville, Howard's garden city was arranged on a circular design with boulevards and avenues surrounding a central park. The compact design gave it a human scale and put most essentials within walking distance of the residents. He thought of every need, even foreshadowing today's shopping malls with elegant glass arcades in each town called a "Crystal Palace." An idealist to the last, Howard hoped that workers would unite to create the vision, "for the vastness of the task which seems to frighten some . . . represents in fact the very measure of its value to the community." He was so fervent in his beliefs that he launched the Garden City Association in 1899 to turn belief into practice.

George Cadbury supported Howard's vision because it coincided with his own ideas on land use. He believed that injustices in the ownership of land "lay at the root of many social evils." If the estimated 9 million households in England were housed in cottages at ten to the acre, he reasoned, they would occupy a mere 900,000 acres of the 77 million acres in Britain. Since tests at Bournville showed that one acre of cottage gardens yielded twelve times more produce than one acre of pasture, it was a much more effective way of meeting the nation's food needs. A massive increase in death duties was needed, he thought, so that it would no longer be possible for most of Britain's land to accumulate in just a few hands. Bournville proved that land was more effectively cultivated "in the hands of the people themselves."

As for the difficult decision to disinherit his own children—the reasoning behind it was set out six years later in an interview that

George Cadbury gave to a committee of the Canterbury Convocation investigating social problems, including the accumulation of wealth. At the heart of it, he explained, was his unwavering faith.

George believed that "every man must give an account of himself to God." According to Matthew 19:24, "It is easier for a camel to go through the eye of a needle, than for a rich man to enter the Kingdom of God." The camel, it is said, had to stoop to go through the Needle's Eye gate into Jerusalem; a rich man can enter if he will humble himself before God. For George Cadbury, it was simply wrong that a lucky few "have a superabundance of wealth . . . and every conceivable comfort and luxury" while countless others in "so-called Christian lands . . . lack things which are essential to health and morality." He felt, moreover, that great wealth was of questionable value. "I have seen many families ruined by it, morally and spiritually," he told the committee. And while money brought no lasting happiness to the rich, it "certainly brought a vast amount of misery upon those who did not have their share."

George and Elsie wanted to contribute more of their personal wealth to develop the community at Bournville. Over the years several handsome public buildings were built around the village green. The first was a meeting place known as Ruskin Hall, which eventually became the Bournville School of Arts and Crafts. It provided professional qualifications such as teacher training as well as many craft skills like dressmaking and metal work. George and his wife also paid for the Bournville Schools. Happy afternoons were spent together perfecting the designs that equipped each school with a modern library, scientific laboratory, and extensive playgrounds. And of course it all had to be in a beautiful setting, something immemorial that evoked a continental style and possessed classical beauty. When staying in Bruges, Belgium, George and Elsie were enchanted by the sound of the cathedral's bells, and they arranged to make an exact copy of the Bruges bells for Bournville. It was a great day when all twenty-two bells were hoisted into position below the domed cupola in the tower of the Infant School, the carillon ringing out around the village green.

The Cadbury brothers had initiated a great many schemes targeted at improving the health and well-being of their staff, and George was dedicated to developing them further. A job at the chocolate factory was not for the physically faint hearted. The men's sports grounds now reached to twelve acres, and there were Bournville teams for every conceivable sport. In the summer months, the outdoor pool for men was popular, and in 1905 an imposing indoor pool was completed for women, and thousands of staff learned to swim. The women also had twelve acres of grounds for sport. Fitness training was compulsory for anyone under eighteen; an hour a week was set aside in the work schedules. Village events were organized on the green, including a maypole for children's dancing in spring, folk dancing, Morris dancing, country dancing, and a youth club.

Should anyone fall ill, a doctor was hired in 1902 for the staff. The medical department expanded over time to include four nurses and a dentist, who were available to all employees free of charge. Free vitamin supplements were provided for those lacking stamina, and a convalescent home in the Herefordshire countryside was built for staff in need of a rest. These amenities may seem quaintly paternalistic by modern standards, but at a time when employees could be subjected to unhealthy or even dangerous working environments, it is small wonder that workers were queuing up to join Bournville. By the turn of the twentieth century, George Cadbury took a further step and asked his son Edward and nephew Barrow to look into creating a pension scheme.

There were the spiritual needs of his community to consider as well. George believed it was not possible to grow morally or spiritually in a slum. Only in the open spaces of the country was it possible for a man to come into touch with nature, "and thus know more of nature's God." At Bournville, apart from the Friends Meeting House, a site was found for an Anglican church, a village hall, and vicarage. George welcomed meetings of different faiths. He was a friend of William Booth, a Methodist, who had founded the Salvation Army in 1865, and he valued Booth's message of a "practical religion" encouraging members to work in the slums. George believed all churches should unite to tackle issues such as helping the poor and created a central library so ministers and preachers could share works from different faiths.

George and Elsie's efforts to help the underprivileged began to show tangible results. In 1919 studies were carried out that compared children ages six to twelve who had been brought up in the poor Floodgate Street area of Birmingham with children of the same ages who grew up in Bournville. The children in Bournville grew on average two to three inches taller and were eight pounds heavier than their counterparts from the poorer districts of Birmingham. Infant mortality in Birmingham was 101 per 1,000 births, twice as high as the rate in Bournville.

Above all George wanted to use Bournville to improve the lives of children from Birmingham's slums. This may well have been due to the enduring influence of his mother, Candia, who in her temperance visits to the poor districts in Birmingham was concerned for the innocent young victims caught in the cycle of deprivation. George revisited those same dirt-encrusted, teeming inner cities, where a dozen families might occupy one house, and practical as ever, wanted to give the children space. In his ideal world, no child would be brought up where a rose could not grow. He arranged to buy sites from the Birmingham City Council and turned them into playgrounds, hoping that other wealthy families in Birmingham would follow suit. Ideally, he argued, there should be a playground every four hundred yards, so that children throughout the city had daily access to spaces where they could play and grow more healthy.

To improve children's health, George and Elsie created The Beeches in Bournville. This large house and grounds were used as an invalid home in the winter, but in the spring, the Beeches was turned into a summer camp where children could enjoy a two-week holiday from the industrial slums. Under the jurisdiction of the endlessly capable Mr. and Mrs. Cole, thirty stayed at a time. They could eat as much as they wanted, sleep in clean beds, and roam the garden and surrounding fields all day. According to contemporary reports, the children enjoyed their stay so much it was not unusual for them to be "unaccountably missing" on departure day. Eventually they were found hiding under beds or in cupboards when it was time to go. Ever keen to document the benefits so other benefactors would follow suit, children were weighed on arrival and departure and found to be two to three pounds heavier after their visit.

No doubt inspired by his father's campaign to help the chimney sweep boys, some of whom were badly maimed, George Cadbury had another scheme in mind for children who were unable to play. He knew that many of the cripples on the streets were the luckless "victim of cruel circumstances or ignorant chance," and especially tragic were those harmed by "the carelessness of their own drunken parents." George bought a grand house known as Woodlands, which was set on six acres of parkland just across the road from the manor house. It was adapted to cater to the special needs of crippled children.

George Cadbury enjoyed making the rounds of these charities. He liked to visit the Barn when a party was in progress. According to his biographer, Alfred Gardiner, he also visited the handicapped children at Woodlands each week, a "large box of chocolates tucked under his arm." Invariably his entrance was greeted "by loud shouts of the children." After chatting with the children downstairs who were recovering their mobility, he would go upstairs to see the children with more seriously injuries whose chances in life were limited. He visited every child handing out gifts, and he hired a surgeon to investigate if anything more could be done for them.

George Cadbury's religious convictions shaped his world. It unified every aspect of his life and gave purpose and energy to his philanthropy.

Walking around Bournville, George could see the results of his endeavor: houses and public buildings where there had once been muddy fields. The improbable dream that he and his brother shared had been turned into solid bricks and mortar, into something powerful for good. And it was all from chocolate. Chocolate, or rather the humble cocoa bean, had created a little Eden. He hoped the success of his charities and trusts would inspire others. "Example is better than precept," he said. "If you can show that your life is happier by giving" than by hoarding, "you will do more good than by preaching about it." So it was with great pleasure that he was approached in 1900 by Joseph Rowntree when he too wanted to create a model village.

In York, Joseph Rowntree, like George Cadbury, found it liberating to delegate part of the business to the younger generation. He had an all-consuming interest in tackling the problems of poverty, a passion shared by his son, Seebohm. Both Joseph and Seebohm had been much moved by a powerful series of books called *Life and Labour of the People in London*, which were written by Charles Booth in the 1890s. Booth popularized the idea of a "poverty line"—a minimum weekly sum that was needed to keep a man and his family at a basic level to maintain health. His study highlighted the levels of squalor and degradation that London's poor endured, and he argued that the state had the means to help them. Seebohm was interested in applying a dispassionate scientific analysis to try to understand the causes of poverty. Despite his duties at the chocolate works, he found time to embark on a groundbreaking study.

Seebohm chose York as a representative provincial town and set out to gather data on 11,560 families on 388 streets—two-thirds of the town's inhabitants, including, he said, "the whole of the working class population of the city." He and his investigators undertook sensitive inquiries house to house, questioning people on their rent, income, number of occupants, number of rooms, access to a water tap, diet, and other personal information.

Seebohm pored over the data. Page after page of case notes revealed a vivid snapshot of poverty in York, each distilling the bare facts of a heartrending family struggle, but how could he use the information to analyze the problem more systematically?

Labourer. Married. Two rooms. Four children. Chronic illness. Not worked for two years. Wife chars. Parish relief. This house shares one closet and one water tap with eight other houses. Rent 1s 7d. . . .

Woodchopper. Married. One room. Parish relief. Wife blind. Mostly live on what they can beg. This house shares one closet and one water tap with two other houses. Rent 2s. . .

Labourer. Married. Four rooms. Six children. Filthy to extreme. This house shares one closet with another, and one water tap with five others. Rent 3s 6d. . .

Husband in asylum. Four rooms. Five children. Parish relief. Very sad case. Five children under thirteen. Clean and respectable but much poverty. . . . This house shares one closet with another house and one water tap with three other houses. Rent 3s 9d. . .

Chimneysweep. Married. Two rooms. Five children under thirteen. All sleep in one room. . . . Man in temporary employment earning 2s a day. . . . A bad workman . . . incapable of supporting his family decently. . .

Polisher. Married. Four rooms. Two children. Parish relief. Wife washes . . . Man not deserving; has spent all large earnings on drink. Fellow workmen have made several collections for him. All speak badly of him. House very dirty. Rent 3s 10d. . .

After consulting with nutrition experts on the minimum requirements for a basic diet, Seebohm Rowntree set a poverty line for a family of five at 21s and 8d—roughly £75 per week today—acknowledging that this allowed for a diet "less generous . . . than that supplied to able bodied paupers in workhouses." He defined "primary poverty" as those below this poverty line. No matter how carefully they spent their wages, this group did not earn enough to cover the minimum basic needs of life, which he described as "the maintenance of merely physical efficiency." Incredibly, 7,230 people (almost 10 percent of York's population) fell into primary poverty, meaning they could not earn enough to feed themselves adequately.

Seebohm's analysis showed a low wage was the biggest single cause of primary poverty. Half the men in this category had jobs, but they worked for such a pittance that they could not meet their families' basic needs. Apart from appallingly low wages, the other key causes of primary poverty were the size of the family and the death or illness of the wage earner.

The next group Seebohm analyzed was the 13,072 people suffering from what he called "secondary poverty"—roughly 18 percent of the population. To the investigators, this group appeared just as poverty-stricken as the first group, despite the fact that its members earned enough money to meet their basic needs. However, they failed to do so because they were spending some of their income on nonessentials, "either useful or wasteful," such as drink. For those in secondary poverty, he considered a number of factors were contributing to their poverty, such as inadequate housing or overcrowding. Taking the two groups together, Seebohm showed that 27 percent—half the working population of York—were in either primary or secondary poverty.

Seebohm Rowntree was "much surprised" that his findings co-incided with Charles Booth's research. Booth had estimated that 30 percent of Londoners lived in poverty. If the findings in London and York could be extrapolated to other towns, reasoned Seebohm, "We are faced with the startling probability that from 25–30% of the town populations of the UK are living in poverty," a result that he thought prompted "great searchings of the heart." Surely, "No civilisation can be sound or stable which has at its base this mass of stunted human life?" For him it was unacceptable that "multitudes of men and women are doomed by inevitable law to a struggle for survival so severe as to cripple or destroy the higher parts of their nature." Seebohm's research was published in 1901 as *Poverty: A Study of Town Life*. One person who read it was Winston Churchill, a Tory MP at the time. Rowntree's study "has fairly made my hair stand on end," he said.

Joseph Rowntree was keen to do what he could to alleviate the situation his son had revealed in York. By 1900 he was in a position to do this; in the five years since moving to Haxby Road, his business had doubled in size with sales approaching £500,000. After discussions with George Cadbury, Joseph purchased 150 acres of land three miles outside of York and hired an architect to design a village on parallel lines to Bournville. He envisaged a similarly idyllic community, a utopia of cottage gardens resplendent with produce and pale children running freely through the woods, taking on the color of health. He wanted his village to be affordable for the poorest slum dwellers of York, many of whom were supporting a family on less than £1 a week. When the lowest weekly rents of 5 shillings proved to be beyond their means, Rowntree commissioned simpler cottages to be built without bathrooms or hot water for £135 each and let for 4 shillings per week.

It took time for his experiment to come to fruition, but gradually, with the addition of the Folk Hall, schools, and playing fields, the pretty garden village of New Earswick took shape. In 1904, sixty-eight-year-old Joseph Rowntree, like George Cadbury, handed over the estate to the nonprofit Joseph Rowntree Village Trust. To complement the work of the Village Trust, he also created the Joseph Rowntree Charitable Trust and the Social Services Trust. These had the remit to investigate social and religious issues and explore problems of "importance to the well-being of the community." He committed one-half of his total wealth to these three trusts.

Discussions between the two friendly rivals brought Joseph Rowntree and George Cadbury together on another issue of keen, shared interest. Joseph Rowntree's older son, John Wilhelm, was beginning to question the Quaker movement and challenge its restrictive practices. He felt that the Quaker movement was stagnating, and the decline in numbers and outdated codes of practice were leading to a withering of the Society. It was in danger of becoming little more than "a hereditary social club!" Where was the spark? What was its mission? John Wilhelm organized a series of meetings to discuss ideas and called for the creation of a permanent college that would develop Quaker thinking. George Cadbury offered his former home at Woodbrooke on the outskirts of Bournville for the Quaker college, the only one in Europe. He and Elsie wanted Woodbrooke College to become a retreat where the spirit might be recharged; they funded scholarships for students from around the world. They hoped the college would contribute to the evolution of the Quaker faith and bring a new understanding reborn from centuries encrusted with obedience to outdated ideas.

Meanwhile, Joseph Rowntree was not the only entrepreneur in England inspired to copy Bournville. Early in the twentieth century, Sir James Reckitt, a Quaker and a successful businessman in household goods, developed a similar garden village in east Hull. Ebenezer

Howard's ideals began to take shape as he founded his first garden city in Letchworth in Hertfordshire, followed years later by Welwyn Garden City. Another friend of George Cadbury, Dame Henrietta Barnett, created the Hampstead Garden Suburb in north London.

Soon there was a stream of visitors to Bournville from overseas. A Frenchman, George Benoit-Levy, returned home to create a garden village at Dourges in northern France. In Germany, Margarethe Krupp, who inherited a fortune from her husband's large armaments firm, gave a million marks to build a big estate at Margarethenhohe in Essen on condition that the architects studied Bournville before drafting their plans.

Word of Bournville's success reached across the Atlantic and to India, China, and even Australia. "Bournville," declared the *Melbourne Age*, "is as important to England as a Dreadnought."

While George Cadbury Sr. was happily absorbed in creating his model community at Bournville, he could not ignore the wider issues in society. The deepening crisis of the Boer War provoked him to action.

In the early autumn of 1900, a rector's daughter from Cornwall, Emily Hobhouse, heard rumors of a new and horrific practice being used by British commanders against the Boers. As a member of the South African Conciliation Committee, she learned of inhumane conditions in a "concentration camp" in the region—so named after the policy of "concentrating" Boer women and children in one location, allegedly for their own protection. The British had fought their way into Boer territory by the summer of 1900. Faced with guerrilla tactics, British commanders applied a scorched earth policy, razing 30,000 Boer homes in the Transvaal region to the ground. Hobhouse heard of hundreds of Boer women, children, and prisoners trapped in a concentration camp in Port Elizabeth on the South African coast. She set sail to help them and to investigate the situation.

Her research revealed that there was not one but thirty-four concentration camps. Worse, it was a mockery to call these "refugee camps." Conditions were so barbaric they were more like death camps. In one camp alone, fifty children died each day, and a third of the inmates perished over one month. There was no provision for adequate food, clean water, or sanitation. Disease was rampant, famine was rife, and many inmates were emaciated. The camp system was "whole sale cruelty," Emily wrote. "To keep these camps going is murder to the children." She denounced the so-called humanitarian system run by British commanders as "hollow and rotten to the core."

Back in Britain, however, the press was speaking in an almost united voice in favor of war and failed to reveal its full horror. When Emily Hobhouse returned to England and tried to explain what she saw, "The press abused me," she said. She was branded "a rebel and a liar and an enemy of the people" and dismissed as "hysterical and even worse."

In England, Lloyd George had not given up on his efforts to find a Liberal backer for the *Daily News*. George Cadbury, shocked by developments in the war, the corruption of the mine owners, and the recent revelations of concentration camps, began to see how owning a national newspaper could have a value. It seemed a matter of duty to use his wealth to influence public opinion. "This war seems the most diabolical that was ever waged," he told Labour MP John Burns. "Just now it seems to me that speculators, trust mongers, and owners of enormous wealth are the great curse of this world and the cause of most of its poverty!"

In 1901, he agreed to Lloyd George's proposal and put up £20,000 to join a partnership to purchase the *Daily News*. By any standards, this was a colossal sum—enough to build more than eighty new houses at Bournville. But in sharing ownership of a national paper, he hoped to expose other social ills, such as inhumane factory conditions. He would have a national voice that could promote the Quaker ideal of pacifism and to speak for the inarticulate and the unfortunate.

But opposing the war was no light matter. Advertisers responded swiftly by removing their business from the *Daily News*, and losses soared. By the end of 1901, his business partner wanted out. George Cadbury faced a tough choice. He could sell his share and run the risk that the paper would be bought by those in favor of war. Or he could put up another £20,000 to buy the paper outright. Despite the rising losses, George Cadbury chose the latter.

As sole proprietor, he appointed an editor who shared his views: Alfred George Gardiner, who would later write Cadbury's biography. Under Gardiner's editorship, the *Daily News* drew attention to the scandal of tens of thousands of Chinese coolies laboring in South African mines in subhuman conditions. With provocative headlines such as "Yellow Slavery," the paper condemned the Tory government for condoning slavery and supporting wealthy British interests.

Gardiner and his team also highlighted the urgent need for labor reforms at home. The *Daily News* was tireless in its exposure of inhumane labor conditions in Britain. The paper funded an exhibition in London that revealed the appalling exploitation of those working in sweated labor. They found women making shirts in their homes for less than a penny an hour, repairing sacks for two shillings a week, and chain-making for six shillings a week, often working more than twelve hours a day. George Cadbury became president of the newly formed Anti-Sweating League and was supported by the indefatigable efforts of his oldest son, Edward. Edward wrote two books summarizing the findings: *Sweating*, which highlighted the need for a minimum working wage, was published in 1907; and *Women's Work and Wages* followed in 1908. The *Daily News* also campaigned for unemployment benefits and old age pensions. Edward and his father helped to create the National Old Age Pensions League to champion the cause of state support for the elderly. It appeared that the dream of creating a chocolate factory to promote social reform and justice was finally coming to fruition.

George Cadbury's attitudes and beliefs were increasingly in step with the new Labor Movement. He agreed with the trade union movement. The campaigns for improved labor conditions, shorter working hours, and better provisions for workers such as sickness benefits: these were steps he had already taken in Bournville. But there were very few Labor MPs. "We want a hundred working men in Parliament," George declared. "Only then will the condition of the people become a living issue."

Cadbury's opinions put him in conflict with the *Daily News*'s chief executive, the journalist Thomas Ritzema, who had strict puritanical views. Not content to promote pacifism and labor causes, the moral-istic Ritzema cancelled the racing pages and betting tips and opposed any advertisements for alcohol. Circulation plummeted further. The paper began to be seen as needlessly moral and censorious. The great philanthropist was finding his venture into public life increasingly troubled. Soon the *Daily News* was costing him up to £30,000 each year. His fortune, cultivated with such parsimony and exactitude, was being drained. Worse was to come.

For a Quaker whose public virtue was much reported and whose own paper thundered about the wrongdoings of others, it proved to be a particularly nasty revelation. George Cadbury began to hear ap-palling reports of a slave trade in Africa. Slavery was rife in the very plantations where he was buying most of his cocoa: São Tomé. This was a moral blow more severe than any business setback.

12

A Serpentine and
Malevolent Cocoa Magnate

The first warning of slavery came when George Cadbury's nephew, thirty-four-year-old William Cadbury, sailed across the Atlantic to visit one of the company's small cocoa plantations in the West Indies. As a leading buyer for Cadbury, he had bought two small estates in Trinidad four years earlier to research improvements in cultivation. William thrived on the outdoor life and eagerly anticipated his annual research trip to the West Indies, where it always felt like summer. But this year, as he toured the shady avenues of trees appreciating the order and beauty of the place, William learned of troubling news.

The growers in Trinidad told him of a rumor they had heard about cocoa plantations thousands of miles away on the other side of the Atlantic. It concerned São Tomé and Principe in the Gulf of Guinea, the two islands that were the first to cultivate cocoa in Africa. The Trinidad growers believed that some of the workers on these West African islands were slaves.

William was worried: In 1900 Cadbury bought 45 percent of its beans from São Tomé and Principe. He knew very little about the islands except that the beans cultivated there were superior to any others in Africa, and production was prolific.

By chance, later that spring, the Cadburys were notified of a plantation for sale on São Tomé. As William read the sales brochure, to his alarm he saw a list of assets that included "two hundred black labourers worth £3,555." "The suggestion behind this statement was obvious and disturbing," he wrote. The workers were referred to as part of the property. He took the matter to the Cadbury board. According to the minutes for April 30, 1901: "This seems to confirm other indirect reports that slavery . . . exists on these Cocoa estates." The board asked William Cadbury to investigate.

The two islands were under Portuguese control, and slavery had notionally been abolished in Portuguese colonies during the 1870s. The abrupt end to the slave trade in São Tomé had come in 1875, when 6,000 desperate laborers simply walked out of the plantations and entered the capital demanding that they be treated like freed men. So how was it possible that a plantation owner could continue this grotesque practice? William Cadbury turned to Travers Buxton, the secretary of the British Anti-Slavery Society, for advice.

William learned the Anti-Slavery Society had received a number of accounts from missionaries and explorers in the years since 1875. In 1891, a Swiss missionary, Heli Chatelain, reported seeing slaves during his travels in Angola who were destined for São Tomé. "Some of them looked healthy," wrote Chatelain. "The majority showed signs of bad fare; some . . . were starved to skeletons." A French traveller in 1900 also observed slave gangs in Angola. "All this trade is done with the protection of the Portuguese government," he claimed in the *Anti-Slavery Reporter*. In 1902 William was introduced to a Scottish missionary, Matthew Stober, who had recently returned from central Angola. Stober was another to claim he had witnessed the slave trade firsthand.

How was this possible when slavery was banned? William Cadbury was sufficiently troubled that he set out in 1903 to Lisbon, Portugal, to meet with the local authorities and plantation owners for himself. Matthew Stober, a fluent Portuguese speaker, accompanied him. He wanted the missionary to describe the horrors he had witnessed directly to the plantation owners and establish the truth. In a letter to Joseph Storrs Fry II in Bristol, who was also buying São Tomé cocoa, William set out his concerns. He wanted to enlist the support of the other leading cocoa buyers to bring the practice to an end.

As Cadbury and Stober made their way by train and carriage across France and Spain towards Lisbon, they had plenty of time to ponder the predicament. Quakers had pioneered campaigns against slavery for three centuries. How was it possible for leading Quaker employers to apparently be involved in a barbaric trade that supposedly did not exist?

From the earliest days of the Quaker movement, Friends believed in the sanctity of human life and the significance of every individual in the eyes of God. In the seventeenth century, the founder of Quakerism, George Fox, travelled to the Caribbean and America to speak out against the cruel trade that reduced men to little more than cattle to be bought and sold. After Fox's death, the Society of Friends continued to denounce slavery. This "Hellish practice," stormed Benjamin Lay in 1736, is a "filthy sin . . . the greatest sin in the world."

Revulsion at the slave trade triggered a high-profile Quaker campaign for reform in the latter half of the eighteenth century. In England, Quakers were not permitted to stand as MPs themselves, but this did not stop them taking the first antislavery petition to the British parliament in June 1783. The politician and philanthropist William Wilberforce was horrified at what he learned of the depraved trade and took up their cause, becoming one of Britain's most prominent abolitionists. In 1787, when the Abolition Society was formed, the majority of its founders were Quakers. One method they used to expose the cruelties of the trade was by publicizing drawings of slave ships that showed slaves crammed into the transports shoulder to shoulder. Their campaign gained momentum and helped to pave the way for the British Slave Trade Act of 1807, which made it illegal to capture and transport slaves across the British Empire.

But enacting a law did not bring an end to the highly profitable trade. The Royal Navy intercepted more than 1,600 slave ships between 1808 and 1860 and liberated 150,000 slaves found on board. Any captain caught carrying slaves faced a fine of £100. It was not uncommon for slaves to be thrown overboard to avoid discovery.

Quakers continued to campaign and created the Anti-Slavery Society in 1823. They wanted not only to stop the slave trade but also to free all existing slaves. Their work culminated in the Slavery Abolition Act of 1833, which paved the way for the gradual emancipation of all slaves across the British Empire. The British and Foreign Anti-Slavery Society then took their campaign to other countries.

As Quakers, many of William Cadbury's forebears, including his great uncles, Joel Cadbury and Benjamin Head Cadbury, the older brothers of his grandfather, John, had been active antislavery campaigners. Joel Cadbury, who immigrated to Philadelphia, told his family about appalling incidents of slavery that he witnessed in America. On one occasion, during a business trip in 1842 to New Orleans, he saw a large crowd gathered around a shed and realized that slaves were being sold inside. As he entered, he saw a black woman on sale. Other slaves, herded into position like animals, waited their turn. Almost naked, the woman was made to stand while the auctioneer pointed out her selling points. She was a mere exhibit—described as healthy and fit for anything. When sold she would become the owner's property, to do with as he wished. Joel was so sickened he had to leave. His wife, Caroline, echoed his concerns and later became treasurer of the Shelter for Coloured Orphans. The English Quakers of Pennsylvania were among the first in America to campaign for the abolition of slavery, a campaign that gradually spread across America.

In Birmingham, William Cadbury's great uncle, Benjamin Head Cadbury, had worked tirelessly for the antislavery movement. After the American Civil War, he continued his work for the Society of Freed People of the Southern States. He collected warm winter clothing for women and children, arranging sewing circles and organizing the transport of essentials such as bedding and shoes from Liverpool to America. William's uncle, George Sr., also joined the Anti-Slavery Society and contributed funds along with other family members. With strong and lasting family ties to antislavery movements, it was hard for William to understand how they may have been unwitting beneficiaries of a secret slave trade.

In Lisbon, he and Matthew Stober hit an impasse. They met ruthless characters such as the Marquis de Valle Flor, the wealthiest São

Tomé trader who was rumored to subject his slaves to appalling treatment and to stockpile cocoa to control the price. He was one of many plantation owners who flatly denied having any slaves. There were others who refused to speak to them, or if they did, objected to British inquiries into Portuguese affairs. After all, they reasoned, what about Cecil Rhodes's treatment of Africans in the mines? Or the British Army's mass slaughter of Boer families during the war? How dare the British preach to the Portuguese about morality in their colonies?

Cadbury and Stober soon determined that British cocoa imports were of only modest significance to the Portuguese, accounting for not more than 5 percent of their exports from São Tomé. If British firms stopped buying, they would lose any leverage they held over the Portuguese, and William Cadbury feared the slavery would continue. Meetings with Portuguese ministers proved more promising. The minister for colonies, Manuel Gorjao, conceded there was an issue and assured his English visitors that the new Portuguese Labor Decree of 1903 would settle the matter. The decree required workers in São Tomé to be paid a minimum wage, started a modest repatriation fund, and implemented measures to stop illegal recruitment.

Once back in England, William Cadbury won the support of all leading Quaker chocolate manufacturers. Rowntree of York and Stollwerck in Cologne, Germany, joined Fry and Cadbury in their opposition to slavery, and a debate began as to the best way to tackle the problem. A boycott of São Tomé cocoa, the Rowntrees wrote, "would mean a serious pecuniary loss to those manufacturers who entered upon it." Joseph Storrs Fry II replied that nothing should stop them from "countenancing a great wrong." As a first step, the cocoa firms agreed to hire an investigator to travel to the islands and confirm the facts.

Optimistic that he was making progress in securing a coordinated response from buyers and that the Portuguese authorities would change their practices, William Cadbury reported to the Cadbury board in 1903 that "things were going to mend."

ANGOLA, DECEMBER 1904

Independent of the cocoa firms' investigation, a young English journalist, Henry Nevinson, arrived at the port of Luanda on the Atlantic coast. He had been hired by *Harper's Monthly Magazine* to make the treacherous journey to the interiors of Angola and investigate the rumors of slavery.

Luanda had once been a key trading center, but as Nevinson walked through the dusty streets, there was little hint of slavery. Everything spoke of departed riches: forts in ruins, rusted guns, and decaying grandeur mingled with "a century of rubbish." It was, he wrote, a bankrupt city, "with one drain, fit to poison a multitudinous sea."

From Luanda he took the steamer south to Lobito Bay, another infamous area for the slave trade. But still, he encountered no direct evidence: no gangs of boys "chained together, their hands shackled, and their necks held fast in forked sticks," he wrote. Instead he was met with blank stares. People shrank from his inquiries. He sensed they were frightened of revealing what they knew. Nevinson suspected that anyone who dared speak out might meet with some mysterious misadventure; poison perhaps or some apparently random act of violence in the bush.

Nevinson and his small party trekked inland, deep into beautiful terrain, "a land of bare and rugged hills, deeply scarred by weather and full of wild and brilliant colours, the violet and orange that bare hills always give." He was heading for the heart of Angola's "Hungry Country," his group wending its way along paths so narrow and sheer he compared them to a "goat-path in the Alps." Still no slave caravan. Did the slavers have advance knowledge of his trip? Could they have changed their route?

But as he made the 450-mile journey inland, Nevinson began to spot worrying evidence. "The path is strewn with dead men's bones," he observed, "the skeletons of slaves who were unable to keep up with the march and so were murdered or left to die." Deeper inland the bones were in such numbers that it "would take an army" to bury them all. Carelessly discarded in the bush, Nevinson saw the crude wooden shackles that were used to prevent escape. Typically a block of wood had holes hacked in them in which the arms or legs of a slave—or sometimes two slaves together—could be held tight in place by a wooden pin. "I saw several hundred of them," Nevinson recorded, "scattered up and down the path."

There were more signs of brutality. He came across the body of a slave who had died recently. "When I tried to raise the head, the thick woolly hair came off in my hand," Nevinson reported. To his horror this exposed "a deep gash made by the axe at the base of the skull just before it merges with the neck." The blow had been so heavy that as he tried to lay the head gently down, it "broke off from the backbone and fell to one side." It is perhaps hardly surprising that Nevinson grew increasingly fearful the deeper he penetrated into this violent land, where life had no value and could be destroyed in seconds with the butt of a rifle or the blow of an axe.

Nevertheless, Nevinson persevered. Near the town of Caiala, he came across a group of terrified boys hiding in the bushes, closely guarded by men with whips. "At the sight of me they all ran away," he recorded, "the men driving the boys before them." This fuelled his suspicion that the boys were slaves. "Men armed with *chicotes* [hide whips] do not hide a group of boys in the bush for nothing." His party came across a larger group of forty-three people guarded by men with guns. One "beautiful woman of about twenty or little more" said she had been sold for twenty cartridges. She had left her home "four moons ago," leaving behind her young baby "who was still suckling . . . when they took her away." The guards described the group as "voluntary labourers." In another village, Nevinson was told of a father who had recently committed suicide. He was out of his mind having just "pawned the last of his children," to settle an extortionate debt with a Portuguese trader.

Gradually, with discreet inquiries, Nevinson gathered sufficient evidence to conclude that people in the interior were indeed being taken as slaves. Some were sold by their own people. They might be "charged with witchcraft," he wrote, or "were wiping out an ancestral debt . . . sold by uncles in poverty . . . or paid as indemnity for village wars." Local customs made the purchase of slaves easier, he observed, partly because of the "despotic power of tribal Chiefs," and because of "the peculiar law which gives the possession of the children to the wife's brother . . . who can claim them for the payment of his own debt or the debt of his village." All too often, however, he found slaves were simply seized by agents for the Portuguese in raids on the frontier or claimed to settle extortionate debts to colonial authorities.

As Nevinson pieced together the Portuguese labor system, he began to expose a cynical system of exploitation that left him simmering with rage. Although slavery had technically been abolished, free men were being turned into slaves with the full knowledge and cooperation of the colonial authorities. It was in coastal towns like Benguala that the "deed of pitiless hypocrisy" that apparently cleared the Portuguese authorities of wrongdoing took place. Here the terrified slaves seized in the interior were herded in gangs into the tribunal. Paraded before the Portuguese officials, "They are asked if they go willingly as laborers to São Tomé." Many were too terrified to speak; those that did were ignored. Official papers were duly completed, which apparently "freed" them but in fact simply changed their status from slaves to "voluntary workers" who had agreed of their own free will to toil in the cocoa plantations of São Tomé for five years. This bonded labor was known locally as "servicais" but was nothing more than slavery.

"The climax of the farce has now been reached," Nevinson fumed. "The requirements of legalized slavery have been satisfied. The government has 'redeemed' the slaves that its own Agents have so diligently and profitably collected. They went into the Tribunal as slaves, they have come out as contracted labourers. No one in heaven or earth can see the smallest difference." But he raged, the "blackest of crimes" has been committed, apparently under the full protection of the law.

Although Nevinson took care to conceal the purpose of his visit, he was convinced he had been poisoned during his stay in Benguala and was suffering from "violent pain and frequent collapse." Nonetheless, he crawled onto the steamer to follow the slaves' journey to São Tomé. He was able to observe them from the upper deck: They were bedecked in "flashy loincloths to give them a moments pleasure," a contemptuous token of their new status as "voluntary" labor. But the *servicais* were not deceived. They knew São Tomé was *okalunga*—hell on earth.

Nevinson estimated there were 30,000 "voluntary" slaves on São Tomé and another 3,000 on Principe. Their conditions were harsh; the work unrelenting. On average one adult in five died each year, "their dead bodies lashed to poles and carried out to be flung away in the forest."

After his six-month investigation, Nevinson published his account in *Harper's Monthly Magazine* in August 1905. It made for harrowing reading. That same year, the Portuguese islands briefly became the world's top cocoa producers, but the cruelty and misery behind the figures was becoming all too transparent. This was not, said Nevinson, "the old fashioned export of human beings . . . as a reputable and staple industry." This he acknowledged had disappeared. Nonetheless, "The whole question of African slavery is still before us," he concluded. It had merely gone underground; disguised, modified, and legalized, but still a loss of liberty. To Nevinson, the enduring horror of it all was "part of the great contest of capitalism."

Cadbury and other Quaker chocolate firms were put on the spot. Their own research had yet to make headway. William Cadbury had met with directors of the other Quaker chocolate firms, and they had appointed an investigator, Joseph Burtt, who was due to leave for Africa. Despite Nevinson's revelations in *Harper's*, the young and idealistic Burtt was keen to press on. He was convinced a second independent report was necessary before they could challenge the Portuguese authorities. Traders in Lisbon flatly denied Nevinson's account. Was it possible, Burtt reasoned, that Nevinson misjudged the situation, perhaps because he spoke no Portuguese or because of "the nervous and overwrought condition of his mind?" Burtt thought this could explain why Nevinson feared he was at risk of murder. Such "a delusion," he said, was common to those "who have been overdone in Africa."

It was not long, however, before Burtt too was "overdone" in Africa. After six months in São Tomé and Principe, he fell seriously ill with tropical disease. His fever was so high he could not walk and had to be transported in a hammock for part of the journey. A doctor was sent from England to help him travel across Angola and on to the Transvaal to investigate labor in the gold mines, but their progress was slow.

In his letters to William Cadbury in 1906, Burtt essentially confirmed Nevinson's findings. It was an undercover operation, he said, that involved deceit and corruption at every level of the Portuguese administration. "No imported labourer in São Tomé has ever been returned to the mainland of Africa," he confirmed. "Children who are born on the estates are the absolute property of the owners." In the villages in Angola, where slaves were seized, there was such dread concerning the fate of any missing person, that his "family go through a service of the dead on his behalf." It was quite clear that the slave trade was every bit as horrific as Nevinson had recounted.

William Cadbury returned to Lisbon to put pressure on the authorities. Once again, he was faced with denials or requests for more time to implement reforms. In response, George Cadbury Sr., Arnold Rowntree, and other cocoa directors appealed to the British Foreign Office to confront the Portuguese government.

On October 26, 1906, William and George Cadbury Sr. secured a private meeting with the foreign secretary, Sir Edward Grey. They told him that the English cocoa makers were united in their desire to act together and were keen to ensure "that any step we take will be in harmony with any premeditated action of the British Government and be of real use in helping to solve the great African labour problem." Grey promised to help and "was very kind and courteous," George noted. In November, however, he received a letter from the Foreign Office urging his discretion on the matter. Grey wanted the Cadburys "to refrain from calling public attention to the question" until he had a chance to read Burtt's report and "to speak to the Portuguese minister himself on the subject." The Cadburys had to contain their impatience.

Unknown to the Cadburys, the Quakerly concern to end slavery immediately was entangled in a far bigger web. Even though the Foreign Office had promised to put pressure on the Portuguese, there were other British interests at stake that affected negotiations—

notably labor problems in the mines in South Africa. The British government was trying to strike a deal with the Portuguese to employ workers from Mozambique in their gold mines in the Transvaal. They were therefore in no hurry to antagonize the Portuguese authorities. The Foreign Office was stalling for time.

Burtt returned to England in the spring of 1907 and reported his findings to the leading cocoa manufacturers. Records show that on May 2, he convinced the Rowntree board "beyond all doubt" that the workers on São Tomé were held in "a condition of practical slavery," and that "cruel and villainous" methods were used to procure the labor. On June 27, leading directors of the Quaker chocolate firms met to discuss the problem. Seated at the table were Seebohm Rowntree, the author of *Poverty*; his cousin Arnold Rowntree; Edward Cadbury, who had just exposed appalling working practices in Britain in *Sweating* and *Women's Work and Wages*; his cousin, William Cadbury; Roderick Fry; and Francis Fry. They debated whether the Foreign Office could be trusted to resolve the issue. Was there any way the British could stop the slavery once and for all? Should the cocoa manufacturers organize a boycott—a move that William and others argued against, claiming that it would achieve nothing but "the comfortable assurance that we have wiped our hands of all responsibility in the matter." At heated meetings on June 27 and again on July 4, they decided to give the Foreign Office more time and try to use their buying power as leverage.

Meanwhile everything that the Quaker brand of chocolate stood for—the promised land of justice and welfare for all—was beginning to be called into question in the British press. Rumors began to circulate that the idyllic Bournville village with its happy workers producing a delicious chocolate bar rested on the unspeakable misery of African slaves. As for George Cadbury, the chocolate "uncle" who created homes for cripples, was it possible that he was in fact nothing more than a "serpentine and malevolent cocoa magnate?"

13

The Chocolate Man's Utopia

DERRY CHURCH, PENNSYLVANIA

While the cocoa magnates of England were preoccupied with Quaker idealism and social reform, the slumbering American market was waking up to a chocolate tycoon of its own.

Hershey had returned to the Pennsylvania haunts of his childhood. Exploring the region around Derry Church by horse and wagon, he found an isolated farming community still lost in the last century, lacking the trophies of modernity such as gas and electricity. While his family and critics were astonished at the idea of building on a massive scale in what appeared to be the middle of nowhere, Hershey could only see the potential. It was good dairy country. His milk chocolate factory would be surrounded by farms that could supply all the fresh milk he needed.

In 1903, Hershey arranged a survey of 4,000 acres and bought parcels of land wherever possible, starting with 1,200 acres. A local architect, C. Emlen Urban, was hired to start work on the designs. The factory alone would provide six acres of floor space filled with the very latest equipment with the capacity to make 100,000 pounds of chocolate each day. It was an extraordinary gamble, but there was no room for caution or uncertainty in Hershey's thinking. His father's advice still echoed in his mind: "If you want to make money, you must do things in a large way." This would be no regional concern such as his rivals were engaged in. Hershey was going to sell his chocolate across America from coast to coast. His chocolate would be more accessible, too; he would sell it at bus stops, in train stations, and from street vendors and cafes as well as sweetshops and grocers. And with mass production, he aimed to lower the price so everyone could afford it. Hershey's would be chocolate for the people.

Hershey delighted in mulling over the plans with his architect. He knew what he wanted. If money could buy beauty and grandeur, then he would have it. The factory—the humming hub of the enterprise— would look palatial with elegant limestone buildings set back from Chocolate Avenue by a sweeping lawn the size of a football field. It would make Cadbury's little cottage factory in the country, in those few green fields known as England, look a little out of date, a little last century by comparison. The town would also be built on a Hershey scale. The ambitious design boasted two main thoroughfares, Chocolate Avenue and Cocoa Avenue, intersected by streets named after exotic locations where Hershey bought cocoa: Areba, Trinidad, Caracas, Java, Para, Granada. . . . Like Bournville, the charming homes would have gardens and be built to differing designs set well back from rows of maple trees that lined the streets. He planned shops, a library, an athletic ground with a grandstand, and a 150-acre park of landscaped grounds with an enormous pavilion for skating and dancing. The world would come just to look.

It was a vision that put the spotlight on Hershey in a new debate about what the fulfillment of the American dream was all about. This was the age of the gilded millionaires: railroad tycoons like Vanderbilt, oil kings such as Rockefeller, meatpacking magnates such as Gustavus Swift and Philip Armour, or William Clark in mining. The sale of Andrew Carnegie's steel company for $200 million in 1901 almost certainly made him the richest man in the world. Wealth on this scale was unprecedented. Newspapers and magazines lapped up stories of the lifestyles of the new millionaires, prompting a moral debate: Was it right for the fortunate few to possess such staggering wealth while millions faced unimaginable poverty? Was this the embodiment of the American dream or a grotesque distortion of it?

John Davison Rockefeller, who was made rich beyond imagining as Standard Oil's kerosene became "the Light of the World," conveniently accepted Calvinist thinking on the matter. Success was his due; it reflected God's will. "God gave me my money," he said. He struck an increasingly controversial figure, caricatured in the press as an industrial emperor and accused of monopolistic practices. But he also gave money to charity and was building a reputation for philanthropy. In the 1890s, he helped to transform the University of Chicago with a donation of $80 million, and in 1901, he founded New York's Rockefeller Institute for Medical Research, which later became Rockefeller University.

Andrew Carnegie spelled out an entire theory of philanthropy. In 1889, he published "Wealth," the first in a series of articles for the *North American Review*, in which he set out his view that the rich had a moral obligation to look after the poor. "The contrast between the palace of the millionaire and the cottage of the labourer . . . today measures the changes which have come with civilisation," he wrote. He contrasted this with older cultures, such as the native Sioux. The wigwam of a Sioux chief, the most senior person in an Indian village, differed very little from the tents of his poorest braves. Carnegie tried to explain how these changes came about in almost Darwinian terms. There was a "law of competition" in the continuing economic struggle as wealth is accumulated in the hands of the capable few. But such laws also served a moral purpose: It was the responsibility of the rich man to give his fortune away. The same effort that had gone into making the millions should be spent on distributing it to benefit the community. Needless to say, his article sparked a furor, with other captains of industry refusing to fall in line with his views.

Ironically, despite Carnegie's professed views on wealth, he failed to put an end to the horrific working conditions in his own steel mills but rather used his theories to justify them. It was his duty, he said—especially if he was going to give his money away—to make his business as profitable as possible. With this in mind, his managers cut wages, increased hours, and ran the mills with ruthless efficiency. According to *Cosmopolitan* in 1903, inside his mills "were pits like the gaping mouth of hell, and ovens emitting a terrible degree of heat. . . . The injuries sustained are of a frightful character." Carnegie continued to preach his "Gospel of Wealth" in speeches, and his series of essays was reprinted, but his views were not always appreciated. A theologian at Dartmouth College, William Jewitt Tucker, was appalled at the patronizing idea that millionaires were the best equipped to dispense the wealth they had made from the labor of others. "I can conceive of no greater mistake, more disastrous in the end to religion if not to society," he wrote, "than of trying to make charity do the work of justice."

Milton Hershey's grand scheme would show them all. He would build the perfect American dream. His workers would benefit from the beautiful surroundings of his model town at Hershey, and his chocolate works would offer every conceivable modern comfort. His staff would be among America's working elite. As the walls of his factory began to rise from empty cornfields in 1903 and 1904, the trim figure of Milton Hershey could be seen everywhere trekking through the mud and the dirt. With each day his utopia became more tangible and real. How could it be other than good?

But the would-be chocolate king was in trouble. Hidden from view in the research department, his struggle to create a milk chocolate recipe was intensifying. Hershey's headquarters for chocolate research was concealed in a test plant behind his old family home near Derry Church. Apart from a Jersey herd, the facility had its own dairy, milk-processing plant, and large warehouse filled with kettles and vacuum pans for testing different chocolate mixtures. The grounds were patrolled by security each night to ensure there were no intruders. Absolute secrecy was essential to guard the humiliating fact that there was little to guard. Success was elusive, but the world must not know.

Like the Swiss before him, Hershey wrestled with the problems of milk processing. Experiments with cream and whole milk failed, so he turned his attention to skimmed milk. The key was to find a way to evaporate the water from the milk in such a way that it could be smoothly mixed with the sugar and cocoa fats. After heating the milk, its flavor almost invariably became poor, burned, or scalded. If the milk managed to condense successfully, it could turn lumpy when mixed with the chocolate ingredients as the cocoa oils mixed with water in milk. Even if the testers succeeded in making a chocolate bar, it could turn rancid. And then there were the potential pitfalls associated with scaling up production. How would they handle the daily input from the milk of 15,000 cows? Could they expand milk processing for mass production? How could they prevent a large batch from spoiling?

With Hershey generous but mercurial, kindhearted but always on a short fuse—shortened still further with worry—his small staff was uneasy. They commonly worked through the night; impromptu sleeping arrangements were set up in the barn so an experiment could be watched through the small hours. While their boss's benevolence was beyond doubt, they knew that just one tiny slipup could be cause for instant dismissal.

There are slightly differing accounts of Hershey's breakthrough. The heroic version has Hershey working late one night with John Schmalbach, a colleague from his caramel factory. After several hours of laborious failures, Schmalbach seized the initiative and tried a very slow evaporation of nonfat milk over low heat. He succeeded in reducing the water content of the milk and added the sugar to create a sweet, creamy concoction with no hint of a burned flavor. Better still, they found the mixture could be blended with the ingredients from the cocoa bean without spoiling to produce a smooth milk chocolate. Hershey was thrilled. In his view, the faintly bitter flavor could not be bettered. When the experiment was repeated with the exact same temperatures and timing, it worked again. Slightly sour, distinctly original: the perfect American milk chocolate bar.

According to a more cynical view, the origins of the Hershey's milk chocolate bar are less romantic. Hershey happened to acquire a large batch of milk powder from Europe, which had slightly soured by the time it crossed the Atlantic. Reluctant to waste such a large amount, he used it to make chocolate and found that it sold well. Company officials have always denied that soured milk powder played any part in the breakthrough formula.

Whatever really happened that led to that distinctive Hershey taste, mass production was the next step. With his factory almost complete, Milton Hershey was poised to become the Ford of chocolate. Ironically, the one person who would have particularly treasured this moment was missing: Milton's father, Henry Hershey. The man who always advocated going for the grand scale, died in February 1904 as the elusive American dream was finally being created all around him. He had a heart attack in the unpaved streets of the half-built town.

BOURNVILLE, BIRMINGHAM, ENGLAND

On the other side of the Atlantic, Hershey's struggles were mirrored by those of twenty-six-year-old George Cadbury Jr. at Bournville. The Swiss, the Dutch, and even their old rival Fry had launched a milk chocolate bar, Fry's Five Boys Milk Chocolate. The Rowntrees, in an attempt to cash in on Swiss success, launched a Swiss Milk Chocolate followed by their Alpine Milk Chocolate and Mountain Milk Chocolate. Although both Rowntree's and Fry's milk chocolate products were still based on milk powder and lacked the quality of the Swiss producers, it was surely only a matter of time before they caught up.

The Cadburys had wrestled with the problem of milk chocolate for fifteen years and failed to find a breakthrough recipe. After a research trip to Switzerland, George Jr. had tried to release an improved milk chocolate bar in 1902 using condensed milk rather than powdered milk, but it fared no better than the previous attempts. Refusing to surrender the challenge, George and his team eventually stumbled on a discovery. They discovered a milk chocolate bar from Switzerland with a unique taste and texture: It was rich and creamy, like chocolate velvet. Tests confirmed that this bar—made on a small scale by the venerable Swiss family firm of Cailler—contained a higher percentage of milk mixed with the chocolate ingredients than Daniel Peter used to make his bars. For George Jr., it pointed the way forward.

Each day, George Jr. drove his Lanchester to Bournville and walked up the steps to the modest room that passed as a chemists' laboratory. The challenge seemed insurmountable: to create and mass-produce a bar that was even milkier and creamier than the competition. He was joined by Booth the chemist; a confectioner, Otto Unger; an engineer, Louis Barrow; and a foreman, Harry Palmer. He and his small team busied themselves measuring, titrating, and boiling the different mixtures. George was so caught up in the process that it is said that one night, sleepwalking and delirious, he "rose in the small hours and trundled his young wife, Edith, around the bedroom under the impression that she was a milk churn!"

Late in 1904, an exhausted George Jr. and his team hit on the exact combination of temperature, pressure, and cooling to condense the milk in such a way that large volumes of milk could be mixed with the cocoa without spoiling. It was indeed a recipe that was creamier and sweeter than Peter's chocolate; rich and very satisfying. Each half-pound bar contained a glass and a half of full-cream milk. George thought it good enough to take to the Cadbury board.

Samples were duly handed around. The principal members of the board were George's older brother, Edward, his cousins, Barrow and William, and his father, George Sr. In solemn silence the bite-sized chunks were chewed, pen and paper at the ready to note any flaws with exacting criticism if disappointed. The seriousness of the occasion was born of so many equally hopeful but abortive trials. Why should this be different? Slowly tongue and taste were wrapped around each other. Five gravely sober faces softened, then showed surprise and then excitement. Another small piece of chocolate confirmed what taste buds knew as tongues licked lips and fingers. This was like Swiss chocolate—no, better! This could be launched on the market with confidence.

The date was set for 1905—the only question was volume. The Swiss were selling thirty tons of milk chocolate a week in Britain. Would the public prefer their product over the Swiss chocolate? The board was inclined to be cautious and suggested they create capacity for five tons of George Jr.'s new chocolate a week. Even this figure seemed optimistic, they reasoned, since it grossly exceeded consumption of any of their milk chocolate bars to date. George Jr. had a different plan. He wanted Bournville geared to twenty tons a week. His idea was to launch in a big way before other firms could copy them.

After some debate, he won the backing of the board. Word of the new and wonderful chocolate spread around the company. The sales team decided to promote the milk content by calling the new bar Dairy Maid. Just six weeks before launch, there was a change of plan. According to the *Bournville Works* magazine, the winning idea came by chance from a Plymouth confectionery shop. The daughter of the shopowners happened to be enjoying a bar of Swiss milk chocolate just as a Cadbury salesman paid a visit. He could not resist telling her about the luxurious new milk chocolate they were bringing out "that will sweep the country—Cadbury's Dairy Maid." The young girl replied, "I wonder you don't call it Dairy Milk; it's a much daintier name." Six weeks later she received a complimentary slab of milk chocolate with the name she had proposed emblazoned across the wrapping: Cadbury's Dairy Milk.

George Jr.'s milk chocolate bar finally rolled off the production lines in June 1905. Oddly, it was given hardly any advertising support and was presented in plain and cheap wrapping to keep the price down. Sales were slow and George's estimate of twenty tons a week began to look reckless. The economy of the launch was not due to Quakerly frugality but a result of the company being stretched to the limit by their prolonged struggle with the Dutch over cocoa, the core of their business. Van Houten's alkalized cocoa had cornered 50 percent of the market in Britain. Sales of Cadbury's Cocoa Essence, their leading brand for thirty years, continued to fall in 1905.

Without knowing Van Houten's formula, George Jr. was once again required to come up with a solution—and fast. It wasn't long before he brought a new taste before the board: Cadbury's very own brand of alkalized cocoa. Once again the board agreed that the new cocoa had a good flavor. The sales teams, however, were baffled as to how to promote this new drink without undermining their old one. Cadbury's name stood for pure, unadulterated food. If they promoted the superior taste and solubility of their alkalized cocoa, they risked drawing attention to weaknesses in Cocoa Essence. Refusing to hesitate, George Jr.'s new cocoa was launched at Christmas 1906. Packaged in colorful chocolate brown tins, its new name was boldly displayed on the side in large letters: Bournville Cocoa.

In the space of one short year, George Jr. had launched the two creations that he hoped would save the company from the Swiss and Dutch onslaught: Dairy Milk and Bournville Cocoa. By this he would stand or fall. By this, the company might stand or fall. Like Hershey in America, all he could do was wait.

VEVEY, SWITZERLAND

As the Americans and the British strived to launch their own versions of Swiss milk chocolate, Swiss businessmen and bankers were already leaps ahead of them. The creator of milk chocolate, Daniel Peter, the man who had struggled with his invention for so many lonely years, found himself greatly in demand.

Since 1896, Peter had not looked back. Investment in his company, Société des Chocolats au Lait Peter, increased rapidly. In the three years since 1900, Peter's authorized capital rose from 1 million Swiss francs to 1.5 million, and his sales reached 6 million Swiss francs. In addition to his chocolate works at Vevey, Peter developed another plant to meet the rising demand for milk chocolate thirty miles northwest in Orbe.

In January 1904, Daniel Peter was approached by another Swiss confectioner, Jean Jacques Kohler, who wanted to join forces. Although Kohler's company was worth less than half of Peter's, his chocolate products complemented Peter's range, and he had strong sales teams in France and Switzerland. For sixty-eight-year-old Peter, it allowed him to step back from the front lines of the business, leaving the capable and likeable Kohler in charge. That same month the

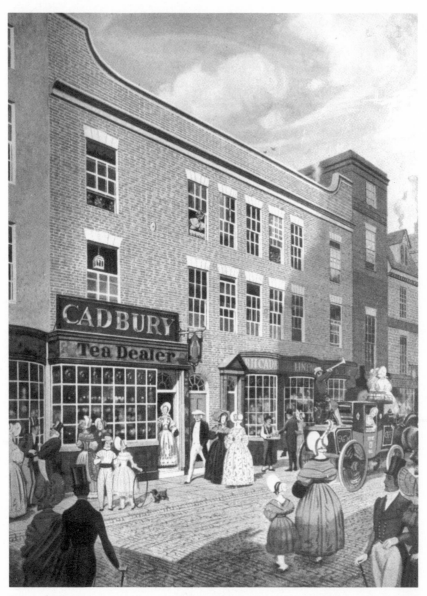

John Cadbury's tea and cocoa shop in Bull Street, Birmingham—the start of the Cadbury chocolate business. From a drawing by E. Wallcousin, 1824.
(Courtesy of Cadbury)

George Cadbury, age 25, taken in 1866 at a time when the family cocoa business was close to failure.
(Courtesy of the Cadbury Family)

Richard Cadbury and his son, Barrow, in 1866.
(Courtesy of the Cadbury Family)

The Cadbury's Bridge Street factory in Birmingham in the mid-nineteenth century. (Courtesy of Cadbury)

Dixon Hadaway—
Cadbury's first "traveller."
(Courtesy of Cadbury)

An advertisement for Fry's cocoa. (Courtesy of Cadbury)

The Fry family of Bristol ran the largest chocolate factory in the world in the nineteenth century. (Courtesy of Cadbury)

The Cadbury brothers breakthrough product: a purer form of cocoa. (Courtesy of Cadbury)

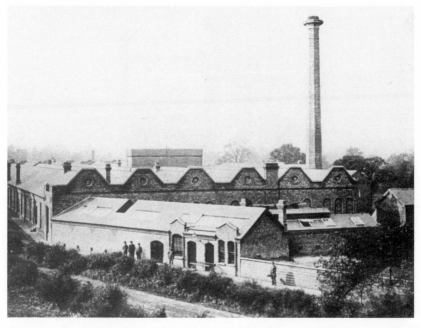

Exterior photo of Cadbury's Bournville, 1879. This is the first known photograph of the Bournville factory. (Courtesy of Cadbury)

In Switzerland, Rodolphe Lindt developed a new technique to grind the cocoa beans. (© Chocoladefabriken Lindt & Sprüngli AG)

A nineteenth-century chocolate conching machine, which made chocolate smooth and velvety. (Mary Evans Picture Library)

Henri Nestlé, circa 1875. Nestlé
created milk powder and mass
produced a new infant formula.
(Nestlé Historical Archives, Vevey)

In the 1870s, Henri Nestlé's neighbor, Daniel Peter, began experiments
adding milk to chocolate at his factory in Vevey.
(Nestlé Historical Archives, Vevey)

Milton Snavely Hershey, age 16, as an apprentice in an ice cream parlor in 1873. (COURTESY OF HERSHEY COMMUNITY ARCHIVES, HERSHEY, PA)

Milton Hershey briefly attended a Quaker School House near Lancaster, Pennsylvania. (COURTESY OF HERSHEY COMMUNITY ARCHIVES, HERSHEY, PA)

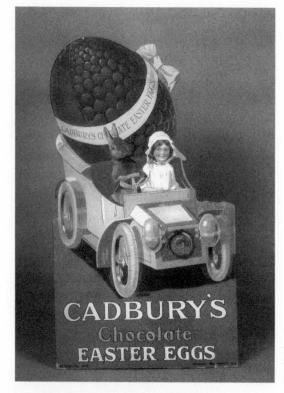

An early Easter egg advertisement.

(COURTESY OF CADBURY)

The village green at the Cadbury brothers model village at Bournville.

(COURTESY OF CADBURY)

Staff play croquet on the womens' grounds at Bournville, 1896.
(Courtesy of Cadbury)

Lily pond in the womens' grounds. (Courtesy of Cadbury)

The girls' dining room at Bournville, 1902. (COURTESY OF CADBURY)

Horses and the first petrol vans at Bournville. (COURTESY OF CADBURY)

Swimming lessons for staff at Bournville, 1910. (Courtesy of Cadbury)

King George greeted by George Cadbury, 1919. (Courtesy of Cadbury)

Vans leaving the factory. (Courtesy of Cadbury)

Bournville: the factory in the garden. (Courtesy of Cadbury)

Kraft cheesewagon, 1921.

(KRAFT®, PHILADELPHIA®, VELVEETA® AND MIRACLE WHIP® ARE REGISTERED TRADEMARKS OF KF HOLDINGS AND ARE USED WITH PERMISSION.)

By 1939, J. L. Kraft had 40 percent of America's cheese market.

(KRAFT®, PHILADELPHIA®, VELVEETA® AND MIRACLE WHIP® ARE REGISTERED TRADEMARKS OF KF HOLDINGS AND ARE USED WITH PERMISSION.)

Milton and his wife, Catherine "Kitty" Hershey, 1910.
(COURTESY OF HERSHEY COMMUNITY ARCHIVES, HERSHEY, PA)

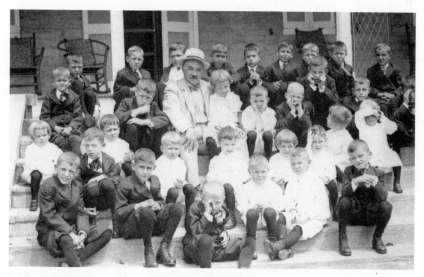

Milton Hershey used his fortune to create The Hershey Industrial School
to help boys from deprived backgrounds.
(COURTESY OF HERSHEY COMMUNITY ARCHIVES, HERSHEY, PA)

Adrian and Dominic Cadbury, the fourth generation of brothers at the helm of the firm. (COURTESY OF THE CADBURY FAMILY)

two firms merged to form Société Générale Suisse de Chocolat with authorized capital of 2.5 million Swiss francs.

The Nestlé company kept a close eye on the deal. No sooner had Kohler and Peter completed their negotiations when they received a call from Auguste Roussy at Nestlé. Roussy had originally declined to help Peter develop his milk chocolate. Now Nestlé was hungry to get into the lucrative milk chocolate market and had plans to launch brands of its own.

During the long summer of 1904, talks took place between Peter and Kohler and managers at Nestlé. The result was a collaboration that favored both sides. Nestlé invested a million Swiss francs with Peter and Kohler and agreed to hand over the manufacture of Nestlé's own brands of chocolate to them. In return Société Générale Suisse de Chocolat was given access to Nestlé's excess milk supplies and the company's considerable expertise in sales and marketing and established position in foreign markets. Effectively the agreement meant that each company specialized in what it did best: Nestlé handled chocolate distribution and sales while Peter and Kohler concentrated on quality manufacturing.

But when Nestlé's deal with Peter and Kohler was announced, Nestlé's main rival, the Anglo-Swiss Condensed Milk Company was spurred into action. Founded by two Americans, Charles and George Page, Anglo-Swiss had been Nestlé's leading competitor for thirty years, and it also wanted to get in on the chocolate bonanza. When it failed to secure a deal with other Swiss chocolate firms, such as Suchard, it approached Nestlé. In 1905 the two companies merged to create a Swiss dynamo. The Nestlé and Anglo-Swiss Condensed Milk Company was a truly international food concern with American and European staff and expertise and eighteen factories worldwide, including five in Britain, twelve in Europe, and one in America.

By skillfully combining their assets and talents, the Swiss had launched a food manufacturing superpower, which could already deliver milk chocolate to Europe and America and had plans to tap into Australia and Asia as well. While the Americans and the British had only recently discovered their recipes, the Swiss deals meant that consumers throughout the developed world would soon wake up to the delights of quality Swiss milk chocolate.

HERSHEY, PENNSYLVANIA

But even the sophisticated Swiss bankers, with their eyes fixed on the American market, had not bargained on the well-honed entrepreneurial skills of Milton Hershey. By 1906 the town of Hershey was on the map. On entering, the visitor was left in no doubt of that fact. The name proclaimed itself with confidence, writ large and bold and frequently. It shone from the towering factory chimneys and blazed above the main factory entrance, reminding anyone who passed through that determination over an indifferent fate by Milton Hershey had created a living fairy tale: A town that made chocolate.

The sheer scale of his operation in America dwarfed the efforts by the Europeans. Apart from his milk chocolate Hershey Bar, he introduced conical chocolate drops called Hershey's Kisses in 1907, followed swiftly by Hershey's Almond Bar. With his leading rivals an ocean away and the voracious American appetite spreading from coast to coast, he had created a chocolate money machine. Net sales soared from $1.3 million in 1906 to more than $5 million by 1911.

Thousands of visitors flocked to see Hershey's miracle and to marvel at the astounding chocolate factory. The factory in a cornfield was not unlike Bournville but it was done on an American scale. Sightseers could enjoy a stroll down the wide boulevards and wander into the center of town, which boasted such novelties as landscaped gardens, a zoo, a miniature railroad, and a band. Shops sprang up along the main avenues, and there were carefully designed homes for the workers to buy or rent. All the while, Hershey continued to buy up thousands of acres near the town, which he turned into dairy farms to supply the factory. The entire region prospered.

At the very heart of this chocolate utopia was Hershey's palatial home, High Point. Approached across a green carpet of lawn, its many wings framed by woodland and a view of the Blue Mountains beyond, it was the embodiment of material success. With its white-pillared porch reminiscent of ancient temples, fine interiors, and echoing halls, the house was so opulent that it could not have been further from the plain homestead of Milton's youth. Hershey's mother, a Mennonite, gave her full approval to her successful son. She had her own large house on Chocolate Avenue, and her financial troubles were over. Known as "Mother Hershey" or sometimes "the Queen mum," she enjoyed a respect in the community that she prized after many long years of struggle. Not content to wallow in her newfound comfort, she combed her grey hair into a starched cap, donned her apron, and continued to wrap sweets for her son as she had always done. Their new wealth and the company's potential seemed limitless.

But no amount of money could solve one very personal problem. After ten years of marriage, it was clear that Milton Hershey's beautiful wife, thirty-eight-year-old Kitty, who had long suffered from ill health, was not able to have children. There would be no son, no heir for his wealth. Hershey felt the loss deeply. "It's a sin for a man to die rich," he told his friends. He found it hard to accept the doctor's verdict that there was no cure for her nervous disorder. Kitty hid the growing signs of her weakness and paralysis to spare him pain, and all he could do was watch as his beautiful wife—decorated with any jewel she wished from Tiffany—deteriorated to the point that she needed a wheelchair.

She began to talk of a new venture, a venture that promised a future: a special orphanage for deprived children. Hershey seized on the idea; it was something they could create together. For both of them, it became a lifeline. They could give something real and useful to those in need. There would be children about the place with their innocence and their fresh way of seeing things. And the orphans would want for nothing that it was possible for Hershey to provide. They would have all the things he had not as a child. In November 1909, Kitty and Milton Hershey signed a deed of trust endowing their orphan school with 486 acres of farmland. According to a close relative, Joseph Snavely, they wanted to make themselves "literally parents to a family of orphan boys."

It was a proud moment when the first ten boys enrolled at the Hershey Industrial School. The teaching was informal at first, with the boys gathered around one large table to learn crafts and skills, but they soon graduated to a converted barn. The children stayed at the local farms, but Milton Hershey made a point to visit every Sunday.

Slowly, the chocolate entrepreneur, a self-made man tied to ticker tape and who lived and breathed the dry air of finance, found the father in himself; he found that long-neglected role at last in the company of these desperately deprived and needy children. It was a bittersweet role. He confided to a friend, "I would give everything I possess if I could call one of these boys my own."

14

That Monstrous Trade in Flesh and Blood

On September 26, 1908, the *Standard* revealed that Cadbury was profiting from slavery. The white hands of the Bournville chocolate makers, said the London paper, "are helped by other unseen hands some thousands of miles away, black and brown hands, toiling in plantations, or hauling loads through swamp and forest." The slaves' wretched lives formed a stark contrast to "the young ladies in the firm's employ" at Bournville who "visit the swimming bath weekly and have prayers every morning."

The *Standard* deplored the hypocrisy: "It is that monstrous trade in human flesh and blood against which the Quaker and Radical ancestors of Mr Cadbury thundered in the better days of England. . . . And the worst of all this slavery and slave driving and slave dealing is . . . to provide a sufficient number of hands to grow and pick the cocoa on . . . the very islands which feed the mills and presses of Bournville."

At the next board meeting at Bournville, the mood was somber. William felt slandered; his years of effort to resolve the issue had been ignored and his planned visit to Angola mocked. Instead the article created the impression that the Cadburys had deliberately delayed resolving the issue of slavery to continue making a profit from São Tomé beans for as long as possible, all the while trumpeting their virtuous practices at home.

For those present at the meeting, this simply was not true. Considerable efforts had gone into resolving the issue. There were, however, questions to be answered. Why had it taken William so long to investigate conditions in São Tomé? Was he too trusting, especially of British politicians such as the foreign secretary, Sir Edward Grey, who appeared to have promised much and done nothing?

George Sr. stood by his nephew. He knew the Cadbury board had agreed they intended "to put a stop to the conditions of slavery— not merely to wash our own hands of any connection with them." If they had stopped buying from São Tomé, they would have lost their leverage over the Portuguese to effect reform. Yet in the eyes of the paper and its readers, they looked hypocritical and as if they lacked integrity. As head of the firm, George Sr. was directly accused. His staunch Quaker principles and utopian creation appeared to rest on the backs of slaves. It was a shaming indictment for a man of God. The board decided to sue the *Standard* for libel.

In October 1908, William Cadbury embarked on a trip to West Africa with the firm's expert, Joseph Burtt. They wanted to find out whether there had been any changes following the years of diplomacy with the Portuguese and British Foreign Office. But the Portuguese seemed to have learned of their visit in advance. They made sure there was nothing to be seen and promised their English visitors that signing up new *servicais* or slaves had been "suspended."

Cadbury and Burtt were not convinced. Although they did not catch the Portuguese red-handed, they were suspicious that new slaves were being smuggled into São Tomé at night. They saw known slave traders with Portuguese officials when they visited Angola, and the ill-concealed antagonism they felt from the Portuguese governor general failed to reassure them that the colonial authorities were genuinely implementing reform. The underground slave trade, they concluded, was being hidden more skillfully than ever. William returned to England in March 1909 and discussed their findings with the management at Cadbury, Fry, and Rowntree. A week later, the British Quaker firms announced they were boycotting cocoa from São Tomé and Principe.

Several European companies followed their lead, but as George Sr. and William had feared, it was soon apparent that a boycott would not stop the slave trade. German and American brokers simply stepped in to purchase beans from São Tomé that were superior to those grown elsewhere in Africa. Working through the Anti-Slavery Society, Cadbury sent experts overseas to Germany and America to alert foreign cocoa companies to the problem.

William Cadbury and the other Quaker manufacturers were keen to investigate alternative cocoa plantations in Africa. The first cocoa seeds had reached the Gold Coast—now known as Ghana—as recently as 1879. Although the climate was suitable, the beans from this region were of poor quality. On his recent trip to Africa, William Cadbury bought a small site at Mangoase in the Gold Coast to research ways of improving production. He soon found that local dealers paid farmers the same low price for cocoa beans regardless of the quality. Bags could be filled with damaged or wet beans, which rotted during shipment and ruined the batch. Working with local producers, Cadbury and Fry representatives made it clear they were prepared to pay market price for quality cocoa. They taught local farmers how to carefully dry and ferment the cocoa, and production from the region soared.

Meanwhile, on November 29, 1909, the case of *Cadbury Bros. Ltd. v. the Standard Newspaper Ltd.* was heard. Crowds gathered in the imposing Victoria Law Courts in Birmingham. The courtroom was packed with press, family members, and curious members of the public. Lining up to represent the two sides were the most renowned lawyers of their day. Sir Edward Carson, a conservative MP and barrister for the *Standard*, was known for his theatrical style and flair for interrogation that had earned him a reputation as "the best cross questioner in England." Magazines such as *Vanity Fair* had a field day printing cartoons of the tall, spare Carson, his chin thrust forward and bushy eyebrows arched in a constant contemptuous question. By contrast, Cadbury had hired the acclaimed liberal barrister Rufus Isaacs. Sober and exacting, he was among the very few who could take on the celebrated Carson.

The case had come to symbolize more than libel. For many it represented a titanic clash over the ethics of the Liberal and Conservative parties, the battle lines neatly described by Carson's biographer, Edward Marjoriebanks: "The greatest Conservative leader of the day (Carson) was engaged for a Conservative organ (the *Standard*), against the most brilliant advocate in the Liberal Party (Isaacs) who was in turn attacking on behalf of the honour of a great Liberal family (the Cadburys) not unconnected with the most powerful Liberal organ (the *Daily News*)." The Tory *Standard* was edited by Howell Glynne, a keen supporter of Cecil Rhodes, Joseph Chamberlain, and the Boer War. Cadbury's Liberal *Daily News* had not only passionately opposed the war but also exposed abuses of British power in South Africa, notably the cruel exploitation of Chinese coolie labor in the mines. This, said the *Daily News*, was British slavery by the back door. Yet now Cadbury's paper and the Liberal establishment were under scrutiny for apparently turning a blind eye to slavery in the São Tomé cocoa plantations.

William Cadbury was the first to take the stand. During four days of questioning, the great barrister made him spell out to the court every detail of his investigation.

Edward Carson: Men, women, and children, freely bought and sold?
William Cadbury: I don't believe, as far as I know, that there is anything that corresponded to the slave market of 50 years ago. It is now done by subtle trickery and arrangements of that kind. I don't think it is fair to say that in Angola there is an open slave market.
Edward Carson: You don't suggest that because it is done by subtle trickery that makes it better?
William Cadbury: I do not.
Edward Carson: But in some cases they are bought and sold?
William Cadbury: In some cases they are bought and sold.

When Rufus Isaacs took over the questioning, William had a chance to demonstrate the steps he had taken since he first became aware of the slavery problem in 1901. The Cadburys wanted to use their buying power to bring about real reform, he explained. They had appointed their own investigator, Joseph Burtt, to present the Portuguese authorities with definitive proof of slavery rather than unsubstantiated allegations that could be easily dismissed. William described the repeated trips to Lisbon to pressure the Portuguese authorities and the discussions that took place with the British foreign secretary. "We went on buying the cocoa," William explained, "because we were absolutely advised by the highest authorities we could consult that it was the best thing we could do in the interest of reform of labour conditions in West Africa."

Heads turned in the packed courtroom as the celebrated George Cadbury Sr. was called next to the witness stand. At seventy, he was still a tall man with a commanding physical presence but he walked more slowly. His wife, Elsie, watching anxiously from the gallery, knew he was feeling the pressure. It was hard for her, knowing her husband's passionate commitment to just causes, to watch as he was subjected to a humiliating cross-examination.

George Cadbury's protests that they were trying to bring about change echoed around the room and came back to haunt him. He seemed frail and did not speak with his nephew's self-assurance. Carson pressed on. As the owner of the *Daily News* and "the great champion of the conditions of labour of South Africa and the Congo . . . why then did Cadburys—those perfect gentlemen . . . pay one million three hundred pounds . . . to the slave dealers in Portugal?" In the close atmosphere of the court, George Sr. failed to communicate his reasons effectively. He relied on honesty, which soon looked foolish or worse in the hands of the clever Carson. There were cries of "Shame!" in the courtroom, and the acclaimed philanthropist appeared reduced to a pitiable old man.

To everyone's surprise, Carson did not call any witnesses to support the *Standard*'s accusations. Justice Pickford summed up the issues for the jury: They were "not there to decide whether Messrs Cadbury took the right course, or whether any better course could have been taken." There was only one question the jury was charged with answering: "Were [the Cadburys] for the purpose of preventing an attack on their character as philanthropists, and at the same time to postpone any final decision as to not purchasing cocoa grown by slave labour, were they purporting to take steps which were of an ineffective nature in order to obtain a mitigation of the evils?" Was this, in effect, a dishonest plot to enable the chocolate firm to profit from slave-grown cocoa?

The jury returned within the hour.

The foreman rose. He announced that the jurors had found in favor of Cadbury. But when the jurors declared the damages against the *Standard*, the result was unexpected.

"One farthing!"

The award was enough for George Cadbury. "It has been a long ordeal," he wrote later to his son Henry. "Mother was there most of the time and I think is thoroughly tired out. . . . How thankful we are for the result." He felt relieved that the "slanders hurled against us had been cleared." He was also spared legal fees since the *Standard* was ordered to pay the costs. For William Cadbury, it was not so easy to come to terms with the result. Although the jurors agreed that Cadbury had been libelled, their contemptuous damages implied they were not satisfied with Cadbury's handling of the slavery issue, notably the long delay before boycotting São Tomé beans.

There was one benefit of the lawsuit, however, at least in the short term. News of the libel case reached America, where chocolate manufacturers joined the fight to urge the Portuguese to end slavery. Caught in the glare of international publicity, the Portuguese authorities finally halted the transport of slaves from Angola in 1909, and according to one account, 14,000 slave-workers were repatriated from the islands. In the longer term, however, the issue was far from resolved. The British Anti-Slavery Society continued to receive reports of labor abuses, and the Foreign Office faced repeated criticism for its failure to persuade the Portuguese to improve conditions for workers on the islands.

In time the new agricultural techniques introduced into the Gold Coast in Africa by Cadbury and Fry brought improvements in production. In 1910 the Gold Coast farmers harvested 26,000 tons of cocoa, more than the notorious islands of São Tomé and Principe. The following year this jumped to 40,000 tons—more than any other country in the world. The food of the gods from the New

World was becoming established as an Old World crop. *Theobroma cacao* made its way west along the high grassland savannahs of the Ivory Coast and Sierra Leone, east into Nigeria and the Cameroons and south into the great Congo Basin, paving the way for Africa to become the world's leading producer of cocoa.

With demand for chocolate soaring in the west, cocoa manufacturers were urgently seeking new sources of beans. Dutch colonialists had already taken seedlings to Java and Sumatra; the British were establishing plantations in Ceylon and India. The seeds of the ubiquitous cocoa tree, carried by eager missionaries and colonists, even graced the shady beaches of far-flung coral archipelagos of the Pacific such as Vanuatu and Samoa. The exotic plant, once a precious currency of ancient civilizations in Mesoamerica, was spreading around the world, following the shadowy blue fringes of the great equatorial rain forests.

George Cadbury Sr. had a stubborn streak. Although there were some in the family who believed that the *Daily News* investigations into labor abuses had goaded the Tory press into making libellous accusations, George regarded it as money well spent. He wanted to use his wealth not just to help his workers and the Bournville community but also to influence society at large—especially now. Since the launch in 1906 of HMS *Dreadnought*—the new terror weapon of the day—the naval arms race between Britain and Germany had accelerated. Military spending by the leading European powers had escalated rapidly. With Europe caught in the grip of a dangerous arms race, George saw it as his duty not just to champion liberal reform at home but also the cause of diplomacy and peace overseas.

Shortly after the court case, George Sr. learned that two Liberal papers, the *Morning Leader* and the *Star*, with a circulation of half a million, were for sale, and he did not want to see them fall into Conservative hands. He confided in his son Laurence, "It seemed a very serious matter to let them go into the hands of those who might seek to promote war with Germany and would oppose measures of social reform." George approached the Rowntree family to discuss the possibility of the two Quaker families buying the papers together. Joseph Rowntree's nephew, Arnold, who already had experience running the *Northern Echo* and the *Nation* for the Rowntree Social Services Trust, was keen to work with George Sr.

When they took over, however, they faced a serious dilemma. Both the *Morning Leader* and the *Star* published gambling news, which provoked condemnation from their Quaker friends. Joseph Storrs Fry's brother and a successful barrister, Sir Edward Fry, led the Quaker charge of hypocrisy. The very men from the Cadbury and Rowntree families who supported the National Anti-Gambling League, declared Edward Fry, were encouraging gambling in their sporting press!

George Cadbury Sr., however, had already tried removing the betting news from the *Daily News* and the *Echo*. In both cases it had led to a catastrophic fall in circulation. There was a real possibility that if he removed the racing from penny and half-penny papers like the *Morning Leader* and the *Star*, the papers might go under. "It was evident that the *Star* with betting news and pleading for social reform and for peace," he explained to Laurence, "was far better than the *Star* with betting and opposing social reform and stirring up strife with neighbouring nations."

It was not long before the Tory press picked up news of the split in Quaker thinking. Journals such as the *Spectator* took up arms against the apparently ever-expanding "Cocoa Press." Quaker virtue was once again on the line. George Sr. was "held up to execration as an odious example of the sleek hypocrite who profited by the degradation and vice of others." George Cadbury was particularly troubled by the continued accusations of fellow Quakers such as Sir Edward Fry, who bluntly implied that he had taken "the devil into partnership to aid the Almighty." It reached the point, declared the *Manchester Guardian* in an editorial, that the Cadburys and Rowntrees "are assailed with such severity" that anyone might suppose "that they had introduced a gambling newspaper for the first time into the white robed company of the London daily press!"

On November 14, 1911, with a view to streamlining the organization of the papers and retiring from active management himself, George Sr. set up the Daily News Trust. In transferring his ownership of the papers, he articulated how he hoped the trust would be run. The document is a testament to his desire to apply Quaker beliefs and Christian thinking to the world of business and journalism:

> I desire in forming the Daily News Trust that it may be of service in bringing the ethical teaching of Jesus Christ to bear on National questions, . . . for example that Arbitration should take the place of War and that the spirit of the Sermon on the Mount . . . should take the place of Imperialism and of the military spirit which is contrary to Christ's teaching that Love is the badge by which a Christian should be known. The parable of the Good Samaritan teaches human brotherhood, and that God has made of one blood all nations of men. Disobedience to this teaching has brought condign punishment on nations; and though wars of aggression have brought honour and wealth to a few, they have always in the long run brought suffering upon the great majority.

For George Cadbury, the verses of the New Testament had a beauty and simplicity that he had used as a guiding principle throughout his life. For him it was simple: If everyone followed the teaching of Christ, people and nations could live in peace together. His faith anchored his thinking and unified all spheres of his life. It speaks volumes for the times that his editors endeavoured to support his view.

Ironically, the political will was already in place that would make such a close marriage of religion and business less urgent—for some, even redundant. That very year, a law was enacted that brought fundamental reform to at least one social issue that had troubled the Quaker conscience for generations: poverty. The impetus for change had come in part from the Quaker community itself, through influential writers such as Seebohm Rowntree.

After publishing *Poverty*, Seebohm had toured the country promoting a new vision of social responsibility. His research inspired prominent politicians such as Lloyd George, the chancellor from

1908, and Winston Churchill, a Liberal MP. "This festering life at home," Churchill wrote of the British poor, "makes world-wide power a mockery, and defaces the image of God upon earth."

Such influential thinking coincided with another forceful voice coming from the workers themselves. Still laboring under the harsh regimes of the previous century, the vast majority of laborers felt alienated. Many endured low pay and poor working conditions that had scant regard for health or welfare. Across Britain, workers were waking up to their own power. Enlightened employers like the Rowntrees had voluntarily set up their own pension scheme in 1906 and provided a host of benefits including free medical care and education, but they found their workers joining unions and making more demands. For Joseph Rowntree, who had put up £10,000 of his own money to start the pension fund, it was an unsettling time, reflecting an uneasy shift in the relationship between an employer and his staff. But his sons joined the growing number of employers who believed union membership was the way forward. Across England, the Labor Party was gaining support, and membership in the new trade unions reached 2.6 million in 1910. All this reflected a widespread recognition that the Victorians' tolerance of poverty had no place in twentieth-century Britain.

This momentum for change led to a series of groundbreaking Liberal reforms. After vigorously lobbying in the *Daily News*, the *National Old Age Pensions League*, and the *Anti-Sweating League*, it was rewarding for George Sr. and Edward to see that change was finally possible. The Old Age Pension Act of 1908 provided a means-tested income of between one and five shillings per week for people over seventy. The majority of those eligible in the first year were women earning less than £31.50 a year. The Trade Board's Act of 1909 created boards that could set minimum wages in trades that were notorious for sweatshop labor such as tailoring. That same year saw Lloyd George's revolutionary "People's Budget," which set out a redistribution of wealth, with higher rates of tax for those earning above £2,000 to fund further reform. With the National Insurance Act of 1911, the state had to provide a basic level of unemployment and sickness benefits. At last, the law of the land decreed that those struggling at the lowest economic rung would be recognized and supported. By today's standards, the amounts they received were modest—but the ambition for reform was huge.

In time these sweeping Liberal reforms would pave the way for abolishing the Poor Laws, which carried the shame of miserly welfare dispensed by the parish under laws that had their origins in Tudor times. Workhouses, thought by many to punish people for poverty, survived until 1930; even then many remained—renamed as Public Assistance Institutions—until 1948. But the grinding poverty and pittance for a wage on which a family could not possibly survive was relegated to the past.

The specter of a Dickensian world, of a large and downtrodden underclass for whom there was no way out other than debtor's prison or workhouses, would become a thing of the past. The need for charitable Quaker businessmen like Joseph Rowntree to provide for workers out of their own pockets became less urgent. The Liberal reforms helped to forge a framework for modern social welfare. What was once the domain of men of God was becoming the official business of the state. It was a step along the road that helped to distance the world of business and religion.

Hostility to Cadbury's and Rowntree's "Cocoa Press" may have been exacerbated by the resounding success of the chocolate firms in the early part of the twentieth century. Far from being damaged by the court case, Cadbury was an increasing threat, even to its Quaker friends and rivals at Fry in Bristol. In 1905 Cadbury's sales of £1,354,948 were only just behind Fry's at £1,366,192 while Rowntree had sales of £903,991. For Cadbury's staff, overtaking their old ally and rival became a realistic goal.

Cadbury at last had a chocolate bar that was a fitting contender in the chocolate wars. The titanic struggle between the Swiss and British milk chocolate producers was being fought in confectioners and

grocers throughout the country. The weapons were irresistible chocolate confections backed by travellers in motor cars, poster campaigns, price wars, and publicity stunts. Swiss chocolate was so prized
that at first George Jr.'s Dairy Milk had trouble meeting the board's
target of two tons per week. Word spread and by 1910, it was the
clear favorite among the British chocolate brands and well on its way
to becoming Cadbury's best-seller as chocolate sales began to catch
up with cocoa. It was a wonderful vindication for George Jr. as sales
approached twenty tons a week. The taste proved so popular that
Cadbury introduced the same Dairy Milk chocolate in other lines
such as the Fancy Box and as a coating on Easter eggs. George Jr.
supervised the creation of a dedicated milk-condensing plant at
Knighton in Staffordshire to satisfy demand. His Bournville Cocoa
was also a great success, overtaking their long-established brand
Cocoa Essence by 1911.

Cadbury's export trade was also growing exponentially under the
meticulous supervision of George Jr.'s older brother Edward. According to his colleagues, Edward worked "at high pressure, made
swift decisions and was not always easy to work with." Yet there was
no doubting his business acumen. When he took over the export department, entire continents were managed by a single traveller. In
just a few years, after extensive trips around the British Empire, Edward established sales forces in China, South America, Canada, and
the West Indies. Shrewdly exploiting the potential of the British
Empire, with its colonies serving as a convenient catalyst for commerce, exports soon made up 40 percent of Cadbury's total sales.

After a chase that lasted half a century, the Cadbury giant finally
overtook Fry in 1910. Cadbury's sales reached £1,670,221 with Fry
lagging behind slightly with £1,642,715. Even Rowntree was becoming a threat to Fry with sales climbing to £1,200,598. The efficiencies
gained by the company in moving to Haxby Road, combined with
the continued success of their gums, pastilles, and Cocoa Elect, had
spurred a period of sustained growth.

Despite this news in Bristol, eighty-four-year-old Joseph Storrs
Fry II, battling against deteriorating eyesight, held on to his power as

company chairman. He had an aversion to change, and his nephews and cousins were powerless to break the mold of his thinking. He failed to inspire his development team to come up with a satisfactory competitor to Dairy Milk. Ignoring the evident rewards that had come to both Cadbury and Rowntree by moving to modern sites outside Birmingham and York, he repeatedly opposed any move from the center of Bristol.

For him, the awkward conglomeration of factories in Bristol was sacrosanct, hallowed by centuries of Quaker tradition, "beautiful" in his eyes. But his eyes were growing dimmer, always attuned to that inner vision of his youth when those in charge at Fry had "waited upon the Lord." New buildings, new products; the modern generation, obsessed with change, missed the point. "Unless the Lord build the house, they labour in vain that build it." The sickly scented busy world of chocolate-making faded. His religious interests became more focused. And at last, sight finally gone, his world lit by faith alone, he met his maker on July 7, 1913, at age eighty-seven. He remained a man of God first; chocolatier second.

Although Cadbury had overtaken its chief British rival, the Swiss were still beyond reach. The merger of Peter-Kohler in 1904 and their marketing agreement with Nestlé had precipitated exponential growth. Swiss interests converged further when, in 1911, the family firm of Cailler approached Peter-Kohler and another deal was signed. Nestlé held a 39 percent stake in the united firm of Peter-Cailler-Kohler, and the Swiss giant that emerged was a colossus, apparently unbeatable. More than half of all chocolate consumed worldwide was Swiss.

But the bitterly fought battle among the European chocolate empires was about to be eclipsed by a far more dangerous conflagration. On June 28, 1914, a bullet in Sarajevo triggered the chain of events that would see the boundaries of Europe—and the commercial empires within them—totally redrawn.

15

God Could Have
Created Us Sinless

In Britain in the summer of 1914, the appetite for war was palpable, but Barrow Cadbury, now vice chairman of Cadbury, joined a delegation bent on persuading the Kaiser against war.

Such pacifist idealism seems otherworldly, even naïve in the face of the mighty German and British military industrial machine. But pacifism was central to the Quaker movement and echoed back to its earliest years. It had its roots in George Fox's rejection of violence in the face of hardship and suffering. "Turn the other cheek," Christ had said. For over a century, Quakers had campaigned for the disarmament of all nations. Yet now the impetus for war was unstoppable. Peace movements were overwhelmed. The tide was at the flood.

On August 1, 1914, Germany declared war on Russia. Two days later, Germany was at war with France. On August 4, Germany invaded Belgium, and Britain declared war on Germany. When Britain joined the conflict, Lord Kitchener, the commander during the Boer War responsible for the policy of herding women and children into concentration camps, was named Secretary of State for War. He launched his legendary poster—"Your Country Needs You"—and hundreds at the garden factory in Bournville answered his call.

At the *Daily News*, Alfred Gardiner saw that George Cadbury Sr. "had never faced so searching a test" of conformity to Quaker doctrine. Unlike the Boer War, which George viewed plainly as unjust and which failed to challenge his religious beliefs, this conflict brought him "face to face with the fundamental tenets of religious persuasion." Pacing the large wood-panelled rooms of the manor house, a set of Quaker rules devised in the English shires during the seventeenth century seemed remote.

The war split the Quaker community in two. For some there were no circumstances, regardless of the outcome, under which a Quaker could deviate from the doctrine of nonresistance. For others like George Sr., this was no longer a simple issue. Although he acknowledged that the causes of the war were complex, and he found fault on the British side, he believed that the prime mover in this world calamity was German militarism. While he remained "a very strong believer in Peace," he insisted that German militarism "must be crushed."

The issue was critical since his children with his second wife had recently reached adulthood. George and Elsie knew their three sons would make their own decisions. Despite the long-standing family commitment to pacifism, their headstrong youngest son, twenty-one-year-old Egbert, known as Bertie, left the Quaker movement immediately to sign up with the Admiralty. In his words, he and his friends "were all in a desperate hurry to enlist because we thought the war would be over by Christmas and unless we were quick we might miss all the fun." His brother, twenty-four-year-old Norman, had trained as an engineer and started work in the Electrical Mechanical Brake Company in West Bromwich. Soon he was swept up in a most un-Quakerly activity: manufacturing bomb parts, shells, artillery hubs, gears, and track links for tanks.

George's oldest son by his second marriage, twenty-five-year-old Laurence, was keen to volunteer for the army but remained committed to the Quaker movement. "I strongly urged—as I am a well known advocate of Peace," George Sr. explained later, "that Laurence should join the Ambulance Section." On August 21, Arnold Rowntree and others had launched an appeal in the Quaker magazine the *Friend* asking young Quakers to form a Friends Ambulance Service to rescue the wounded on the front lines. Laurence left with the first unit, one of forty-three volunteers.

As soon as they reached France, they learned that wounded from the Battle of Yser in southwest Belgium were in need of help in the sheds of the Dunkirk railway station. According to the Friends Ambulance Unit records, when Laurence and his Quaker friends opened the door, "a terrible sight met their eyes." Light filtered through the windows revealing thousands of men lying where they had been left with appalling injuries. Many had been there for three days and nights, "practically untended, mostly even unfed, the living, the dying, and the dead side by side, long rows of figures in every attitude of slow suffering or acute pain, of utter fatigue or dulled apathy, of appeal or despair." Gangrene was the terror quietly poisoning torn flesh; the air was thick with the sickening smell of it. Working day and night, the Quaker volunteers treated the wounded and organized transport for 6,000 to be transferred to hospitals.

By early November, the Quaker ambulance convoy was on the road again. The next stop: An ancient town in west Belgium caught under intense bombardment: Ypres.

HERSHEY, PENNSYLVANIA

During the autumn of 1914, as the prime of European manhood faced the horror of warfare in the industrial age, Milton Hershey's forty-three-year-old wife, Kitty, was also struggling to survive. Her assailant was unseen, an enemy unknown to modern science but just as deadly.

With each passing day, Kitty seemed a little more diminished; her smile fragile, her breathing difficult. Swaddled in the most expensive furs, she was still cold; pampered with every conceivable diversion, she did not have the strength to lift a book. Slowly her mysterious nervous ailment robbed her of her last vestiges of dignity; despite her husband's devotion, she was utterly helpless. On a trip to Philadelphia in March 1915, Milton Hershey, forever attentive to the woman he could not do without, left to get champagne to cheer her. When he returned, he was too late. Kitty had died.

Milton was utterly distraught. Here was a man who apparently could do anything, who had built a nationwide brand, a multimillion-pound business, and a celebrated town—but his massive wealth could not save Kitty. With his wife lying in a bronze casket, fresh flowers ordered to decorate her vault for years into the future, he returned to Hershey and threw himself into what he knew best.

Work was his world. In the months after Kitty's death, he cut a mercurial, frenetic figure, with an occasional unpredictable streak that made employees worry about getting on his wrong side. At times, a complete stranger was the recipient of his unexpected goodwill, such as a cripple he spotted from the window of his car who suddenly found himself with sufficient funds to pay for the necessary surgery. At other times, a committed and long-serving employee might find himself on the firing line over something that was not his fault. Hershey's Chocolate Company continued to mint money with sales approaching $10 million by 1915. The queue of vehicles waiting to load up with goods was unending; some four hundred a week. Hershey's influence over the district was spreading as his farms extended to almost 9,000 acres. Appreciative visitors arrived by the hundreds to gaze at the wonderful sights of the famous chocolate town.

It was not enough for Hershey. In early 1916 he removed himself from the many poignant reminders of his life with Kitty and found a retreat in the Caribbean island of Cuba. Cuba had recently been liberated from Spanish control, and America was flexing its own imperial muscle, seeking colonies of its own and bringing American style and commerce to the island. Hershey seized the opportunity. With the war posing a threat to Atlantic shipping, he feared a sugar shortage might sabotage the comforting routines of his chocolate money machine. As Hershey settled into a luxurious hotel in Havana enjoying distant ocean views over Havana Bay, he forced himself to focus on business: Was there a way he could control his own sugar production?

What began as a modest trip with a Cuban guide through the sugar plantations culminated in a gamble on a typical Hershey scale.

Milton toured the northern coast between Havana and Matanzas with the boundless enthusiasm of a young man. Tirelessly he trekked through fields of sugarcane, not noticing the heat, viewing the growing green, the vigor of the canes, the flowing water, the rich earth. The whole glorious fecund island was growing money. Hershey was in a buying mood: 10,000 acres thirty-five miles east of Havana were a start. It was like beginning anew and required all his energy, and he had energy to squander while trying to blot out memories.

Hershey raised the funds for his venture by selling securities and creating a new company, the Hershey Corporation. This put him in a position to proceed simultaneously with a giant sugar mill, a grand hotel, and of course, another model town, Hershey Cuba, with over 180 cottages with their own gardens. He wanted his workers to have the best of the new technology. His model houses would boast such extravagances as taps with running water and electric lights. He continued to buy land—eventually some 65,000 acres—and made plans for an electric railway that would cross it from Havana to Matanzas: the Hershey Cuban Railway. While eyebrows were raised back in Hershey, Pennsylvania, at the incredible extravagance of the venture, Milton felt invincible as sugar prices continued to climb.

Milton Hershey became a familiar figure in Havana: He was the very image of wealthy benevolence as he strolled through the tropical landscape in his white suit and panama. His mother sometimes accompanied him on trips, when they stayed in old-world haciendas and enjoyed the view of Havana Bay. Milton continued to spend his way through his grief, and gradually the isolated, expatriate society in Cuba afforded him some relief. Millionaires he had long admired, such as Henry Ford, also relished the privacy of the Caribbean island. These were Havana's boom years, when exotic luxuries were always available to the super rich, and the tropical air was fragrant with the scent of money.

Milton's business continued to expand exponentially, and he was now in a position to control the price of one of his main raw materials. The very rich Mr. Hershey, almost cursed with the Midas touch—widowed, childless, as he drank champagne, smoked fine cigars, and gambled in Havana's nightclubs—had no one to whom he could bequeath his vast wealth, and all the while his chocolate money machine grew daily.

EUROPE 1916

On May 31, the greatest navies the world had ever seen confronted each other in the the North Sea near Jutland, Denmark. The two mighty fleets, glittering with an array of weapons sufficient to blow each other out of the water, squared up to each other. With a horrible inevitability, soon all was chaos, the dark shapes of the dreadnoughts and battle cruisers barely visible in the smoke of battle as they spilled out thunderous gunfire. The noise was deafening, the smoke alternately obscuring and revealing scenes of horrific destruction as shells ripped into men and machine. Fourteen British and eleven German ships were lost in the Battle of Jutland, and 8,500 young men gave their lives. Soon numbers were to become meaningless, when a month later, one of the bloodiest military operations ever recorded began to unfold at the Somme in France. In one fateful day, July 1, 19,240 British men died and more than 35,500 were injured—the greatest losses in a single day in the entire history of the British army.

News from the battlefields in France and Flanders reached George Cadbury and his community at Bournville through journalists at the papers and letters from Laurence in the Quaker convoys. For George Sr., the war proved to be a considerable test of faith.

How could anyone make spiritual sense of the depths of suffering that the new technology left in its wake? The poisonous yellow-green plumes of chlorine gas floated like clouds over the trenches at Ypres, burning eyes, dissolving lungs, and causing a slow and terrible death by asphyxiation. Fighter planes, the new terror of the skies, were armed with machine guns and rained bombs on the innocent as they darted through the skies like deadly thunderbolts. Then there were tanks that crushed the vestiges of civilization into the mud beneath their treads. Young men torn to shreds in the barbed wire defenses of No Man's Land. All this evil handed out so impersonally demanded an explanation. The industrial age, which had brought so many benefits, had also unleashed a monster: killing on an industrial scale never before seen in human history. World order, it seemed, was slowly collapsing. This orgy of mindless killing was incomprehensible.

George Cadbury felt a pastoral concern for his flock at Bournville. Faith was at a crisis point. How could God allow such evil? Although he too had unresolved issues arising from the conflict, he felt it was his duty to visit the families who attended the Bournville Morning and Evening Meetings. They wanted to discuss their worries and fears; they wanted reassurance. The argument usually went, "If God reigns, it would be impossible that all the sin and misery culminating in this terrible war could be permitted."

George, wrestling with the same thoughts, gave no sign of any underlying schism and spoke of faith: "If there were no sin, there could be no free agency. God could have created us sinless; then there would have been no freedom of choice and no test of our obedience and love for him." Then he asked if they "had ever been tempted to evil and resisted temptation?" Drawing on his experiences in the Adult Class, he explained that he had seen many times that "yielding to sin brought no real or lasting happiness, but resisting temptation did." He quoted from the Bible: "Blessed is the man that endureth temptation for when he is tried he will receive the crown of life, which the lord has promised to them that love him."

It is hard to imagine the impact of these visits or whether they were appreciated. According to his biographer, George Cadbury had a "patriarchal relationship" with the inhabitants of Bournville. Doubtless they were in awe of their employer and benefactor; some may have been moved by and helped by the strength of his own faith. George himself saw it as his duty.

But there was growing hostility to pacifists in Britain, and the Cadbury family made no secret of their views. In November 1916, a military inspector was ordered to examine George's activities to find out if he was funding antiwar or anticonscription campaigners. The inspector even insisted on going through George's personal accounts, so he duly fetched his checkbooks. He had nothing to hide; three-quarters of his income was given away to philanthropic causes but none were antiwar campaigns. His family supported the war effort.

Twenty-year-old Molly, his youngest daughter, had followed her older brother, Laurence, to France soon after the outbreak of war to work in a military hospital. Laurence was building a reputation in the Friends Ambulance Unit with eighty vehicles under his control. Their sister, twenty-two-year-old Dolly, worked as a nurse at Fircroft Working Men's College, which had been hastily converted into a hospital, along with The Beeches. George's youngest son, Bertie, was initially posted to Yarmouth on minesweeping operations in the North Sea. "Don't tell Mother or Father," Bertie told Laurence after a particularly reckless trip where his unit unknowingly sailed straight through a minefield, "or they will have hell's own needles." Nine months later Bertie transferred to the Royal Naval Air Service. His task was to attack the German airships, or Zeppelins, which brought a new terror to the towns of Britain. At first the British were hope-lessly ill-equipped. The Zeppelins flew on dark nights, but there were only two searchlights along the East Anglian coast. Even when the British got airborne, the Zeppelins had a faster rate of climb and could move out of range all too easily. Bertie spent long hours patrolling over the North Sea. On one particularly dark night, losing control for a few crucial seconds as his goggles slipped, he crashed into the sea—and was lucky to escape with minor injuries.

Meanwhile, George Sr.'s much older sons by his first marriage, Edward and George Jr., were dealing with rapidly changing circum-stances at Bournville. All the horses at the factory had been com-mandeered, and parcels could no longer be easily delivered. The trained workforce gradually disappeared. The brothers found it diffi-cult to recruit people who could operate the specialized machinery. Soon raw materials were in short supply.

Even under these austere conditions, what chocolate they could produce emerged as the high-energy comfort food of choice for troops on the move. Far from an anticipated downturn, Dairy Milk and Bournville Cocoa were in such demand by the British government that the Cadbury brothers had to streamline the chocolate works to gear up production of their two most popular brands. The seven hundred different types of chocolate products they were making at the start of the war were reduced to two hundred within two years. They did, however, introduce a much-loved innovation in 1915: a chocolate assortment sold in special five-pound cartons named Milk Tray.

As the effects of German U-boats and the naval blockade intensified, the government ordered the production of essential foods at Bournville. The milk-processing plants at Frampton and Knighton developed for Dairy Milk production were hastily adapted to churn out butter, condensed milk, milk powder, and cheese. Sections of the factory at Bournville now made biscuits, dried vegetables, and fruit pulp in addition to the core chocolate lines. "George is having a very anxious time at Bournville," George Sr. confided to a friend on February 24, 1916. "We have lost some 1,700 out of 3,000 men that were with us when war began . . . to the Army and Navy." Within a year he reported that another seven hundred of his workers had been moved to munitions factories. It was increasingly hard to find skilled engineers to repair machinery. George Sr. remarked that women were taking over men's jobs and "were doing remarkably well."

The remaining staff contributed to the war effort long after the Bournville bell signalled the end of their workday. Women set up the Bournville Nursing Division, often working in local military hospitals at night. The Bournville Girls Convalescent Home at Bromyard in Herefordshire was transformed into a Military Convalescent Home. Sixty members of the Works Ambulance Class supported the Birmingham division of the St. John Ambulance Brigade; their role was to transport the wounded who arrived at Birmingham's Snow Hill Station to local hospitals. Bournville volunteers set up stalls at the station and greeted soldiers returning from the front with hot drinks and food. The Works War Relief Committee helped the families of men in active service. The Education Department of Bournville sent books to the troops in the trenches. Wartime spirit saw even the Bournville Dramatic Society keeping up the show with plays performed on improvised stages.

Edward and George Jr. were invited to meet with Fry's directors in Cheltenham, Gloucestershire. The Frys were seeking greater collaboration between the two firms, especially on pricing. As months of war turned into years, chocolate companies were facing shortages of milk and sugar. The government's Sugar Commission introduced quotas in 1916 to ensure that essential foodstuffs had priority. The Frys found their decision to concentrate primarily on the cheaper end of the market had cost them; they could not produce volume and were losing market share to Cadbury and Rowntree. They were also hit by the loss of exports, which had become prohibitively expensive to insure or simply too dangerous. The struggling house of Fry began to fear being taken over by the predatory Swiss.

During the war, the Swiss firms stood to lose the most. Their home market in Switzerland was small, and production and sales across continental Europe had been disrupted. The naval blockade made it dangerous to secure supplies and export to lucrative foreign markets like Britain. By 1916, faced with a shortage of fresh milk, some factories had to be closed. But Nestlé's directors devised a brilliant strategy for getting around the crisis. They knew that dairy and chocolate production in many countries was soaring to meet large government orders. Their solution: Nestlé went on a spending spree.

The Nestlé directors borrowed on a large scale to invest in setting up companies overseas or buying a controlling stake in foreign companies. Through their American branch in Fulton, New York, they acquired interests in firms in North and South America. Their shares in milk-processing companies in Ohio and Philadelphia alone brought them control of twenty-seven factories. Nestlé's production in America rapidly became five times greater than its entire Swiss production before the war. Soon company directors were in Australia hunting down similar deals, and it was not long before the hungry Swiss set their sights on the lucrative British market: They would target Fry.

It was in the Quaker chocolate firms' interests to help each other repel foreign rivals. At Cheltenham, Fry, Rowntree, and Cadbury voluntarily agreed to limit production of less essentials lines such as confectionery in favor of basic foods like cocoa and milk. By cooperating, they hoped to pull through the war without falling into Swiss hands.

By early 1917, German submarines were having a devastating effect on supplies. Sugar quotas plummeted 50 percent. The British chocolate houses rushed to adapt recipes of their remaining core lines to reduce the amount of sugar. Fancy Boxes and other luxury lines disappeared. At Bournville, milk chocolate production stopped altogether. There was a shortage of basic food for the public. "We are sending 20,000 gallons of milk each week from Frampton to Birmingham as there is a great scarcity in the poorer districts," George Sr. told a friend. Cadbury was forced to abandon its leading line, Dairy Milk.

Over in Switzerland, thanks to the support of Swiss banks, Nestlé's worldwide acquisitions grew exponentially—but so did their borrowing. Loans of 12 million Swiss francs in 1912 increased to 54 million by 1917.

Isolated from the horrors of global conflict, Milton Hershey continued to thrive. "Hershey town was so peaceful and serene a community that all the horrors of war one read about seemed strangely out of tune with the course of life," wrote Hershey's relative, Joseph Snavely. "Even the prospect of war with Germany seemed far-fetched."

Nothing seemed to tarnish Hershey's Midas touch. He continued to benefit from his Cuban spending spree as sugar prices rose with the threat to shipping. By January 1917, German submarines began targeting merchant ships in the Atlantic directly. On April 2, President Woodrow Wilson spoke to a special session of Congress setting out the case for war. "German submarine warfare is a warfare against mankind," he declared. America joined the war four days later.

Almost immediately the U.S. government placed an order for 2 million Hershey bars. The firm's sales soared from $10 million in 1915 to $20 million in 1918. Amidst wild rumors that the Germans would find a way to sabotage the factory, Hershey set up a Home Guard. "A finer squad of soldiers never before carried broom handles," said Snavely, since the workers were not permitted to carry arms.

In contrast to the hive of activity in Hershey's chocolate works in America, in Britain, parts of the great Fry citadel in Bristol fell silent. The firm was struggling. Fearing that Fry—or even Rowntree— might be tempted to sell out to their rich Swiss rivals, Edward Cadbury came up with a radical solution: a merger of all three companies to create a Quaker giant. Such a large Quaker enterprise, he argued, "will aim not only to make profits, but also serve the community." Continued competition under wartime conditions is wrong, he reasoned, if together they could give "better service to the public and create better conditions for our workers."

On February 5, 1918, at a solemn Rowntree board meeting in York, the younger members of the family, Seebohm and Arnold Rowntree, argued earnestly in favor of the three Quaker firms joining forces. But Joseph Rowntree was resolutely against it. Some believe this was a matter of stubborn pride; others attribute it to his vision. As a Quaker, he wanted Rowntree to survive independently in order to pioneer a profit-sharing scheme for its staff. "The present industrial organisation of the country is unsound," he said, because it causes a class division "between the holders of capital on one side and workers on the other." He wanted to use the family firm to test out how to "minimise the evils" of the capitalist system. As a Quaker, Joseph saw it as his duty to nurture the guiding light within each member of staff. The real goal for an employer "was to seek to secure for others . . . *the fullest life* of which an individual is capable." An amalgamation between firms he thought would lead to a colossus: a moneymaking behemoth that lost sight of Quakerly ambitions.

Although the Rowntrees opposed the merger, they joined the Frys, Cadburys, and other Quaker colleagues for a Conference of Quaker Employers that April. They wanted to discuss steps to realize such high ambitions. "War has revolutionised the industrial outlook," declared the conference chairman, Arnold Rowntree, in his opening address. During a time of crisis, there was an urgent need for Quaker leaders—whether shareholders, employers, or workers—to examine the way their religious faith could be given "even fuller expression in business life." He asked all friends to consider the Quaker *Book of Discipline*. Citing the section on "The Stewardship of Wealth," he warned against "the spirit of greed . . . unchecked by a sense of social responsibility" and urged the conference to find ways to express the Quaker view "that all human life should be reverenced as capable of the highest distinction."

Seebohm Rowntree led a session on wages that explored the ethical principles that should be used in determining wages. It was a "monstrous thing," he declared, that millions still lived below the poverty line, and he encouraged Quaker employers to "strongly press for State action in that direction." He argued that employers should ensure "that *every* man should be entitled to a Basic Wage," set at a level that "should enable a man to marry, live in a decent house, and provide the necessaries of physical efficiency for a normal family." If a business could not afford to pay such wages, its management "should very strictly limit" what they pay themselves while they improve the efficiency of their company. George Cadbury Jr. led a session on the factors that affect a worker's peace of mind: security of employment, quality of environment, and so on. Other speakers addressed such topics as industrial injury, pensions, and even the democratization of industry: schemes for profit sharing or other forms of copartnership and training to enable junior staff to aspire to senior positions within a firm. The result was a visionary report setting out a template for applying Quaker principles to business life. Years later, after the Second World War, some of these ideas were enshrined in British law with the formation of the Welfare State.

But at such a time, it was not easy to apply Quaker ideals when the war brought real issues of business survival to deal with. Talks about Fry joining forces with Cadbury continued over the spring of 1918. At a directors meeting in Bournville, George Sr. opposed a merger of the chocolate houses but for different and more commercial reasons than his rival in York. "If we fought off the foreign competition once, I have no fear of doing so again," he said. His voice may have sounded frail, but his fighting spirit was intact. With ingenuity and drive, he was certain they could take on their overseas competitors. As part of a merged entity, he felt there would not be "the same energy thrown by either firm into their business." As someone who had forged the business from the start, he recognized the significance of that immeasurable, indefinable fighting spirit.

The younger generation of Frys and Cadburys listened to their Quaker elders, but they were keen to proceed. The Great War had exposed fundamental weaknesses in Fry's operation, and Barrow and Edward Cadbury, calling the matter "urgent," feared "the Frys might be tempted to take offers from other quarters." If Nestlé bought Fry, they would gain an "insurmountable advantage" in the British market. Over the spring and summer of 1918, the chocolate companies were valued by two different city accountants as a first step towards a potential merger.

By now, letters from their younger brothers brought news of turning points in the war. Laurence's Quaker convoy was at the Second Battle of Marne, seventy-five miles northeast of Paris. At the front line in late June 1918, "There was great uneasiness," Laurence wrote. "Everyone knew an attack was coming—but where?" On July 15, "The Hun made his greatest and last push over a 50 mile front," he wrote. Convoys from the Friends Ambulance Unit were positioned to help the French Army at the hottest points. By late July, the tables had turned. "We had regained the initiative and were attacking." At a certain point, the French found there was no one in front of them. They started in pursuit, recounted Laurence, "and kept the Hun on the run giving him absolute hell." It was the first in a series of Allied victories.

Bertie was also beginning to glimpse victory. In April 1918, he had been promoted to captain in the new Royal Air Force and was put in charge of a squadron at Great Yarmouth that was responsible for patrolling for U-boats and Zeppelins. He wrote to his father on August 6, 1918: "You will have heard . . . that my lucky star has again been in the ascendant, and that another Zeppelin has gone to destruction, sent there by a perfectly peaceful live-and-let-live citizen, who has no lust for blood or fearful war spirit in his veins. It all happened very quickly and very terribly."

Bertie was at a concert with his fiancée when he was summoned to the RAF station at Yarmouth. He heard three Zeppelins had been sighted fifty miles to the northeast. Knowing full well that there was only one machine left with the necessary speed and climb, he wrote, "I roared down to the station in an ever-ready Ford, seized a scarf, goggles and helmet, tore off my streamline coat, and semi-clothed, with a disreputable jacket under my arm, sprinted as hard as ever Nature would let me, and took a running jump into the pilot's seat. I beat my most strenuous competitor by one-fifth of a second."

As soon as he left the air field, Bertie saw the Zeppelins and maneuvered into a position where his gunner, Bob Leckie, could target one. The explosive bullets ripped a massive hole in the airship, flames ran along its length, and it plunged in a great fireball into the sea. "The action was very short," he wrote. "She lighted after a few rounds and went hurtling down to destruction from a great height." He and Leckie gave chase and managed to start a fire in a second airship, but it was extinguished and the Zeppelins moved away at high speed.

Their luck had run out. Bertie's engine stopped. Leckie's gun jammed. "Our sting had gone. . . . I think that half hour, driving through 12,000 feet of cloud in inky blackness on a machine that I had been told could not land at night, even if I ever made land again, was the most terrible I have ever experienced." When he did successfully land, "in a machine which I thought certain to crash and catch fire," to his horror, he found that his bombs had failed to release and he had "two 100lb bombs on board; also my live saving belt had been eaten through by acid from an accumulator."

Afterwards they learned that the airship they destroyed was an L70, the best in the German fleet. They had brought down Peter Strasser, the chief of the German Airship Service, Fuhrer der Luftschiffe. After this raid, there were no further Zeppelin attacks.

As the guns of the Great War finally fell silent in November 1918, belief in European civilized supremacy had been thrown into question. Thirty countries had battled in a conflagration that was fought on five continents. The Austro-Hungarian and Ottoman Empires had been destroyed; Germany and Russia had been defeated. The Versailles Peace Treaty brought 13 million more people into the British Empire and added 1.8 million square miles. But the price was terribly high. More than three-quarters of a million British fighting men had died. At Bournville, of the 2,000 men who left to join the forces,

218 never came back. In a solemn ceremony, a memorial tablet was raised in their honor.

Those who did come home to Bournville returned to a different commercial landscape. In the final weeks of the Great War, the Cadburys' once great rival, Fry, had partnered with them in a new holding company called the British Cocoa and Chocolate Company. The Fry family, believing that both firms were of equal value, was shocked when the valuations were completed. Cadbury's assets were worth three times more than Fry's. Consequently, although both firms were subsidiaries in the British Cocoa and Chocolate Company, Cadbury held the controlling interest. Shares were issued in relation to the valuations of the two companies. Chairmanship of the whole enterprise fell to Barrow Cadbury. Keen to "do the right thing" by the Frys, he valued their shares generously. The great Bristol chocolate house was now effectively a subsidiary run from Bournville. It was the first in a series of mergers and takeovers that would transform the British chocolate industry over the next century as the pace of globalization quickened.

It soon became abundantly clear that far from being the dynamic rival the Cadburys had envisaged, Fry was something of a white elephant. Twenty-six-year-old Bertie, honored with a Distinguished Flying Cross for his war record as a fighter pilot, was eager to take on the challenge of the Bristol firm. He returned from the war to find there was no room for him at Bournville. Instead he took an offer from Fry at £300 a year, but when he turned up at Union Street in Bristol for his first day in May 1919, the state of the firm shocked him.

He was greeted by the legacy of failed investment by Joseph Storrs Fry II. "Partially manufactured goods were transported by horse drawn box vans through narrow congested streets," he wrote home, "between 24 different factories." The doors from the many buildings opened directly out onto the street, making it impossible to track who came and went; goods disappeared without trace. With a pub on every street, the calm discipline that characterized Bournville was lacking. Equally curious for Bertie, "It was impossible to shake the then directors out of their complacency and their false sense of security." For a reason best known to the director of confectionery and the director of chocolate-making, the two men were "hardly on speaking terms." Since they both required large teams of almost identical staff, the inefficiencies multiplied, as did the confusion. Worse still, reported an amazed Bertie: "Fry's never had much regard for quality, but during the War they abandoned any pretence of maintaining it and they opened up their refiners and let them rip." The inevitable result was that they had a "terrible reputation" and were producing "unpleasant" chocolate. Could anyone be surprised they were failing, he thought, "with a divided and hopelessly inefficient and out of date factory, a sales force split in two, and a reputation for poor quality?"

As for the Swiss rival that had prompted the move in the first place, as George Sr. had forecast, they had nothing to fear. Nestlé's bold growth strategy came with a high price. They had continued their aggressive spending, acquiring twenty-two more factories in Australia and America in 1920 alone. They had eighty factories worldwide when the postwar downturn kicked in. The combination of plummeting government orders, stunning levels of debt, a crisis in foreign exchange, a rise in costs of raw materials, and panic selling of Nestlé shares in 1921 brought the company to a crisis point. In 1921, for the first time in the company's history, Nestlé announced a substantial deficit of 1 million Swiss francs.

Ever practical, when George Sr. and Elsie learned there were children starving in Austria after the war, they made arrangements to bring fifteen of them to stay in Bournville village. Quaker friends organized "cocoa rooms" to feed orphaned children in Vienna. George became known as "the chocolate uncle" on account of the numerous boxes of chocolates that he sent to the children.

Gradually George reduced his duties, and when he appeared in public it was invariably with Elsie at his side. King George V and Queen Mary came to visit Bournville in 1919 and toured the almshouses built by Richard Cadbury. Although still tall, spare, his head held high, George Sr. had a certain fragility; he moved with the careful, measured pace of a man who knows his days too are measured. His eyes "gleamed with visionary light" as though fixed on the New Jerusalem that had inspired him.

George may have found that the evil of war was utterly incomprehensible—far removed from his understanding of God—but ultimately nothing could destroy his faith. He heard only one voice and focused on the vision that drove him: a liberal vision of toleration, unity, and a world at peace. On January 18, 1922, he and Elizabeth visited the latest developments of the Selly Oak Colleges, which he had helped to found. Woodbrooke and other Selly Oak Colleges aimed to advance spiritual and theological understanding, and George felt it was urgent to do all he could to bring religions together and encourage churches to work side by side. He and Elsie were touring a new church within the Selly Oak system when he was taken ill. His doctors advised rest.

Even at eighty-three, George was not a man who would readily succumb to doctor's orders. Confined to the upper floor of the manor house, he could hear the familiar sounds of staff moving around the house, the whirring of the electric lift between floors, and outside on the terrace, the water cascading on the stone fountain. Peaceful hours passed in his study, commenting on the minutes from Bournville or meeting with visitors, happily engaged in discussing causes about which he was still passionate. His voice was weak and frail, reported a friend, Lady Frances Balfour, who saw him that summer, but his indomitable spirit never left him as he talked enthusiastically of his "vision of what cities should be."

Even when defeated by the exertion of visitors, from a balcony at the front of the house, he could look over the little empire he had created, still unspoiled. He always maintained that the view from his garden window was a universe in miniature. To see that perfect landscape was enough; even if he travelled beyond the western star, he could not be more enchanted. Across the lake and the herbaceous gardens, in a blaze of early autumn color, he loved to watch the children playing in the fields beyond. That year he and Elsie invited a record number of children for the holidays.

In the other direction towards Birmingham, beyond the trams of Bristol Road, lay the rapidly expanding model village at Bournville, now with more than 1,000 houses and almost 2,000 acres of land, all thriving and at peace.

George Sr. was well enough to visit Bournville in October, but any hopes that he would see another Christmas were short-lived. On October 20, he slipped into unconsciousness. There was a brief rally the next day, when he and Elsie, joined by their belief in the eternity of the spirit and soon to be separated by the great divide opening up between life and death, seized their chance for one more brief reunion and farewell.

On October 24, 1922, Elsie entered in her diary: "Go early to see my darling. Breathing difficult all day. . . . Just as the Bournville bell signalled the end of the day, one sigh, and he too went home after work. Such triumph and joy. Much desolation." She told her friends, "It was the going home of a conqueror."

The sun rose on October 28 on a clear autumn day. Bright sunlight streamed through the leaves on Bournville Green, the trees like brilliant flowers. It was the kind of glorious fall day that George Sr. had always loved. But it was the day of his memorial service.

Sixteen thousand people gathered silently on the village green to pay their respects. Bouquets of flowers engulfed the Rest House. Tributes poured in from around the world. There were messages from thousands of people whose lives had been touched by George Sr. in a personal way—the young Viennese woman rescued after the war, the criminal whose life was transformed by his Adult Class, the cripple who first experienced swimming at the farm.

The Bournville choir sang hymns. The twenty-two bells of the carillon that had once enchanted George and Elsie rang out across the village. Eyes were on Elsie, her grief and loss staunchly masked behind a veil of formality as well-wishers offered their condolences. "He was very much more than a captain of industry," declared Henry Hodgkin in his eulogy. "He was much more than a large-hearted philanthropist, he was much more than a far-seeing builder of the future, though he was all these things. Pre-eminently we think of him today as our friend . . . and we think of him even more as a man of God, whose religion was his life and whose life was his religion. . . . He was a man of wide sympathies. . . . It seemed as if none lay outside his great heart. The world was his parish. He had a universal spirit."

People mourned not just the loss of a pioneer but the loss of all that George Cadbury had come to symbolize: the practical mystic whose visions of utopia, of garden cities and factories, whose love of nature and the simple things in life, whose overpowering faith and desire to do good informed every aspect of the enterprise he created. Above all, said Hodgkin, "He was a man who loved. The inspiration of his life was love. . . . Can any epitaph be more worthy than this—'He loved greatly'?"

Perhaps George Cadbury would have marvelled at the fuss. He believed he was merely doing his job and fortunate to be in such a position. His faith had always pointed the way—even when faced with the meaningless horror of the Great War. His conviction that your own soul "lived or perished according to its use of the gift of life" had guided him from the outset and never wavered. Neither he nor Richard, innocents at business when they took over the factory from their father, had any conception of the embarrassment of riches that following this course would provide. But business for them had always been just a means to an end. As Quakers, they knew the rewards were for their fellow men and for the glory of God.

Soon afterwards a similar scene played out in York when George Sr.'s friend and rival, Joseph Rowntree, died at the age of eighty-nine. Right to the end, according to his private papers, he was puzzling over the question of poverty and whether, through rigorous scientific inquiry, poverty could become a thing of the past. In York, as in Bournville, people mourned not just the passing of the man, but everything he symbolized that had brought such unexpected good to the world of business on such a scale.

For although the Quaker pioneers had died, they left behind enterprises in York and Bournville that were larger than the individuals themselves. People spoke of the "spirit" of the Quaker chocolate firms as though a mantle had gently enveloped each one, granting them a life and character of their own. Each seemed charged with the mysterious purpose of the men who created them, as though even the bricks and mortar were bent towards some stoic Quaker quest. What hope was there that their iconic creations would live on in the changed landscape of the post-war world? Would the dedicated altruism and idealism falter now that the leading lights were gone?

On November 18, 1923, the front page of the *New York Times* carried a startling revelation about America's chocolate millionaire. Mindful of Kitty's wishes and inspired by the philanthropy of Quakers and others, the cigar-smoking, gambling candyman had discreetly given away his massive fortune. "I decided to make the orphan boys of the United States my heirs," Milton Hershey told the *Times* reporter, James Young. Hershey had turned his company stock, worth $60 million, into a trust to benefit the orphan boys of the Hershey Industrial School. "He picked out the boys who never get a chance and decided to give them one," wrote Young. "The biggest chance they've ever had in the history of the world." The reporter found Hershey to be a practical man of few words; nonetheless, Hershey managed to convey his message.

"Our boys are our finest possession," he said to Young. "They are the future itself, growing up before our eyes."

"Suppose you had had two or three sons?" Young asked. "Would you still have felt the business should go to the orphan boys?"

"Well, my wife and I decided that we ought to do this," he replied. "She . . . did not live to see the plan completed. It was hers and mine." He hesitated. "Too much money is an evil influence. Money spoils more men than it makes. . . . Yes, I think even if I'd had those sons you mention I still would have wanted the poor boys to get the business. . . . Because they are all our boys, you know, after all, whether we happen to be their dads or not."

PART
IV

16

This Company Isn't
Big Enough for Both of Us

CHICAGO, ILLINOIS, 1920s

The Roaring Twenties—brash, hedonistic, jazzy—exorcised some of the horrors of the Great War. There was new hope, new ideas, and lovely new toys for all those shimmying, Charleston-stepping moderns, high-heeling it into the golden twenties, where you could live in a modern house and fill it with objects of wonder that banished drudgery with the touch of a button. Many households owned a car, a radio, sometimes a refrigerator, and even a toaster. This new world of consumerism and easy credit seemed a world apart from the frugality and self-restraint of the Quakers. Only a few years had passed since the death of George Cadbury, but the chocolate companies were about to be thrust onto a different planet: planet Mars.

Forrest Mars was born in America in 1904 but grew up in a remote mining community in North Battleford in Saskatchewan, Canada. His entry into the world of confectionery happened by chance in Chicago in 1923, when he met his estranged father, Frank.

Frank Mars had come to success late in life after struggling for years with a succession of failed candy businesses in the frontier towns of the Midwest. Chicago in the early twentieth century was the battleground that produced such winners as William Wrigley Jr., a salesman who worked the city streets, peddling his new ideas for chewing flavors: Spearmint and Juicy Fruit gum. Chicago also produced the Curtiss Candy Company, creators of the Baby Ruth and Butterfinger. Then there was George Williamson, who launched the delicious Oh Henry! candy bar—named, according to the *Chicago Tribune*, after a pretty company employee who went into such a flutter when her boyfriend arrived that "all the young lady could exclaim was 'Oh, Henry!'"

But for Frank Mars and his wife, Ethel, there was no quick breakthrough, and the hardship led to the collapse of their marriage in 1910. Frank was ordered to pay $20 a month to support six-year-old Forrest, but he often failed to make the payments. Ethel felt she had no choice but to send her son away. She worked as a sales clerk while Forrest lived with his grandparents in Canada.

Forrest worked hard and eventually enrolled at the University of California at Berkeley. He took casual jobs to fund his education and rapidly discovered his talent for business. Pushing the boundaries as he tested his entrepreneurial skills, he soon landed in prison. His "crime" was an overzealous advertising stunt. Working as a salesman in the summer of 1923, he plastered the central street of Chicago with posters for Camel cigarettes, completely ignoring such niceties as payments and permissions—and ended up with a lot of explaining to do. The person who turned up at the Chicago prison to bail him out was none other than his estranged father, Frank Mars. Perhaps even more galling for Forrest, the father who had so carelessly abandoned him was now a success. After years of struggle, the upturn had come slowly for Frank Mars with the launch of his third candy-making company, known simply as Mar-O-Bar.

With characteristic opportunism, Forrest seized the moment to discuss the confectionery business with his father. In the 1920s, Frank Mars employed over 125 in staff and had a large house in Minneapolis, home to his second wife who was also called Ethel, and their young daughter, Patricia. But his Mar-O-Bar company was not yet well known beyond the state of Minnesota. Forrest urged his father to think big. Surely they could come up with a new type of confection that they could launch from coast to coast like Hershey?

Forrest was undoubtedly aware from his childhood of the potential of a particular type of confectionery, usually made by combining cheaper ingredients, such as toffee or caramel, with chocolate. In Canada, this type of candy had been on sale for many years, often handmade with maple fudge or marshmallow coated in chocolate. It was becoming known in the trade as a "countline" since the bars were sold by count and not by weight, like blocks of chocolate. During the First World War, countlines had been developed for the U.S. army when it was discovered that the chocolate coating kept the high-energy confectionery ingredients fresh. While leading manufacturers such as Hershey and Cadbury were focused on producing solid chocolate bars, no one was making chocolate-coated bars in factory quantities.

Forrest sensed an opportunity. "My father and I walked into a Walgreen store," he told Don Gussow in a rare interview for the *Candy Industry and Confectioners Journal* in February 1966. "Looking over the candy department, I said to him: Why don't we find a way to make just one piece of candy instead of so many different items?" What Forrest suggested next was essentially a countline for mass production: "a chocolate center with some malted milk and coated in milk chocolate."

Frank Mars was evidently impressed by his son's suggestions. Once back in the factory near Minneapolis, it did not take him long to come up with a mouthwatering concoction made by covering a bar of nougat and a layer of sweet caramel with a thick coating of chocolate. The bar was satisfyingly chunky compared to a Hershey chocolate bar and could be sold more cheaply since the confectionery ingredients cost less than cocoa. Equally important, the chocolate coating kept the nougat filling fresh, making it possible to transport the product around the country. Frank cheekily approached Hershey to purchase a supply of chocolate for the coating. By early 1924, he was ready to launch his new bar. He called it the Milky Way.

The Milky Way was an overnight sensation. In one year, Frank's dreams came true. Sales at the Mar-O-Bar Company leapt from $72,800 to $792,900. Frank was ready to expand beyond Minnesota.

Within three years, he had started construction of a stylish new factory in Chicago that won much praise: "An outstanding bit of architecture," enthused the *Chicago Tribune*. When Forrest joined his father at the new Chicago plant, there was just one problem. Forrest, like his father, "was more than a little brash," observed Harold Meyers in *Fortune* in May 1967, and he "had definite ideas on how things should be done." His father, now feeling his years, tried to smooth over the cracks.

Father and son sold a staggering 20 million bars from coast to coast by 1929. It seemed nothing could stop them—even the financial drought of the Great Depression. In 1930, a year when 26,000 businesses failed and 10 percent of the population was out of work, Frank and Forrest Mars rode out the crash on a wave of innovation. That year they launched a peanut, caramel, and chocolate sensation called Snickers, allegedly named after the family horse. Their 3 Musketeers bar soon followed.

In Pennsylvania, Milton Hershey wasn't worried—yet. He had the foresight to spend his way through the Depression, giving generously. From the backseat of his gleaming sixteen-cylinder Chrysler, he cruised Hershey town, watching work progress for a new school, a grand hotel, offices, factories, and a sports hall. Working with his closest ally, William Murrie, the president of the Hershey Chocolate Company, Milton found $10 million to spend on new facilities and more importantly, to create jobs. Even though sales of Hershey's block chocolate dropped by almost a half during the Depression, he was easily able to withstand the effects of the crash of 1929 protected by his venture into Cuban sugar.

Sales for Mars's countlines like Snickers, Milky Way, and 3 Musketeers were also reduced during the years of long queues for any kind of work, soup kitchens, the exodus from Dust Bowl farms. But the years of depression put Mars at an advantage. His countlines were satisfying snacks that could fill empty, hungry stomachs and were cheaper than block chocolate. Frank and Forrest found ways of improving efficiency by standardizing ingredients. They made sure their candy was priced within the reach of millions. Just eight years after father and son had reunited, Mars was the second largest confectioner in America. Not only did the obliging Mr. Hershey have to wake up. The upstart new company was soon casting its long shadow over the flourishing garden factory at Bournville.

It was a family rift that launched young Forrest on his own path to success. "Frank Mars was proud as punch of his son," insisted a colleague, "but he wasn't about to let him run things." In 1933 they had an intense quarrel. Father and son stopped talking almost as abruptly as they had begun. According to an article in *Fortune* in 1967, Frank sent his son packing, claiming "this company isn't big enough for both of us. Go to some other country and start your own business." Forrest walked out of the Chicago factory with the foreign rights to the Milky Way and never saw his father again.

Free to dedicate himself to business, Forrest began his research in Switzerland. He worked first for Jean Tobler and then for Nestlé. When he had learned all he could of the Swiss secrets, he came to England. His plan: to enlist the help of the benign and unsuspecting Quaker gentlemen at Bournville to launch his own chocolate company. Unencumbered by religious idealism, he was free to bring his own driven business style to the quaintly philanthropic and paternalistic world of English chocolate making.

BOURNVILLE, BIRMINGHAM, ENGLAND

During the 1920s, the Cadbury cousins worked relentlessly to fill the great void left by George Cadbury Sr. There were more family members in the company than ever before: Barrow Cadbury was the figurehead at the helm of the British Cocoa and Chocolate Company, and several others from his generation held key roles on the Cadbury board.

Barrow's younger brother, William, who had been instrumental in setting up cocoa production in Ghana, contributed to developing the world-famous *Cadbury* script logo. Well before the concept of marketing was fully established, the Quaker directors understood the need for an instantly recognizable icon for the firm. In 1921, William's signature was adapted to create a logo for the company, which appeared on the delivery trucks, in catalogues, and on some of the brands. Barrow and William's cousins, Edward and George Jr., joined the board as well. After the early struggle to create Dairy Milk, George Jr. had the satisfaction of seeing it overtake the sales of all other British chocolate products. As for Edward, with his painstaking attention to every aspect of the business, he was emerging as a natural successor to Barrow.

After the Great War, the Cadbury cousins were joined by a younger generation eager to master the business. This included Barrow's son, Paul, and Edward and George Jr.'s half brothers: Laurence, who was awarded a military Order of the British Empire, and Bertie, decorated with a Distinguished Flying Cross. Edward, always keen to nurture the next generation and capitalize on its energy, saw with some satisfaction that his younger brothers had demonstrable leadership skills. Laurence joined the board of directors at Bournville while Bertie remained preoccupied with Fry in Bristol.

They faced a tough new business world. The export market, built up over decades by Cadbury travellers, had collapsed with the gradual imposition of tariffs around the world. The Cadbury directors realized they needed a completely new strategy overseas. They aimed to team up with local partners and build foreign factories of their own. Cadbury's first venture was in Australia with a local confectioner, James Pascall. They built a factory at Hobart in Tasmania in 1921, and Cadbury-Fry-Pascall was soon planning its assault on the Australian market.

At home the Cadburys feared the return of Nestlé, Menier, and other foreign rivals. To counter this threat, they embarked on a vast program of modernization. Much of the chocolate at Bournville was still handmade, but the Cadbury cousins understood what Forrest Mars had glimpsed: The future lay with the mass manufacture of fewer lines. Supply rationing during the Great War had forced efficiencies on Bournville. The Cadbury cousins knew it was possible to produce volume more cheaply and then pass the savings on to the consumer with lower prices. Adopting this strategy seemed imperative for survival.

The Cadbury cousins oversaw the largest transformation of the chocolate works since it had been built by George Sr. and Richard fifty years earlier. Laurence, as a skilled engineer, supervised the designs of automatic production lines that were tailor-made for virtually every stage of chocolate making: molding machines, blending machines, wrapping machines—each one electrified. The scale of mechanization was so great that an entirely new building had to be built. The old blocks—some just a single storey—were knocked down to make way for a chocolate factory of the future that covered eighty acres. Over the course of the 1920s, Laurence watched with satisfaction as imposing red brick facades some five or six storeys high replaced the darker, smaller buildings of Victorian days. While making his mark on Bournville, he also settled into home life. He married Joyce Mathews in 1924, and soon a young family was on the way. Julian was born in 1926, followed by Adrian in 1929.

At Bristol, the modernization of Fry was more of a challenge. "The Frys were having to fight very hard to keep their head above water," recalled Bertie. The British Cocoa and Chocolate board identified a radical solution: They would abandon the centuries-old Union Street site beloved by Joseph Storrs Fry II and invest in a brand new factory in the country. In 1920 Bertie and the Fry directors walked along the railway lines leaving Bristol until they found a perfect location near Keynsham. They bought over two hundred acres bounded by the River Avon and the main Bristol-to-London Railway and initiated a massive construction plan. They decided to hold a public competition with a £1,000 prize to choose the site's name: Somerdale was the winner.

Against the background of the Roaring Twenties, the Quaker chocolatiers in Bournville held their own. They continued to show great flair in devising tantalizing new confections: the crumbly-textured, extra-light Flake was launched in 1920; Cadbury's Fruit and Nut bar made its entrance in 1926; and the Cadbury Creme Egg, which came in a multitude of mouthwatering varieties, became a fixture at Easter. In Bristol, Fry's Chocolate Cream and Fry's Turkish Delight were still popular, but the company, particularly hard hit by the loss of export markets, was short of new products. Confections devised by the Cadbury development team were passed over for manufacture in Bristol: notably the honeycombed Crunchie covered in a thick layer of milk chocolate.

All the while, the feared return of powerful rivals failed to materialize. Nestlé was slower to recover from the effects of the Great War than anticipated. Their share price crashed in the early 1920s, when it was revealed the company had debts approaching 293,000,000 Swiss francs. To tackle the emergency, the firm's "outdated status as a family or pseudo family concern" was abolished, according to Jean Heer in a company history commissioned by Nestlé. New executives were appointed based on proven talent, not their relationship to the founders. Financial advisers were brought in to reschedule the debt and sell assets. With their expertise, the crisis was resolved.

Rowntree in York was also struggling, and there too family management was blamed. Wages spiralled 150 percent between 1914 and 1924, but there was no corresponding rise in output and no dazzling new products to win over the public. The Great Depression brought matters to a head. Faced with plummeting trade, the company chairman, Seebohm Rowntree, feared for the survival of the business. For a while, the workers at Haxby Road were put on a three-day work week. In the early 1930s, the board decided that "all new directors were to be appointed on the basis of merit," according to business historian Robert Fitzgerald. Family members would no longer have preference; there was no room for part-time directors with their "aesthetic form of entrepreneurship." Fitzgerald notes, "There was no parallel year of crisis" at Cadbury. "The competence of family members like Paul, Edward, and Laurence was widely acknowledged in the industry."

But while their established rivals struggled, there was a newcomer that Cadbury had not bargained on, an American with ideas of his own. In 1933, Cadbury's sales team was soon made aware of a fledgling company operating from a tiny flat in Slough, twenty-five miles west of London. Forrest Mars approached Cadbury directly for a supply of chocolate to coat his new confection. To Forrest's delight, Cadbury's coatings department agreed.

Even today, Laurence's second son—Sir Adrian Cadbury—smiles and shakes his head as he looks back on that decision made by his uncles. "Why ever did we do that?" he asks. Growing up in the 1930s with his brother, Julian, he points out that at the time, the family "would not have seen Forrest Mars as a direct competitor. The basis of our business was moulded bars of chocolate. Mars was different."

In the summer heat of 1933, Forrest Mars set out to reconfigure the Milky Way into a chunkier, more satisfying bar. He hired four assistants and they set to work in an old building in Slough. On one occasion, he was nearly ruined when rain leaked through a roof onto sacks of raw materials, but Noah's Flood would not have deterred Forrest Mars. He worked long hours until he had the perfect formula, combining a layer of soft caramel and a wrapping of the ever-popular Cadbury milk chocolate around a whipped fondant center. The resulting Mars Bar proved to be one of the most successful snacks of all time. In just one year, he sold 2 million bars.

In York, a new director at Rowntree, George Harris, was paying close attention to the novel idea of mass-producing countlines. Although he had married into the Rowntree family (his wife was Friede, the granddaughter of Henry Isaac Rowntree, the company's founder), he had his own ideas about moving the business forward. Harris recognized that Rowntree could never challenge Cadbury's supremacy in block chocolate. Dairy Milk was so dominant that it was outselling Rowntree's milk chocolate ten to one. But could Mars's countlines offer a way forward? Harris went to Slough to meet Forrest Mars. The two men found they had a lot in common: both were seeking to tackle the Cadbury juggernaut.

Under Harris's pioneering charge, the research department at Rowntree was kept very busy. The results took everyone by surprise. Hundreds of tests were carried out on a new chocolate box to compete with Cadbury's leading King George assortment. They came up with Rowntree's Black Magic, which launched in 1933 to immediate success. When Forrest Mars debuted the Milky Way bar in Britain in 1935, followed by Maltesers in 1936, Rowntree had something else up its sleeve. Big things were not expected of the little bar called Chocolate Crisp, which was introduced without advertising in September 1935. It was only a wafer covered with chocolate, a wisp of a thing. But it carried all the promise of crispy crunchiness and melting chocolate—and it was an affordable treat. It proved to be a winner and soon got a catchy new name: Kit Kat. That same year Rowntree surprised the market with the bubbly Aero that teased the palate with a deceptive lightness. In 1936 came Rowntree's Dairy Box, full of soft-centered chocolate temptation. Cadbury countered with intense promotion of its popular Milk Tray brand and launched a new assortment known as Cadbury's Roses—supposedly named after George Sr.'s passion for the flower.

But Harris had still more tricks up his sleeve. Soft chocolate beans coated in crispy sugared shells were repackaged in an eye-catching cardboard tube and sold as Smarties in 1937. To cap it all, in 1939 Rowntree came up with a round mint with a hole in the center and called it Polo. To create so many distinctive brands in such rapid succession was almost unheard of. At last Rowntree's fortunes was turning, and the confectionery wars were intensifying.

But soon the Swiss giant, Nestlé, entered the fray, making the competitive skirmishes of England's Quaker gentlemen look like a children's game. Nestlé's collaboration with the Swiss chocolatiers Peter, Cailler, and Kohler found its stride in the 1930s, and chocolate was now its second most important product. Nestlé and Peter, Cailler, and Kohler had sealed their alliance in 1929 with a full merger that brought six more chocolate factories in Europe under Nestlé's control. As a result, in the year of the crash, Nestlé's profits actually rose from 23 to 30 million Swiss francs. During the 1930s, Nestlé's block chocolate, enhanced by an impressive array of promotional tools—prize schemes, coupons, collecting cards for children—was seizing new ground in British grocers.

In the shadow of the European giant, Forrest Mars used any means possible to expand his operation—and he did not confine himself to selling chocolate. Mars bought a small British pet food concern, the Chappel Brothers, and within a couple of years, it was so profitable that he had more money to invest in his chocolate enterprise. The next step: a small chocolate factory in Brussels to make Mars bars. Soon he was generating sales across the continent.

By 1935, however, the modernization of Bournville was complete. The new Cadbury factory was unlike anything that had been seen before: a vast mechanical palace where sugar and fat and cocoa were metamorphosed into "food of the gods." Every process from molding to wrapping was fully automatic. The cocoa building had over a mile of conveyer belts that carried the beans from trains at one end and churned out cocoa tins ready for loading at the other. The scope of the reorganization was so huge that only a quarter of the works that existed in the days of George Sr. still remained. At Bournville in the late 1930s, a million bars of Dairy Milk and 2 million Chocolate Assortments rolled off the lines every day. The sheer scale of the operation meant the Cadbury cousins could afford to cut the price of Dairy Milk by a staggering 70 percent.

But it wasn't plain sailing. "Grandfather was absolutely right about Fry," says Adrian. "We hampered ourselves with Fry." Cadbury dominated the chocolate and assortment market to such an extent that Fry could make no headway. "We were stuck with the Fry sales force. What were they going to do?" recalls Adrian. The board decided that Fry must challenge Mars's lead in the new area of countlines. "But they were the weaker sales force and the weaker brand. So the area where we should have been growing, we had in fact handicapped ourselves by feeling that we had to look after Fry."

And soon there was another worry. Rowntree began promoting Aero in a way that challenged Dairy Milk head on. Aero, they claimed, "digests twice as fast as old-fashioned milk chocolate." Technical drawings appeared to show the rough texture of ordinary milk chocolate compared to the smoothness of Aero. Rowntree decided to seek a patent for its production process. Cadbury mounted a legal challenge, arguing that some of the processes involved were already in use at Bournville.

As both Cadbury and Rowntree directors hurried to meetings with lawyers, the two Quaker firms appeared to have reached an impasse. Quaker solidarity and allegiances shared over a century evaporated in the face of the intense struggle to win market share.

Seebohm Rowntree, perhaps uncomfortable with the strained situation, chose this time to retire from the board. Cadbury found a common interest with Nestlé, which was also losing customers to Rowntree's Aero. Warily, the two rival firms of Nestlé and Cadbury began to liaise over legal challenges to Rowntree's patent for Aero.

News of this collaboration reached the Rowntree board on April 20, 1937. The possibility that the dispute could be settled before the Society of Friends was briefly considered. This was, after all, how Quaker firms had resolved their differences in the past. But such a meeting never happened because the Society of Friends had ceased to be a relevant or enforceable forum for modern business negotiations. All parties resorted to lawyers, and it was late summer before an agreement was reached on patents and promotions that required Rowntree to back down.

Under the cutthroat conditions of an increasingly saturated market, the moderating Quaker influence declined. In York the Quaker voice diminished in the Rowntree boardroom as independent managers replaced family directors who left or retired. At Bournville, the Cadbury cousins found themselves straddling a widening gulf between business pressures and religious values.

George Cadbury Sr. had pointed to a way forward when he created the Bournville Village Trust, and many of his and Richard Cadbury's children built on his legacy. As Quakers they did not wish to accumulate large personal fortunes; instead, they created trusts or made gifts on a formidable scale. Due to the Quaker influence, wealth from the chocolate works was effectively diverted into the community and wider society.

Barrow Cadbury, Richard's oldest son, gave away much of his inheritance. He fulfilled his father's ambition of creating an institute for the local Adult Schools in Moseley Road. Barrow and his wife, Geraldine, were local magistrates, and they set up a Children's Court and Remand Home to help young offenders. In the 1920s, they used their shares in Bournville to establish two large charitable trusts. Apart from contributing to religious causes, they particularly wanted these trusts to help missionaries, charity workers, and those who had spent their lives helping others. Barrow and Geraldine also gave several former Cadbury houses to the community, such as the home for sick children at Cropwood and the Copeley Hill Hostel for young adults.

Barrow's brother, William, and his cousins Edward and George Jr. continued this tradition by setting up large benevolent trusts. Edward and George Jr. also donated sizeable chunks of land: two hundred acres on the Lickey Hills near Bournville went to the City of Birmingham and four hundred acres with the Chadwich Manor Estate, near Bromsgrove in Worcestershire, went to the National Trust. They gave buildings and funds to Birmingham University and the Queen Elizabeth Hospital Centre at Edgbaston. George Jr., with his love of horticulture, endowed an agricultural college at Offenham, near Evesham.

For some family members, the desire to give up material possessions went to extremes. Richard's youngest daughter, Beatrice, a missionary who inherited a considerable shareholding in Bournville, saw it as her duty to "mitigate the acute suffering caused by the capitalist order of society." She and her Dutch husband, Cornelius Boeke, felt they should give away everything. And they tried to live with no money. When Barrow visited his sister and her eight children, he was shocked to find them living in tents. He insisted on setting up a trust to provide a modest home in Bilthoven for the young family.

The "capitalist order" that Beatrice questioned was bringing a stunning array of luxuries to the consumer. In Britain by the late 1930s, chocolate was no longer a rare indulgence but a routine purchase. Almost everyone was eating chocolate, compared to just 3 percent of the population in 1900. Cadbury's Dairy Milk at two ounces for two pence was the most popular chocolate bar by a large margin. Beatrice's brothers and cousins were riding the wave of mass production and worldwide distribution. Their factories in Tasmania, Canada, and New Zealand were beginning to bring chocolate to the Commonwealth. Bournville, at the hub of it all, the largest and most modern chocolate works in the world, was nominated by a British newspaper as one of the Seven Wonders of Britain.

The Cadbury cousins, however, were not alone in their global vision. Forrest Mars, fast rising to become Britain's third largest confectioner, had devised a cunning scheme to challenge Hershey in America. It took the outbreak of the Second World War to spur him into action. In August 1939, the British government implemented plans to tax all resident foreigners. Forrest Mars left England that same month.

Forrest did not use his father's factory in Chicago as his springboard. He knew that since his father's death, it was being run by his stepmother, Ethel, and his half sister, Patricia. In arguably his cheekiest move yet, he went directly to his rival in Pennsylvania. Forrest Mars was obsessively secretive, but journalist Joël Glenn Brenner revealed the deal he struck in *The Emperors of Chocolate: Inside the Secret World of Hershey and Mars*. Forrest Mars turned up at Hershey and demanded to see the president of the company, William Murrie. Forrest Mars had a canny proposition: If the Hershey Company would supply the chocolate for his next venture, he in return would employ William Murrie's son, Bruce, as vice president of his new company. As for the product, he had a plan allegedly inspired by a candy he had seen in Spain in the 1930s: chocolate drops coated in a brightly colored sugary shell.

The deal was sweet enough for William and Bruce Murrie. As a symbol of the collaboration with Forrest Mars, they decided to call the new candies M&M—for Murrie and Mars. And so it was that Forrest Mars launched his assault on the American market from a warehouse in Newark, New Jersey—without the support of his own family—but with the support of his leading rival: Hershey.

17

I Pray for Snickers

BOURNVILLE, BIRMINGHAM, ENGLAND

August 1939: With daily news reports suggesting that war was imminent, the Bournville and Somerdale chocolate works, gleaming showcases of mass manufacture, were examined as potential sites to make munitions. Somerdale, gutted of its new chocolate technology, was hastily converted for use by the Bristol Aeroplane Company. At Bournville, firms that could meet military needs like Lucas and Austin moved in. Gone were the lines of rosy girls in virginal white tending to the nation's sweet tooth, replaced by the gun-metal colors of war. May 1940 brought a massive German offensive and the fall of Holland, Luxembourg, and France. With the looming prospect that Britain would be invaded after the crisis at Dunkirk, a large area of the chocolate works became Bournville Utilities. Laurence, often working through the night and not stopping for air raids, took charge of manufacturing war materials for the Ministry of Supply.

The chocolate factory was unrecognizable. One young boy, ten years old when the war started, was struck by the difference. "It was a weird place," recalls Adrian Cadbury. "It was covered in green netting and there were workers on the roof scouting for enemy aircraft. . . . Inside it was strange because parts of it were exactly as they had been and others transformed." The Chocolate Molding Department made gun doors for Spitfires and cases for aeroplane flares. The Chocolate

Packing Department created gas masks. The Metals Department produced aircraft parts. Elsewhere millions of jerricans, gas tanks for Spitfires and Lancasters, and gun mounts were in production. "Q block became Q metals run by Lucas," Adrian recalls. "My older brother went in there." To his immense frustration he was not yet permitted to join his fourteen-year-old brother, Julian, who was working on the production line. He had to stay at home with his young sisters, Veronica and Anthea, and the new arrival, a baby brother named Dominic.

The Cadbury family was soon split up by war. Adrian's sisters and baby Dominic were evacuated to Canada. When the Germans invaded Russia in June 1941, Laurence was asked by the Minister of Economic Warfare to fly to Moscow. His task: to lead a British mission to find out what materials the Russians needed and to work with the British Ambassador, Sir Stafford Cripps, towards an Anglo-Soviet pact. Adrian followed his father's progress in the letters he sent home. "For the signing ceremony we went along again in a procession of cars to the Kremlin," wrote Laurence. "As usual we all shook hands with Uncle Joe [Stalin]. . . . He smoked an occasional cigarette and if it went out before he had finished it, economically lit it again. All Russian cigarettes have a piece of cardboard tube, and as Russians do, he kinked the tube to make it act as a bit of a filter."

Back in Bournville, Adrian's uncle, Edward, was running a much-reduced chocolate works. Initially there were large government orders to meet for the army, navy, and air force. But as milk supplies came under government control and imports of cocoa and sugar were threatened, core lines could no longer be made. To eke out precious sugar supplies, Economy Red Label Drinking Chocolate with added saccharin was introduced in July 1940 in plain grey wrapping. In place of Dairy Milk came Ration Chocolate in 1941, a dull and dreary substitute formed with dried skim-milk powder. With state control over rations and supplies and also the movement of foodstuff within transport zones, the chocolate works struggled. The confectionery ration per person per week was gradually reduced to two ounces. Every resource possible was diverted to the war effort. Bournville's recreation fields were dug up to grow vegetables. Sheep grazed on the village green. Older workers at Bournville formed their own Home Guard unit.

At the manor house, Adrian's grandmother, Elsie, turned the farm into a training camp for the Friends Ambulance Unit. A slightly formidable presence, her eyesight failing, she would not leave the manor even when bombs fell nearby and windows were shattered. She and her companion, Elsa Fox, both dressed in hat and garb reminiscent of an earlier age, dedicated their remaining time to the charities that she and George Sr. had valued: the National Peace Council, the YMCA, the World Congress of Faiths, and countless others. Elsie had been awarded the honor of Dame Commander of the British Empire in recognition of her years of service. One night in November 1940, the home for cripples just over the road at Woodlands was struck directly. A wing of the hospital was obliterated, two staff members were killed, and more than thirty children had to be transferred. Even at eight-two, Dame Elizabeth—as she was formally known—threw her energy into rapidly restoring a normal routine for the remaining 140 patients.

Adrian, hankering after a "proper job" at Bournville, was finally permitted to join his older brother. "My first job was a post boy. I must have been thirteen . . . and my last job with Julian was to do the blackout in the chemist's department. The blinds were huge and there were curtains to put in place before we left for the day." As the military operation expanded in 1941, Adrian remembers huts were hastily assembled by the canal where workers packed explosives into anti-aircraft rockets.

The war reshaped the chocolate business, randomly creating winners and losers depending on accidents of geography or birth. One winner was Forrest Mars.

From his factory in Newark, New Jersey, Mars was uniquely placed to benefit under the nurturing wing of his rival, Milton Hershey. William Murrie did all he could to help his son, Bruce, and Forrest secure a foothold in the market. When M&Ms were launched in 1940, many firms faced shortages of cocoa and sugar, but William Murrie made sure that his son was never short of chocolate.

Despite this support, sales of M&Ms were slow to take off, and Forrest could not restrain his volatile bad temper. According to *Fortune* in 1967, just the sight of an ill-wrapped candy bar could provoke outrage. Once he became so incensed that staff watched in astonishment as "Mars hurled candy bars one by one against the glass panel in the board room." The *Washington Post* reported, "He would abruptly sack any worker who failed to meet his exacting standards." No one was spared the explosive tirades, not even his partner, Bruce.

Forrest Mars finally had a chance to meet Milton Hershey, now a frail old man in his eighties, who was perhaps touched to recognize a fleeting image of himself in the enthusiastic entrepreneur. "It is strange how some ideas stay with you," Forrest told Don Gussow in an interview in 1966. "I remember how Milton Hershey admonished me: 'Don't ever go public!'" Forrest took the sober warning from America's chocolate king to heart.

Nestlé also scaled up their American enterprise during the Second World War. The versatile Swiss, equipped with lessons from the Great War, made a radical decision when war broke out. The management team was simply divided in half: Senior staff, including the company chairman, Edouard Muller, moved to offices in Stamford, Connecticut, to expand operations in North and South America. The other half stayed at Nestlé's headquarters in Vevey to run European operations as best they could as the horror of war approached the Swiss border.

The Nestlé staff in Vevey struggled with an extraordinary set of circumstances. Nestlé's Tempelhof works in Berlin fell within the borders of the Third Reich. Nestlé's premises at Lisieux, France, were bombed. They were shut out of their most profitable European market in Britain. Europe belonged to Hitler. Strategies were changed over night as armies were moved like chessmen. Produce was requisitioned; food was in short supply. How different were the fortunes of the Nestlé group in America. They thrived thanks to a remarkable reaction to a very novel product: Nescafé. Instant coffee was such an instant success that by the end of 1940, 6,000 cases a month were being sold in fifty-three of America's largest cities.

DECEMBER 7, 1941

The war reached a new crisis. Japanese bombers sunk or damaged eighteen American warships in Pearl Harbor. The next day America joined the war—an event Milton Hershey had long anticipated. As young men left Derry Township to enlist, Hershey and Murrie stepped up production of a unique kind of chocolate bar called Field Ration D. Crammed with vitamins, the Ration D bar could be drenched with tropical rain and remain dry; it could bake in the sun and not melt. Other types of specially adapted chocolate soon followed, such as Ration K chocolate. With one billion bars supplied to the troops over four years, it is hardly surprising that Hershey's profits nearly doubled during the war, reaching $80 million in 1944.

Milton Hershey was once again at the heart of this chocolate bonanza—but his time was running out. His heart was weakening, and his days were increasingly confined to two rooms he had kept for himself at High Point, surrounded by photographs of Kitty. He still enjoyed experimenting with new products, and his staff was baffled by some of his more eccentric ideas: a sweet potato fudge, a soap with medicinal properties, a nondairy ice cream. His nurses found him quixotic and playful. Harkening back to his Cuban days, he might dress up smartly, mask his grey hair and wrinkles with sunglasses and hat, and have a flutter on the racetrack or in the casinos. With the carelessness of someone who no longer considered the outcome, he ignored doctor's instructions on drink and rich food and enjoyed champagne whenever he was in the mood.

He still delighted in visiting the Hershey Industrial School, which had expanded rapidly and was home to over a thousand boys who lived in surrounding farms and homes. Many had been rescued from extremes of poverty and hardship and felt deep gratitude to Milton Hershey. On one occasion when he attended the school assembly, he

rose to speak. The room erupted in clapping and cheering. Hershey was overcome, and tears rolled down his cheeks. The man of few words could not speak at all: He simply waved his exit.

When eighty-eight-year-old Milton Hershey died in October 1945, 10,000 people passed by his open casket, mourning the loss of a "fairy god-father." Inspired by the Quakers and other philanthropists, he had given away most of his wealth and had earned legendary status in America. Eight graduates of the Hershey Industrial School served as pallbearers in a procession that stretched almost a mile to the Hershey cemetery. Everyone in town wanted to pay their respects as his casket was taken to the vault where he was reunited with his beloved wife. "When we thank God for his life," said the Reverend John Treder in the eulogy, "it will be for the vision it held of a better life for other men." For most there was a certainty that his utopian dream would survive and "his spirit would live on."

The loss of such a giant among the superheroes of the industrial age in America left a vacuum. And there were plenty whose sights were set on filling that void—no matter what it took.

At Bournville in the final months of the war, an exhausted seventy-one-year-old Edward Cadbury stepped down as chairman and handed the reins to his younger brother Laurence, the fifth family member to assume the role. Laurence's family, now reunited, welcomed another new arrival, Jocelyn, born in 1946.

The thrill of pulling down the blackout curtains was quickly gone. Although the war was over, the state tightened its grip on the economy. The country was on its knees. Britain accepted Marshall Aid from America. There was nothing to buy. Everything was rationed from food to furniture. It was still austerity Britain.

At Bournville, any expectation of relaunching much loved brands like Dairy Milk evaporated with a shortage of supplies. Total output was less than half prewar levels, while rationing of only three ounces per person of confectionery a week continued. In York, George Harris was impatient to reintroduce his popular prewar countlines. Rowntree's milk Kit Kat made a brief appearance in 1945 only to be replaced with wartime plain Kit Kat the next year. Harris was obliged to work with Paul and Laurence Cadbury to negotiate with the Ministry of Food on joint supplies for years to come.

Recovery was slow. Four years elapsed before the government lifted confectionery rationing on April 24, 1949. The result took everyone by surprise. There was such pent-up demand that sweetshops simply ran out of stock. Faced with a shortage of supplies, they had to close for weeks on end. Rationing was reintroduced in August. With ten years of no growth at home, the British confectionery companies struggled.

Laurence looked to develop opportunities overseas. "It was quite a long haul to get Australia profitable," recalls Adrian, who was then doing military service in the Coldstream Guards in Tripoli. He knew his father was facing stiff competition from the local firm, MacRobertson's. "New Zealand—absolutely fine, but Canada," he shakes his head. "We got there first. Our milk chocolate set the standard." Yet with such a small market in such a large country, it was hard to build a profitable business. But there was one other obvious target. "The New World," continues Adrian. "It was emerging as a superpower. It was clearly such an important market in terms of size and wealth. Given that we were up against entrenched competitors in Europe, America must have looked tantalising."

While leading European chocolate firms were crippled by rationing, in America, the Hershey Company was in a unique position to expand. During the war, American troops had introduced the delights of Hershey's chocolate across the world. Yet Hershey executives remained focused on the home market and failed to exploit their advantage. In fact, the Hershey bar was so popular they did not even see any need to advertise.

In 1948, Laurence Cadbury had a very good reason to feel confident. Research in six American cities showed that 60 percent of Americans tested preferred the taste of Cadbury's Dairy Milk to the stronger taste of the Hershey bar. Everything augured well for Cadbury to do battle with the American icon with an icon of its own: a five-cent bar of Dairy Milk. They started on the West Coast and sales began to grow. But for Laurence, the excitement of the American initiative was disrupted by terrible news.

On July 26, 1950, his oldest son, twenty-four-year-old Julian, died in a motorcycle accident in France. At the time, Adrian, like his older brother, was reading economics at Cambridge, and he found his student days were "overshadowed" by Julian's death. "Not only had we always been close," he said, "but I suddenly became the eldest member of the family with responsibilities I had never envisaged." His older brother had been an intrepid athlete, and Adrian now threw himself into sport representing the university in the Oxbridge boat race and skiing championships. "I knew it would mean a great deal to my father," he said. As responsibility slowly settled on his shoulders, he found himself eager to start at Bournville.

His father's plans for America were not going well. Building on their success on the West Coast, Laurence organized a major launch of Dairy Milk in 1951 supported by a large advertising campaign. But it was soon clear that something was wrong. They were reliant on distributors who failed to get the stock into the shops. Vast quantities of chocolate were left unsold in various depots. When Dairy Milk was available, the public preferred what they knew, the familiar taste of Hershey. The Cadbury name was unknown in America and the launch failed.

Forrest Mars noted Cadbury's difficulties with interest. He too had a plan to take on Hershey—and in a curious twist, he had a head start. Estranged from his father for much of his life, in death, the terms of his father's will acknowledged his only son. When Frank Mars's second wife, Ethel, died in 1945, Forrest inherited half her shares in the business. At last, he had a stake in his father's Chicago firm—approximately one-third of the business. Forrest also bought out his own partner, Bruce Murrie, thereby gaining complete control of the M&Ms plant in New Jersey. His plan was to bring the two Mars enterprises together into one great empire that would be a fitting challenger to the Hershey giant.

There was one obstacle: his half sister, Pattie. She held another third of the Chicago stock and influenced by her uncle, Ethel's brother, William Kruppenbacher, she had no interest in selling her shares to Forrest. In the bitter family battle that ensued, Forrest at one stage was banned from the Chicago offices by his step-uncle. But Forrest was not one to give up easily. The feud became so acrimonious that Kruppenbacher ultimately gave way and permitted Mars control of a third of the board.

With his hard-won influence, Forrest argued for a complete overhaul of the Chicago factory. Just as Cadbury had mechanized the production of block chocolate, he wanted to mass-produce countlines. It took five years to carry out his plan, but by 1959, Snickers, Milky Way, Mars bars, and 3 Musketeers could be made at breakneck speed as strips of toffee and nougat were hurtled through sprays of chocolate and guillotines to the automatic wrapping room. Manufacturing time per bar was reduced from one day to less than one hour. Meanwhile his own brand of M&Ms finally caught on, becoming the best-selling confectionery in America. But it wasn't enough. Forrest wanted complete control of his father's factory. Nothing less would satisfy him.

In Britain, the sense of living in a twilight world made grey by stultifying shortages at last came to an end. Rationing was stopped in 1953. Hard on the heels of the wave of consumerism that followed came a new medium to promote it: television. Commercial television was launched in September 1955, and Cadbury was on air the very first evening with an advertisement for drinking chocolate.

The Rowntrees were equally quick off the mark. They ran a succession of memorable campaigns as countlines finally made a big comeback: "Have a break—Have a Kit Kat," "Don't forget the Fruit Gums, Mum," "Polo: The mint with the hole," "Wotalotigot," and many others. The slick one-liners of TV advertisements favored individual brands with a simple playful message—perfect for Mars's and

Rowntree's large portfolio of countlines. Within three years, commercials accounted for more than 60 percent of all chocolate advertising. As countlines began to take a share of the market for block chocolate, Paul Cadbury and the marketing team fought back with an innovative series of advertisements. While supermodels promoted the superlight Flake, a romantic James Bond–style action hero delivered a box of Milk Tray against the odds with the slogan: "All because the lady loves Milk Tray."

Not content with just growing the countlines sector, Forrest Mars planned another attack on Cadbury. It was 1959, the year that Laurence stepped down as chairman and handed the reins to his cousin Paul, who had led some of Cadbury's most famous sales campaigns, including "2oz for 2p" and the "Glass-and-a-half" slogan. But Forrest Mars's next move took Paul by surprise. Mars had excelled at creating countlines where the chocolate was mixed with other confectionary ingredients, but now he used television for a direct assault on Cadbury's block chocolate lead by launching a block chocolate bar of his own: Galaxy. It was the largest British television ad campaign for chocolate yet. Cadbury hurried to reposition Dairy Milk, but it was clear that television was changing the rules. One effective TV campaign could shift decades of customer loyalty in a matter of weeks. In a reversal of the views of nineteenth-century Quaker founders such as Joseph Fry and Joseph Rowntree, by 1960 the chocolate and confectionery firms were among Britain's largest advertising spenders: Cadbury at £3.2 million was fifth, Mars at £2.9 million was sixth, Rowntree at £2.8 million was seventh, and Nestlé at £2.3 million was eighth.

In 1961 Paul faced another critical issue much closer to home. There was growing pressure from the wider Fry and Cadbury family members to take the company public. The Cadbury firm had been a private Quaker concern for 140 years. Such a move would be one of the most significant transitions in the firm's history. Adrian and his younger brother Dominic soon learned of the predicament. Adrian had recently joined the board as a director, and Dominic, having completed his degree at Cambridge, was working toward an MBA at Stanford Business School in America.

"The problem was that we had family shareholders, particularly the Fry family, whose capital had been tied up in the business since 1919," Adrian explains, "and they did not have an open market for their shares." By the 1960s this was becoming a significant concern. Although there were about ten Cadbury family members in the business, there were no Frys involved, and in the wider Fry and Cadbury family, several hundred held shares in the firm. There was a desire to "do the right thing by the Frys," says Adrian, and by the growing number of Cadbury family members who could not access their capital.

"'There is no way the handful of family members who were in the business could have bought out those who were not," adds Dominic. More than 50 percent of Cadbury shares were owned by benevolent trusts, he explains, such as the Barrow Cadbury Trust and the William Cadbury Trust. Because Barrow and William had given away most of their wealth, their sons, Paul and Charles Cadbury, "were never what you would call very rich people and could not possibly have bought out the hundreds of Cadbury and Fry members who did own shares."

The family members who wanted to sell were keen to have an objective cash valuation of their shares. With a private company, an independent firm of accountants typically sets the price per share. "But this was clearly different from having an open market in which they knew that the price they got for their shares was the way the market valued it," says Adrian.

To solve this problem and to allow Fry and Cadbury family members access to their capital, Paul and the Cadbury board agreed to go public. The British Cocoa and Chocolate Company was floated in 1962. For the first time since its founding in 1824, the chocolate enterprise was no longer under direct Quaker family control. The management had to report to independent shareholders, who demanded a broad-based and profitable business.

It was immediately clear to Adrian that the firm had to change. "There were teething problems," he says. "For a time the Cadbury board continued running as if we weren't a public company. Paul found the transition extremely difficult." For years, Paul had managed to sidestep the top management in the British Cocoa and Chocolate Company board and instead ran the business through the subsidiary Cadbury board. "But once we floated the British Cocoa and Chocolate Company, we couldn't go on with what was in effect the subsidiary running the business." Adrian knew they needed to have a proper annual general meeting and formal procedures for reporting to the board. "I was concerned," he adds. Shareholders had become the new owners. "Things had to change."

Just how much they had to change is shown by what was happening in a rival's boardroom two thousand miles away on another continent. Forrest Mars continued to battle for complete control of his father's factory. Tragically for the family, a key turning point came when his half sister, Pattie, was diagnosed with terminal cancer. At last she agreed to sell him her shares. He now had two-thirds of the business but he wanted it all. This was his father's life's work, and strangers had a voice on the board. Forrest Mars worked unceasingly to persuade other share owners to sell to him until he finally achieved full control in 1964.

What happened next was reported by Harold Meyers in *Fortune* in 1967. Forrest, whose obsession with the family business was now "bordering on religious zealotry," called a meeting of leading executives shortly after he gained control of his father's Chicago factory. Sixty-year-old Forrest Mars did not walk into the boardroom, "He charged in." He had a youthful appearance despite his age and thinning grey hair. The senior staff members in the room were a little unsure what to make of him. His appearance made no concession to current fashions: "His English suit had wide lapels and his tie was unstylishly wider still." Yet he communicated his intensity with a power that was unsettling. After a brief and wary exchange, he presented his vision for Mars confectionery. "I'm a religious man," he declared. He dropped from his chair to his knees as though the conference table were a church pew. The others watched mesmerized as he began his sermon.

"I pray for Milky Way," he said.

Long pause.

"I pray for Snickers . . . "

No one said a word.

His message was clear. His prayers were for profit. He expected nothing less than the same religious fervor from his staff. It was a very different scene from the one, almost a hundred years earlier, when George Cadbury asked his Bournville staff to join him in prayer to seek guidance on a difficult business issue. But Forrest Mars confirmed what everyone knew.

Money was the new religion.

American Tanks
Were on the Lawn

It would fall to a fourth generation of Cadbury brothers to manage a period of spectacular change. In 1965, three years after taking the company public, Paul stepped down and was succeeded by Adrian, who at thirty-six became the firm's youngest chairman. His younger brother Dominic had just started working at Bournville. It wasn't long before the two brothers had a firsthand experience of Forrest Mars.

"I met Forrest Mars Sr. in London and he offered me a job right *in front of* Adrian," says Dominic, smiling as he recollects the scene. Mars and his wife, Audrey, were holding a drinks party at the Dorchester, one of London's smartest hotels. "They had the best suite of rooms, at the top. We were all invited because as families we were close." Dominic and Adrian's parents were friends with Forrest and Audrey.

A slight hush followed Forrest's job offer. Adrian, forever the diplomat, was quick to step in and diffuse the situation.

"Whatever you offer Dominic, Forrest, we will pay him more," he said mischievously.

Of course, that wasn't true, says Dominic, but he had no intention of working for his brother's most dynamic rival. "Forrest Sr. was that sort of chap," Dominic adds. "He was an interesting man. . . . He had a real wicked smile about him. . . . We knew his employees saw a different side of him. He could be a complete tyrant."

While Dominic started his training in South Africa, Adrian was grappling with turning a 140-year-old private Quaker business into a modern public company. A number of strategic issues had to be resolved—namely, improving the geographical spread of the business, expanding the foods division, and reducing their dependence on cocoa. As cocoa is susceptible to many different diseases and thrives only in one kind of climate, running a massive enterprise based on this one product carried inherent and substantial risks. Cocoa prices had been known to double in just a few months. And there were changes afoot that were transforming the business: notably the rise of the supermarket.

For a century, the backbone of the Quaker business had been the corner shop. In the 1960s, Cadbury had more than 250,000 direct accounts across the country. While the corner shops thrived on a variety of lines, the new supermarkets wanted fewer brands backed up by TV advertising. For the first time, the distributor had begun to determine the manufacturer's range. And while the corner shop would pay on time, the supermarkets had the power to extend their terms of payment. It was a major shift in the balance of power.

Adrian Cadbury also had to find a way to improve the return on capital. Forrest Mars held no stock: He ordered cocoa and sugar to arrive at a certain time on a certain day to minimize the amount of capital tied up in the business. By contrast Cadbury had money tied up in its large inventories.

The young chairman soon found he did not have the right organizational structure to meet these new challenges. He had inherited a business rooted in traditional ways of operating but lacking clear lines of accountability. "We had a ponderous organisational system that was wonderful at involving everyone because we had a great number of committees, but it was slow in coming to a decision," he recalls. "Everyone had a chance to put their pennyworth in, which was very good, but took time." For example, there was a strong participatory system of Men's and Women's Works Councils. These dealt with everything from discipline to bonuses. The councils were a hive of industry that produced a lot of paper "but had little time for work."

The collaborative nature of the business reached all the way up to the Cadbury board. "There were twelve managing directors," Adrian recalls, and they met every week and discussed every last detail. "Even the issue of donkey jackets was a board matter!" The entire organization had to change.

In contrast to the collaborative style of Quaker management that had evolved over a century, Forrest Mars claimed to be "a practitioner of scientific management." In Britain and America, he threw out conventional working practices. Staff members were taken out of their comfort zone. He pioneered the idea of the open plan office. Special privileges disappeared. Luxurious offices with fine art and soft carpets vanished. The objective "was to smash any barriers to communication and inhibit narrow functionalism," reported Bill Saporito for *Fortune* in September 1988. Desks had to be spotless. Even Mars's dog food factories, revealed one executive, "are cleaner than some hospitals I've been in." Everyone had to clock in. Punctuality was so highly prized that employees received a 10 percent bonus just for being on time. Forrest Mars intended to achieve a culture of "egalitarianism and individualism."

Despite an estimated personal fortune of around $250 million, there was no letup for Forrest Mars. Now he had united the two arms of the Mars Empire into one kingdom in America, he wasted no time in putting his own stamp on it. Mars aimed for huge economies of scale by streamlining production to serve a few blockbuster brands: 3 Musketeers, Snickers, Milky Way, and Mars bars. For this to work, he had to shift volume. Executives' success was judged by the returns they made on each brand. He was determined to take on the Hershey enterprise. The goal: to be the number one chocolate confectionery giant in America.

Unlike Hershey, which was content to sell principally in America, Forrest Mars could see a bigger future for Snickers, M&Ms, and Milky Way. In continental Europe, he continued to clash against Nestlé's unstoppable rise. While Mars typically looked to build new businesses tailored to local conditions, Nestlé strengthened its international presence through a policy of acquisition. After purchasing Maggi in 1947, it bought the British food group Crosse and Blackwell in 1960, which included chocolate in its portfolio as well as soups and tinned vegetables. Nestlé was fast becoming one of the world's largest firms. "To protect these characteristics," wrote Jean Heer in Nestlé's company history, "the management proposed that the issuing of registered shares—whose registration would be subject to authorization by the board of directors—be *limited to Swiss citizens*." This, they argued, ensured "stability and balance" in the way the company shares were distributed "both inside and outside Switzerland." Meanwhile, Forrest Mars, sticking to his strategy of building businesses rather than buying and selling them, gave Nestlé a run for its money in Europe.

The creator of Galaxy also had dreams that went beyond the borders of America and Europe. Forrest Mars wanted to find a way into the burgeoning markets in South America and Asia. He had a conversation with Dominic Cadbury around this time, which gives insight into his thinking.

Mars asked, "What is the population of South Africa?" Dominic told him about 20 million.

"It's not large enough to be interesting," Forrest replied.

And sure enough, Mars did not try to find a way into South Africa.

The Cadbury brothers were making modest headway. Shortly after becoming chairman, Adrian had taken a trip to South Africa during the time of apartheid. The two brothers wanted to go to Soweto, but their sales manager was uncertain. "He had never been and he was a local man," recalls Adrian. "Apartheid was so strong that there was a feeling that maybe Africans lived a different life."

The Cadbury van set off as a great plume of dust rose from the wheels like a banner. They made their way into the township, "the sales manager's eyes popping out on stalks."

"Our van was filled with chocolates," says Dominic. "We went into little shops and tiny bars. Everyone loved chocolate."

They realized they had been neglecting a market in South Africa—and another thing was clear: Nestlé was there already. "Apart from chocolate, they had lots of different milk products. The man who ran Nestlé was an important businessman in South Africa."

At Bournville, Adrian wanted to launch Cadbury as a global brand reaching into markets well beyond the Old Commonwealth. Cadbury's food division had already developed breakthroughs such as instant milk, Marvel, in 1964, followed by instant mashed potatoes, Smash. To build on this success, he was looking for a partner to expand the range and reach of their products. He talked to American companies about selling each other's products in their respective territories. While nothing came of these discussions, Lord Watkinson, chairman of Schweppes, a soft drinks company, approached Adrian about a possible merger.

Schweppes had come a long way from its origins in Geneva in 1783, when the watchmaker and amateur scientist Jean Jacob Schweppe refined a method to carbonate water. By the 1960s, the company had grown into an international concern specializing in fizzy drinks such as bitter lemon, ginger ale, and tonic. "Schweppes had a strong branded drinks business," Adrian recalls, "and we had a strong branded chocolate business. In addition both companies had food divisions which could become more of a force in the grocery trade through amalgamation." Combined they would have greater resources for research and development, and the geographical spread of each business complemented the other.

The management of Schweppes was particularly keen on a merger as they feared a takeover. "Even then, size was the only real protection against being taken over," says Adrian. In 1969, General Foods, the American food giant, was shopping for British firms. General Foods made a £37 million ($89 million) bid for Rowntree, which was rejected. Rowntree swiftly merged with Britain's leading toffee manufacturer, Mackintosh of Halifax, which was also well known for such chocolate treats as Quality Street, Rolo, and Toffee Crisp. Adrian was less concerned about a takeover than his counterparts at Schweppes—in part because of the Cadbury benevolent trusts.

In the 1960s, the Cadbury trusts held such a large share of the chocolate firm that potential buyers were put off. And not without reason. The sons of those who set up the trusts worked in the business. "There was a seamless link between the people running the trusts and the business that kept Quaker values at the heart of the company," Adrian explains. "This was wrongly perceived as a barrier to takeover." Adrian knew full well the trustees' legal duty was to the trust—not the company—and trustees could not have protected the company against takeover if a bid was to the advantage of the trust.

For the traditionally Quaker firm of Cadbury, there was just one obstacle to a merger with Schweppes: Its soft drinks were used in alcoholic drinks. Schweppes even distributed an alcoholic brand, Dubonnet. It appeared something of a reversal of the passionate aspirations of the original founders.

Several older members of the family voiced opposition. Adrian's great-grandmother, Candia Cadbury, whose inheritance had been instrumental in launching the business in the first place, had in all probability given her life to the temperance cause. The tuberculosis that killed her was almost certainly a result of her trips around the poor houses and pubs of Birmingham, exhorting anyone who would listen to give up drink. She came from a tradition so steeped in Quaker idealism that one of her forebears was burned at the stake. Some family members were worried. Adrian "spent a lot of time talking to those who had concerns. I explained to them we needed to be bigger. This was absolutely about extending our reach in a fast moving world."

Adrian Cadbury pressed ahead with the merger and in 1969 became joint managing director and deputy chairman of the global enterprise, Cadbury Schweppes, under Lord Watkinson as Chairman. Cadbury Schweppes was a global giant, one-third the size of Nestlé and with turnover approaching £250 million.

The implications of the merger soon rippled out to their overseas divisions. With its commonwealth links, Cadbury had businesses around the world in Ireland, New Zealand, Canada, Australia, South Africa, and India. "At that time, we were really a British company with a lot of businesses dotted around the place," observes Dominic, "rather than a proper international company." He describes his early years in Cadbury's business in Port Elizabeth in South Africa as "wonderful . . . we were left entirely to our own devices." There was an international conference each year when the overseas divisions came together to compare experiences. "But at this stage we weren't yet thinking internationally—looking at all aspects of the business on an international basis."

After the merger with Schweppes, overseas operations stepped up a gear. "There was this pressure to show shareholders that there were real benefits of the merger," says Dominic. Enforcing a unified international policy, however, was not straightforward. The idiosyncrasies of the Indian market highlight the difficulties. India had a potentially vast market, but Cadbury had to adapt to maintain a foothold. At first there was not even an Indian dairy industry. Cadbury set about creating their own dairy herd by inseminating cattle that were accustomed to the heat from Rajasthan in northern India with imported Ayrshire semen from England. Adrian remembers visiting their dairy farm near Poona, south of Mumbai.

"It was the first time I'd seen a cobra," he recalls. "At the dairy farm, they insisted on having their own hens as well as cows. I said, 'No, we don't want to do that.' They got them anyway," he laughs. "They had masses of hens, then they got rats, then cobras came and kept the rats down. The Indians didn't worry too much about them." But they did worry about the cows when they stopped producing milk. It was not acceptable for them to go to slaughter. Cadbury Schweppes found themselves in possession of a growing herd of nonproductive "sacred cows." Small wonder that the corporate finance director could see no prospect of a viable Indian business.

The suffocating heat in India was another obstacle: The chocolate melted. The production team there found it could improve the quality by making slight adjustments to the recipe: They reduced the milk fat and increased the cocoa butter, which is slightly harder. They eventually developed products that were less affected by heat, such as toffee-covered chocolates called Éclairs.

Just as they were making headway, the Indian government introduced restrictions against foreign companies. "We had a period where we could not take dividends," recalls Adrian, "and a period where we had to sell 51 percent of the company to Indian shareholders. We changed our name to Hindustan Cocoa Products." Under this name they found themselves in the surprising position of being protected by the Indian government, which decided that no more foreign brands would be allowed into the country. Coke and Pepsi-Cola could not get in. Nor could chocolate rivals: Suchard tried, and Mars tried, but they both failed to get in. Hindustan Cocoa Products was protected "because we were effectively Indian."

Eventually Cadbury regained control of the company, which was renamed Cadbury India, and developed a new manufacturing plant in Thane near Mumbai. "We still had Indian shareholders," says Adrian, "which was great except for the Annual General Meetings. They would turn up in force and all ask questions so that their names could appear in the minutes. At least one AGM went on for two days!"

Taking the long view eventually paid off. In time more shops were air-conditioned and the sale of block chocolate began to rise. Working closely with the local community, they developed a series of temperature-tolerant countlines especially adapted for the Indian market, such as multicolored chocolate sweets known as Cadbury's Gems and a satisfying nougat and chocolate bar called 5 Star. These successes were established before rivals like Mars arrived, and Cadbury India was soon exporting to other hot climates in the Middle East, Singapore, Sri Lanka, and Hong Kong. "When I went round I found a number of Indians believe Cadbury India is Indian," says Adrian. "For me that's wonderful." The business is efficient but has adapted to the values and customs of the local people.

The Cadbury brothers grew their businesses overseas in steady, incremental steps, working their way across the globe and tailoring products to local markets. Sometimes they were first and were able to establish the taste. Mars's attempt to venture into New Zealand in the early 1960s was quickly countered with a series of successful Cadbury countlines culminating in Moro, which became so popular it was hard for Mars and Nestlé to gain ground. In Australia there was a clash with Mars when both wanted to buy the leading Australian firm of MacRobertson in 1967. Cadbury succeeded, and it wasn't long before Cadbury-MacRobertson secured 60 percent of the Australian market.

Of all the commonwealth countries, Canada was the hardest market to crack. "You've got this three-thousand mile breadth of country, quite a small market and a lot of competition," says Dominic. Cadbury could not afford a dedicated Canadian sales force and were much more dependent on wholesalers to distribute their products. "And we were competing with just about everyone except Hershey who hardly existed in Canada." Local companies such as Neilson were strong; Rowntree and Nestlé were also involved. "Everyone had about 20 percent of the market. Nobody ever made any money. Canada was always a graveyard for confectionery manufacturers."

The overseas businesses remained human scale. "I appointed all the people who ran our businesses outside this country," says Adrian. "I knew them all, I visited, there was a link—if you like, we belonged to a family."

Of all the markets in the world in the 1960s, the real prize was America, still dominated by Hershey. Around the time of the merger with Schweppes, Adrian Cadbury sent executives to speak to the management of Hershey Foods. For Cadbury, Hershey's chocolate company was potentially an ideal partner. A merger would give Hershey an entrée into global markets and Cadbury a way into America. More important still for Adrian, there was a cultural and an ethical fit between the two companies. For both, the business was about more than making money; they had close links with a loyal workforce and their local communities.

But Milton Hershey's chocolate company was protected by the Hershey Trust. The Hershey Trust managed his cherished Hershey School and held approximately 80 percent of the chocolate company's voting power. Nothing could happen without the support of the Hershey Trust, and for years this arrangement had protected his chocolate company from a takeover or merger and safeguarded the community and the school—which had more than 1,100 residential pupils. The Hershey Trust, notoriously conservative and cautious, rejected any merger.

The conservatism of the Hershey establishment would soon play right into the hands of Forrest Mars. After a rapid rise in cocoa prices in the early 1970s, Hershey executives were looking for savings. Their first move was to slash the advertising budget. The Mars sales team, inspired with near religious fervor, went on a crusade to promote Mars products in every possible store at Hershey's expense. Mars was fast overtaking its long-standing rival.

In a surprising twist, sixty-nine-year-old Forrest Mars chose this very moment to walk away from the firm he had put so much into. In 1973, at the peak of his achievement, he handed the reins to his sons, John and Forrest Jr., and left them to run the company. His sons continued the sales battle that he had begun. The following year, in a blaze of triumphant headlines, Mars dethroned Hershey as the leading confectioner in America.

The Cadbury team still had their eye on America. "The challenge was that the American market was 70 percent owned by Mars and Hershey," says Adrian Cadbury, who succeeded Lord Watkinson as chairman of Cadbury Schweppes in 1974. The British firm began by building a factory in Hazleton, Pennsylvania, just sixty miles from Hershey town, from which Cadbury's chocolates began to enjoy modest sales. They needed to increase volume to make the new factory economical, a problem that was solved with the purchase of the Peter Paul Candy Company for $58 million. Peter Paul had a tenth of the American confectionery market with such established countlines as Mounds, Almond Joy, and York Peppermint Patties. Building on Peter Paul's sales, Cadbury hoped to bring in its own brands and effect a massive reorganization with much of Peter Paul's production moving to Hazleton.

Meanwhile, Cadbury's global strategy was stepping up. As international marketing director from 1976, Dominic Cadbury toured the world and found huge variations in the presentation of the different brands. Even the name *Cadbury* was written in different ways. He replaced the numerous typefaces used on Cadbury's packaging with William Cadbury's signature logo to create a worldwide house style. "We also produced international brand logos that set down the colour and the script," says Dominic, "and unified the whole presentation of the Cadbury business across the globe."

Back at Bournville, the results of the merger were evident as a succession of new products rolled off the production lines in the 1970s. The unique Curly Wurly was swiftly followed by new chocolate bars—Grand Seville, Golden Crisp, Ice Breaker—and innovative countlines such as Double Decker and Caramel. Cadbury countered successful Mars and Rowntree advertising campaigns, and sales for Flake quadrupled. But however inventive they were, continued pressure from Mars and Rowntree made it hard to make progress in their home market. Rowntree's launch of the Yorkie bar in 1976 was a major setback for Cadbury. With its satisfyingly thick and chocolatey bite, Yorkie dented sales of Dairy Milk, their flagship brand, and Cadbury's share of the UK market declined to 20 percent.

Dominic was concerned about falling off a "marketing precipice." Below a certain market share, Cadbury could lose its position on the counter. He knew they needed a massive modernization program to compete effectively with their rivals. Dominic organized the greatest transformation of Cadbury's factories since his father and uncles oversaw a renovation between the wars. "We had to introduce a new plant and went through a period at Bournville in the early 1980s of slimming down operations and not trying to do everything for ourselves." There were still many ancillary crafts at Bournville from box making to printing, labelling, carpentry, and sheet-metalworking. While Mars had no unions, Bournville had representatives from forty-one unions. "We took out Trade Street, as we called it, and put up Cadbury World. We had to do some very tough things," says Dominic. The number of brands was reduced from seventy-eight to thirty-three, and state-of-the-art technology was installed.

By 1980, Cadbury's research team had created something new with which they hoped to reclaim their market share. Small-scale consumer trials of their idea showed they were on to a winner: a light-textured chocolate bar in a chunky shape. They immediately withdrew the new bar from store shelves while they made plans for a massive British launch. Secrecy was everything. Existing machinery was adapted to make the new bar, the parts wrapped under black covers until ready for assembly. A huge TV campaign was prepared. In 1983, a nationwide sales conference took place. The sales staff was briefed to speak immediately to retailers to ensure the new deliveries would be in the shops. Within days, the new product—Wispa—was everywhere, and it was an overnight sensation.

"The Wispa launch went incredibly well in Britain," says Adrian, "and we were concerned Mars could copy it in the States." So Cadbury invested in a major new plant that would make Wispa in the Hazleton factory. They planned a major U.S. launch of Cadbury's chocolates, including Wispa. Unlike Mars and Hershey, Cadbury could not afford a direct sales force to blanket the country and relied on wholesalers instead. They arranged generous incentives to persuade wholesalers to stock large quantities of their goods. To seal their success, they improved their most popular brands to suit American tastes: thicker bars, extra almonds, and raisins. By 1984, the plans for the major relaunch were in place. They awaited the verdict from the American consumer.

That same year, Dominic was promoted to chief executive of Cadbury Schweppes, working alongside Adrian, who was now the chairman. They were the fourth generation of Cadbury brothers at the helm of the company. "It really worked because I understood Adrian and he really understood me, and we probably got the best out of each other as a result," says Dominic. But the brothers soon faced a predicament unlike anything their predecessors had encountered.

In a hostile move, the American company General Cinema, which owned a nationwide chain of movie theaters, acquired 18 percent of the shares of Cadbury Schweppes. The American leisure firm was hoping to engineer a hostile takeover. "They were trying to put us into play," says Dominic. "We went through uncertain times." For the first time, the independence of the company was at stake.

General Cinema was able to take advantage of the fact that Cadbury's American campaign was not going smoothly, which depressed the share price of Cadbury Schweppes. Cadbury managers discovered that their chocolates—including the beloved Dairy Milk and Wispa—were simply not in stores. With literally hundreds of lines to sell, wholesalers had failed to give Cadbury's products an extra push to secure orders from retailers. As long as Cadbury chocolates languished in stockrooms and warehouses, there was no way to see if Americans liked the taste. Profits from the U.S. market plummeted.

"Did I lose sleep? Yes very much," says Adrian, "over the factory and over Peter Paul. They were nice people and I felt we had taken them over in the hopes of building their business and it hadn't worked out. I felt responsible."

On July 22, 1988, Cadbury U.S. was sold to its rival Hershey for $300 million. The press spelled out the end of Cadbury's American dream. The press was also critical of Mars: "The Mars Universe," observed *Fortune* in September 1988, for so long "the black hole" of the industry, "so powerful that it influences all the other objects in its system," was now "locked in a time warp." Forrest Jr. and John were described by *Fortune* as struggling "to escape the influence of their innovative father" as they failed to act while Hershey collected the benefits that stemmed from Cadbury's difficulties. The Hershey giant reclaimed its position as the number one confectionery company in America.

General Cinema retained its 18 percent stake in Cadbury Schweppes. If General Cinema could find a bidder, over 160 years of independence could come to an end. Noting the presence of American "tanks on the lawn," the *Guardian* pointed out on October 10, 1990, that General Cinema "did not intend to be passive shareholders." There were repeated rumors that a bid was imminent. General Cinema failed to deny them.

It was an anxious time for Adrian and Dominic. But the brothers and the Cadbury Schweppes management team had a strategy to raise the share price to protect them from the American predator.

CHAPTER 19

The Quaker Voice
Could Still Be Heard

The year 1988 was a critical one for the British chocolate industry.

The saga began to unfold on April 13, 1988. The Swiss-German firm of Jacob Suchard made a "dawn raid" on Rowntree, acquiring 15 percent of the company's shares. Jacob Suchard had already snapped up smaller European confectioners such as Belgium's Cote d'Or and the Dutch Van Houten. Now it had set its sights on Rowntree. But Nestlé's directors were watching closely. On April 26, they made a rival £2.1 billion ($3.82 billion) hostile bid for outright ownership of the great Quaker firm.

It was now possible to measure global market share, and Rowntree was the fourth largest chocolate maker in the world, after Cadbury and the American firms of Mars and Hershey. Like Cadbury, Rowntree was well established in the old Commonwealth and was exporting to over 130 countries. In addition to its merger with Mackintosh, it had also merged with the oldest French chocolate company, Chocolat Menier, as well as Laura Secord in Canada.

Not surprisingly Nestlé's bid to buy Rowntree was greeted with outrage in Britain. People were appalled at the idea of a much-loved British chocolate icon falling to foreign hands. There was a real fear that Nestlé would move production to cheaper plants overseas. And what about the different values and culture of the two firms?

In stark contrast to the high Quaker standards that Joseph Rowntree had once set for his firm, Nestlé was being boycotted over allegations of unethical practices. In question was the very issue about which Joseph Rowntree felt so strongly: unprincipled advertising and promotion. This first came to light when the antipoverty charity War on Want published *The Baby Killer* in 1974—later published under a different title in German, *Nestlé tötet Babies*. The publications claimed that babies in the world's poorest countries were dying because mothers were inappropriately encouraged to favor infant formula over breast-feeding when poor sanitation and lack of clean water could spell a death sentence. Nestlé sued for libel and won the case—but the issue did not go away. Eventually the World Health Organization developed international guidelines for marketing breast-milk substitutes, but allegations that Nestlé breeched the code prompted further boycotts.

With opposition to the takeover mounting from all quarters, Rowntree's management rejected Nestlé's offer. At Bournville, chief executive Dominic Cadbury could see a potential solution. Cadbury would keep Rowntree British—but only if local competition rules could be relaxed. "The idea that Rowntree and Cadbury together were going to hold the British public to ransom through chocolate prices was just absurd," he said. "The supermarkets were already strong, Mars was strong." Cadbury's management approached the Department of Trade and Industry. "We said if you look at Cadbury and Rowntree's market share on a global basis—which is how you should look at it—there is not a competition problem." But he soon found that British government thinking was purely local. "Civil servants in 1988 did not think about global market share." He was told that if he proceeded with the acquisition, he would be referred to the Monopolies Commission.

Cadbury's proposal won no government support. On May 25, Margaret Thatcher's Conservative government announced a foreign group could take over Rowntree. The next day Jacob-Suchard topped Nestlé's bid with an offer of £2.3 billion ($4.19 billion). This was trumped in mid-June when Nestlé raised its bid to £2.5 billion ($4.55 billion). The Rowntree Trusts, which had once held a 51 percent stake in the company, now possessed less than 9 percent. This was partly due to the Rowntree Trusts diversifying their share portfolio but also due to their holdings being diluted in size following successive share issues. The decision was down to Rowntree's shareholders—a diverse group—and they voted to accept. Overnight, Nestlé became one of the world's top four chocolate confectionery firms, and a famous Quaker company had a taste of unfettered shareholder capitalism.

For Dominic Cadbury, the decision was a disaster. The idea that Nestlé was allowed to buy Rowntree and not Cadbury was "ridiculous." "That was a big fork in the road. We as a country have always shot ourselves in the foot here. Had we been more forward thinking about global market share, we would have pushed Cadbury and Rowntree together."

In the aftermath of the takeover, some of the assurances Nestlé made to Rowntree's management appear to have been quietly put aside. Staffing at Joseph Rowntree's great factory at Haxby Road has declined to 1,600. The manufacture of famous brands like Smarties was moved overseas. Even the name Rowntree has been discreetly dropped from the packaging on many brands.

Nestlé continued to grow: It was the world's largest food company and had 7 percent of the confectionery market. Protected for years by Switzerland's federal and local governments, it was immune from takeover. Today, its presence is felt in almost every country in the world. Its company literature considers developments in food in the context of feeding the global population. Questions about its size and market dominance seem to dissipate under the sheer might of the company itself.

General Cinema still held almost a fifth of Cadbury Schweppes's share register, but the Cadbury brothers had a plan to strengthen the company's independence. Dominic wanted to focus the business on its strongest global brands in confectionery and drinks.

At the time, Cadbury Schweppes owned a household products division and a food business that included Typhoo tea, Kenco coffee, biscuits, preserves, and canned goods. For the Cadbury brothers, the most satisfactory outcome was that their managements should be their future owners. Both divisions were successfully sold to their respective managing teams.

Although Cadbury could not grow the chocolate division of the business through mergers with its natural partners—Hershey or Rowntree who shared a similar heritage and ethical values—it was able to expand the confectionery division by acquiring strong sugar confectionery brands: Lion confectionery in 1988, followed by Bassett and then the Trebor Group. This brought in popular brands like Bassett's Liquorice Allsorts, Bassett's Jelly Babies, Trebor Mints, Trebor Extra Strong Mints, and many others.

Cadbury was also keen to find ways to make the drinks side of the business more dynamic. Schweppes had nowhere near the share of the drinks market that Cadbury had in confectionery, but Dominic could see a solution. "We signed up with Coke to create a new bottling company called Coca-Cola Schweppes." This was four times the size of Cadbury Schweppes's original bottling business in Britain. The company soon acquired soft drink brands in America, including Canada Dry. "The aim was to buy a local company, get a local presence, and bring in the global brands off the back of that."

As the brothers refocused the business, the share price recovered. Despite the efforts of General Cinema, no bidder came forward. "At no stage did we agree to meet General Cinema for any negotiation over the future of the firm," Dominic recalls. At the time hedge funds were less of a factor. The share register remained stable. Eventually after three worrying years, General Cinema sold their shares. "It was hugely satisfying to see this threat to the company disappear," he says. "One of the best moments of my life."

In the years following Adrian Cadbury's retirement in 1989, another astonishing opportunity opened up. The collapse of the Soviet Union unlocked an enormous new market. Mars was first to venture into the "Wild East." In the deadly winter of 1990, Moscow citizens gratefully succumbed to what became known as "Snickerisation," when eager buyers waited patiently in queues almost half a mile in length. When Cadbury began exporting chocolates to Russia in 1992, the products sold out almost immediately. Soon Cadbury executives learned that Mars was converting a former military base at Stupino into a chocolate factory. Cadbury was also planning to build a Russian chocolate works—in Chudovo, near St. Petersburg. Two years later, Cadbury and Mars were in Beijing tackling the largest market of all.

"Renowned as a marketing whiz," reported Andrew Davidson in August 1997 in *Management Today*, Dominic has helped to position a company with good Commonwealth links "into a truly global multinational." While Cadbury chocolates were selling around the world, the company also had a major presence in America through its soft drinks. Under Dominic's era as chairman from 1994 to 2000, Cadbury Schweppes acquired Dr. Pepper and 7UP for £1.6 billion ($2.48 billion), swiftly followed by Sunkist, Mott's apple juice, and Snapple. This meant that Cadbury Schweppes could compete with Coke and Pepsi globally, "with astonishing audacity," observed Davidson.

When Dominic stepped down in 2000, for the first time in the firm's 170-year history, there was no longer a member of the family on the board, and less than 1 percent of Cadbury Schweppes shares were in family hands. Over the years, the shares held by the Cadbury benevolent trusts had also declined. The trust's financial advisors had recommended they diversify their holdings. "That is simply a prudent decision by the trusts," Adrian says, "and in my view the wealth which the company produced for the family continues to be used for the causes that the family holds dear." Recent figures show that the Barrow Cadbury Trust, valued at £53.7 million, gives roughly £2.5 million in annual grants. Edward Cadbury's trust, William Cadbury's trust, and several other family trusts give a combined 250 grants each year. All the while, the Bournville Village Trust, still run by family members, continues to flourish.

The shareholders in Cadbury Schweppes, however, were increasingly made up of investors who had no direct personal links to the business and its values and whose priorities were purely to maximize profit. The Quaker voice no longer held sway in the boardroom, but could it be heard anywhere in the modern drinks and confectionery giant?

Dominic argues that it could, proudly citing his brother's role in developing the first code of corporate governance. "Adrian's Quaker background influenced his whole career at Cadbury and his understanding of how a company best operates," he says. "I think you can say the Quaker DNA has shone through the Cadbury company in terms of the work that the former Cadbury chairman has done to help develop the first code of best practice."

Adrian Cadbury was invited to chair a Committee on Financial Aspects of Corporate Governance in 1991 when he was working as a director of the Bank of England. At the time several sensational business scandals had undermined the public's confidence in how companies were run. For Adrian, "The proper governance of companies was becoming as crucial to the world economy as the proper governing of countries." The Governance Committee set a code of best practice on critical issues, among them: honest disclosure, excessive executive pay—especially when not correlated to performance—improving the quality of financial reporting, balancing short-term and long-term interests, and who should be considered stakeholders in the process. The code was the basis for effecting widespread reform of corporate governance.

"Eleven years and twenty-eight countries later," wrote Simon Caulkin in the *Observer* on October 27, 2002, "Cadbury is the elder statesman of the corporate governance movement and Britain is the corporate governance capital of the world." The Cadbury Code recommendations have influenced governance in twenty-eight countries and the World Bank. Although Quaker values were not explicitly mentioned in the Cadbury Code, for Adrian, they were crucial. The aim of the code was to bring "greater transparency, honesty, simplicity, and integrity to the process of running a company," he said.

Even as a global corporation, the company tried to stay faithful to its Quaker heritage, says Todd Stitzer, Cadbury's chief strategy officer in 2000. A Harvard-educated lawyer, Stitzer worked for the British chocolate company his entire career. "I admired the culture," he explains. "It's the appeal of the head-heart relationship that existed within the business. It mattered hugely to me." In 2000, Stitzer points out, Cadbury had a major role in Business in the Community, the organization within the Prince's Trust that Cadbury helped found that focuses on mobilizing business for good. "Cadbury had a very significant role in Help the Homeless and many other causes. And there was a continuing relationship with HIV AIDS and other health projects in Africa." That year, he says, they launched a program to build wells in Ghanian villages that had no fresh water. To date, they have built over nine hundred of them.

In the new millennium, the confectionery industry faced seismic shifts as a fresh wave of consolidation hit. The Hershey Company, so long protected by the Hershey Trust, became the focus of unwelcome attention once more. Just as the Cadbury trusts had diversified their holdings, directors of the Hershey Trust began to question whether the Hershey School would be better protected with a more diverse source of income. They consulted lawyers to find out if the Hershey Trust could sell its controlling stake. "They literally decided that they would auction the Hershey Company," recalls Todd Stitzer, "and they had a line of potential buyers."

Wrigley, Cadbury, and Nestlé began separate negotiations with the Hershey Trust. Now that Nestlé owned Rowntree, they wanted to win back the license to the Kit Kat brand in America—which was owned by Hershey. Wrigley wanted a stake in the chocolate market. Cadbury had always seen Hershey as its closest cultural fit. When news of the secret negotiations was leaked, there was an immediate outcry. The Hershey community felt betrayed. Posters were printed warning, "Wait 'til Mr. Hershey finds out!" Residents and workers paraded down Chocolate Avenue reminding anyone who would listen of Milton Hershey's proud heritage. The state attorney general, Mike Fisher, who was campaigning to become governor of Pennsylvania, was deluged with complaints and mounted a legal challenge to any sale. On September 3, 2002, the case came before the court in Harrisburg, Pennsylvania. The judge ruled no sale could happen without his approval. By that point, however, negotiations were virtually complete and bids were in. "Much to our surprise, at the very 11th hour, 59th minute plus 30 seconds, the trust decided they did not want to sell," recalls Stitzer. Once again, Hershey's chocolate company remained independent.

After spending three months in hotel rooms in New York "trying to put this thing together," Stitzer politely describes the U-turn as "remarkable." But his disappointment was quickly forgotten because "literally the day after it happened, the Pfizer people came over to the UK and said, guess what, we are having an auction for Adams." Adams, an American firm, was the world's second largest chewing gum concern, and its portfolio included gums like Trident, Dentyne, and Chiclets, bubble gums like Bubbaloo and Bubblicious, and other popular brands like Halls cough drops. Stitzer, who was promoted to chief executive in 2003, was charged with growing Cadbury's confectionery business, and it was increasingly clear that there were very few public chocolate companies left to acquire. He changed strategy, buying sugar confectionery and gum businesses in different parts of the world. The acquisition of Adams for $4.2 billion made Cadbury Schweppes the world's largest confectionery giant.

The business was growing so fast that Stitzer was concerned that it might lose touch with the company's core values. "We consciously said in 2003 that we were going to magnify and modernize the George Cadbury principle that doing good is good for business," he says. Even if the corporation was number one in world confectionery, he wanted to try to embed Quaker values in the business. The Quaker founders weren't just philanthropists, he argued, "They were *principled* capitalists." They worked as long-term stewards, committed to all the stakeholders in the business—the staff and the wider community—not just to gains for themselves as owners.

Stitzer acknowledges that modern capitalism is often seen as a "force in opposition to development—a one-way relationship in thrall to profit margins and shareholder returns." He points out that this takes many forms. "True," he says, "unbridled capitalism can be a destructive beast." Equally true, however, is that overregulated capitalism constrains creativity and innovation. "But principled capitalism is a wonderful thing." He defines this as the result of business leaders "purposefully creating an interdependence between two imperatives"—the need "to create long-term value for shareholders" and doing this in a "socially responsible and values-orientated way."

To embed the values of the company in the business plan in a way that could be applied in all countries, Stitzer set a target of 1 percent pretax profit to be committed to social responsibility. "We consistently achieved 2 percent or more," says Alex Cole, director of global corporate affairs, "and it's quite a good measure of to what extent a company considers other things than profit." The company soon launched other industry leading initiatives, such as Purple Goes Green: a commitment to reduce absolute carbon emissions by 50 percent throughout the company by 2020. Ambitious plans were also in progress to ensure ethical sourcing of cocoa and to provide help to farmers. "In the face of escalating cocoa prices and a 40 percent decline in crop yields in Ghana," says Stitzer, "if you create a program that helps you get higher crop yields of better quality in Ghana, and it helps the farmer have a better life, the whole thing joins up, right?"

For those share owners taking a long-term view, such policies did indeed join up. But others took a different view.

In 2007, the American billionaire Nelson Peltz bought 3 percent of Cadbury Schweppes. "Nelson Peltz is a force of nature," declared Shawn Tully in *Fortune* on March 19, 2007. Even at sixty-four, he was described as "relentlessly competitive." As an activist investor, Peltz had identified a way to unlock value in the business and bring immediate returns to shareholders: a separation of Cadbury from Schweppes.

Separating the drinks and confectionery businesses had been under discussion by the Cadbury Schweppes board as a possible move to release value to shareholders. The combined company was worth around £12 billion ($22.8 billion). Separately the drinks arm was estimated at £7 to £8 billion ($13 to $15 billion) and the confectionery business at £9 billion ($17.1 billion). But there was a catch—a vital one for those who wanted an independent Cadbury Schweppes. The sheer size of the drinks and confectionery giant protected it from takeover; a potential buyer would find it hard to raise enough money. It was an awkward combination, too; any buyer would almost certainly choose to break up the company. But if the drinks half were already spun off, Cadbury's confectionery would be a tasty takeover target. Some on the Cadbury Schweppes board argued that it only made sense to proceed with the drinks sale with another confectionery acquisition lined up. With no deal in place, whenever asked in public by investors about a possible drinks sale, Stitzer and the Cadbury Schweppes chairman, John Sunderland, said it was not going to happen.

Behind the scenes, Stitzer drove yet another initiative to unite Cadbury and Hershey in 2007. This time they got close. There was a measure of agreement between the Hershey Trust and Cadbury, but the management of Hershey Foods persuaded the trust not to go through with it. Meanwhile, Nelson Peltz ramped up the pressure, publicly agitating to split Cadbury Schweppes in two.

John Sunderland, who had been with the company for forty years, recalls Roger Carr, who was then deputy chairman of Cadbury Schweppes. "Man and boy, literally straight from university. The concept of separation was more challenging for John—but the recognition that it had to be done I think was very much where he came to." Stitzer concedes that there were differing views on the board. "There were board members who would rather have seen the businesses stay together, but that was a very difficult thing to do in the face of significant pressure from a large number of shareholders." The timing was critical: "We got to a juncture where the pressure to sell the beverage business in the absence of a confectionery transaction was the only course of action we could take," he says. Roger Carr's view is that Peltz did not change the thinking; "he changed the timetable for the announcement, that's all."

Facing wide-ranging pressure to enhance shareholder value, in the spring of 2007, the board of Cadbury Schweppes reached a unanimous decision to split the company just as the global credit crunch began to take hold. As the financial crisis escalated, the sale of the drinks business, now called Dr. Pepper Snapple Group, collapsed. "We were literally three weeks short of selling our beverages business," said Stitzer. Suddenly their private equity buyers could not raise the anticipated £7 to £8 billion ($13 to $15 billion) price tag for Dr. Pepper.

Nelson Peltz was determined to unlock the value in the two companies. If a sale of the drinks division wasn't possible, he wanted to refashion the transaction as a de-merger of the two companies. Above all he wanted higher margins. On December 18, 2007, he sent an open letter to the Cadbury Schweppes board. Management "had nowhere to hide," Peltz said, and its credibility with shareholders was "very low." He demanded that the board appoint several new directors and immediately name a new chairman to replace Sir John Sunderland, who was due to retire.

In February 2008, the board announced that Roger Carr would become the chairman of Cadbury's confectionery when the de-merger was completed. Carr had joined the board of Cadbury Schweppes in 2001. He was well known in the city as chairman of Centrica, and he had held board positions at several other leading companies.

"Nelson literally lobbied our major shareholders to remove the management of Cadbury," Carr explains. "He put the case that the Cadbury management were completely inept, why they should be removed, why all of these failures demonstrated their incompetence, and why he or his representatives should be installed to extract value from the company. All of this went on in my first three months of chairmanship."

Carr went round to see all the shareholders, reminding them that the existing management under Todd Stitzer had bought Adams and transformed the business. "So don't let's suddenly decide we want to throw out the chief executive and finance director," he said, "but let's agree, chairman to shareholders, that the executive team will be given the headroom and support of shareholders for a period to demonstrate their competence and ability to deliver the required performance levels."

Stitzer accepts that his job was threatened but says that this was not related to the beverages de-merger. "It was related to the margin generation and the management's ability to control costs," he says.

He admits that in 2006 Cadbury had a salmonella scare and an accountancy fraud in a factory in Nigeria. "We didn't deliver the margin we said that year and that caused a stir among some of the shareholders, saying, you know, this is the gang that couldn't shoot straight."

Stitzer's frustration with the short-term interests of shareholders is palpable. "It is outrageous. We'd grown revenues six years in a row by 6 percent. We grew margins six years in a row for 6 percent. . . . [The business] was doing everything right, consistently right. It was best in class on most measures for several years . . . but because of this narrow slice of time, people were—as short-term shareholders can often be—just focused on give us cash, give us margin. And we were trying to do it the right way."

In the spring of 2008, the costs of the de-merger soared to an estimated billion pounds—a staggering 10 percent of the value of Cadbury Schweppes. Much of the cost was related to the complexities of a UK-to-U.S. separation and listing and also taxable gain. Some investors began to protest that this was too high a price "for a bit of focusing." Peltz, who now owned 4.5 percent of Cadbury, continued to agitate for a split. The company pressed ahead with the de-merger—ironically the very month that there was further consolidation elsewhere in the confectionery industry. In May 2008, Mars merged with Wrigley, the chewing gum giant. The $23 billion deal toppled Cadbury from its No. 1 slot. Mars-Wrigley became the world's largest confectionery giant.

By contrast, was Cadbury—now shorn of its drinks division—a potential sitting duck?

Roger Carr thinks not. "The de-merger was the right thing to do," he says. "We weren't a sitting duck. The role of companies is not to remain independent at all costs but to create value for those who own them. . . . Certainly by being smaller you become more vulnerable to takeover, but there is nothing wrong with that—that is one way that value is created." He explains that the benefits of being a pure-play confectionery business became very visible in the company results, and "the board has a fiduciary duty to deliver value for shareholders, which should never be forgotten."

This begs the question: shareholder value over what period? If the board prioritizes the creation of short-term value for shareholders, where does that leave the wider interests of the company: the workforce, investment for the future, and the creation of long-term value? And if short-term value comes at the cost of breaking up a company, there may be long-term consequences that include sacrificing a company's independence.

It wasn't long before Cadbury had an unwelcome approach.

"I was at the airport coming back from Lisbon," recalls Carr, speaking of one afternoon in late August 2009. "There was a voice mail on my mobile saying, 'I'm Irene Rosenfeld. I'm in the UK next week and wouldn't mind coming and having a cup of coffee.'"

Irene Rosenfeld was chairman of Kraft Foods, America's largest food giant.

20

They'd Sell for 20p

CHICAGO, ILLINOIS, AUGUST 2009

Irene Rosenfeld had been watching Cadbury, waiting for the right moment. According to the *Times* on September 9, she had once dreamed of becoming the president of the United States and was acclaimed as one of corporate America's most powerful women. "I began studying psychology at Cornell University," she said, "and I found researching consumer behavior fascinating." After earning her BA and an MBA, she spent a large part of her career working her way up the corporate ladder, becoming chief executive of Kraft in 2006 and chairman a year later. Known to colleagues as "charming" but "steely hard," for her a takeover of Cadbury would be the jewel in the crown of a brilliant career.

Cadbury had a large slice of the British market but potentially even more valuable to Rosenfeld was its position in global markets—especially in fast-growing developing countries. Cadbury was the foremost chocolate brand on two continents, Australia and Africa, the subcontinent of India, and in numerous other countries such as Malaysia, Singapore, and New Zealand and it was developing a presence in Russia and China. Now separated from the Schweppes division, Cadbury's confectionery business was valued at over £10 billion ($16 billion), with annual sales of £5 billion ($8 billion). For the American food giant, which was five times larger, Cadbury was a tempting target.

Rosenfeld had become chairman of Kraft at a critical point in the firm's history. Much of the transformation of Kraft into the second largest food giant in the world had happened between 1988 and 2007 under the nurturing wing of America's leading tobacco giant, Phillip Morris. Kraft gained full independence from the tobacco firm in 2007 and emerged fully formed as America's largest food and drink manufacturer and a fitting challenger to Nestlé. Kraft operates 168 factories worldwide, has 98,000 employees, and generates annual sales of over £26 billion ($40 billion). Nestlé, the number one food company in the world, has 500 factories and 250,000 employees with annual sales of over £72 billion ($104 billion).

The story of Kraft Foods Inc. began in 1903, when a twenty-nine-year-old Canadian entrepreneur, James Lewis Kraft (known as J.L. Kraft), opened a wholesale cheese business in Chicago. Originally from Stevensville on the shores of Lake Erie in Ontario, he struggled in America to make ends meet and was down to his last $65, which he invested in a horse called Paddy and a rented wagon. His idea was to buy cheese in bulk from wholesalers in South Water Street in Chicago and resell it to individual grocery stores across town, but his plan did not go smoothly. "Paddy and I were equally discouraged," he told the *St. Petersburg Times* years later. "My small capital exhausted, my hopes for tomorrow nonexistent . . . I was a failure."

But he persevered and gradually won the confidence of the local grocers. After a year he could invest in more horses and carts. As the business prospered, his brothers joined him, and by 1913 they were selling thirty different types of cheese. They were inventive with their advertising: Kraft cheese was promoted on the Chicago elevated railway, on billboards, and in magazines. The turning point came with the onset of the First World War. J.L. Kraft was particularly interested in how to extend the shelf life of cheese by processing it. He found that when cheese was heated with emulsifiers, whey, and other dairy products, it did not need refrigeration and could travel long distances—exactly what the U.S. Army needed. Kraft provided 6 million pounds of tinned and processed cheese to the military and did not look back.

By 1930, J.L. Kraft had captured 40 percent of the American cheese market and was operating on three continents. He bought other companies, notably the Phenix Cheese Company, makers of Philadelphia Cream Cheese. He expanded his own line of convenience foods, including Velveeta cheese spread in 1928, Miracle Whip salad dressing in 1933, and a boxed Macaroni and Cheese Dinner in 1937—sales of which took off in the Second World War when dairy products were rationed. Kraft had another success on his hands when he introduced the first ready-sliced processed cheese in 1950; it was an instant hit combined with that all-American icon, the hamburger. "It was truly revolutionary," says Kraft archivist Becky Tousey. "They had to have in-store demonstrations before customers could believe the slices would easily separate." Later Kraft hit on the idea of wrapping each slice of cheese in cellophane for convenience. By the time J.L. died in 1953, his company had become a household name in America.

The dramatic transformation of Kraft from a successful American firm to the world's second largest food company started in 1988 when it was bought by tobacco giant Phillip Morris. Phillip Morris—now known as the Altria Group—makes some of the world's best-selling cigarettes from Marlboro to Virginia Slims and Chesterfield. The tobacco giant had very good reasons to diversify its business. In 1954, in one of the earliest cases of tobacco litigation, a Missouri smoker who had lost his larynx to cancer, filed suit against Phillip Morris. The tobacco company won the case in 1962, but the problem did not go away. As evidence mounted suggesting a link between cigarette smoking and cancer, so did the costs of litigation. In 1988, after a long-running court case, the judge said he found evidence of a conspiracy by three tobacco companies—including Phillip Morris—that was "vast in its scope, devious in its purpose, and devastating in its results."

That very year, Phillip Morris diversified further into food, buying Kraft for $12.9 billion in one of the largest non-oil corporate takeovers in U.S. history. Phillip Morris had already bought General Foods for $5.6 billion, owners of America's oldest chocolate confectionery, Walter Baker, as well as other famous brands like Birds Eye. Irene Rosenfeld had begun her own career at General Foods, progressing through various managerial roles. "I was one of the first two female general managers at General Foods," she recalls.

The mergers and acquisitions continued on a grand scale. In 1989 General Foods merged with Kraft and soon acquired Jacob Suchard, which brought with it Suchard chocolates and the Tobler company, makers of Toblerone. In 1993 Kraft General Foods bought the historic British chocolate confectioner, Terry of York, acquiring Terry's Chocolate Orange and other much-loved treats and expanded further into Europe with the purchase of the Scandinavian confectioner Freia Marabou. In 2000 Phillip Morris bought Nabisco Holdings, America's number one cookie maker, for a staggering $18.9 billion and merged the company with its Kraft division. Phillips Morris, apart from being one of the largest cigarette companies in the world, was rapidly becoming a colossal food concern.

Then in 2000, Phillip Morris and R.J. Reynolds were ordered to pay $20 million to a smoker who was dying of lung cancer. It was the first ruling to hold cigarette makers responsible for the health of people who took up smoking in spite of the package's compulsory warning labels. On June 7, 2001, Phillip Morris was ordered to pay $3 billion to a smoker with terminal cancer—a record-breaking individual damage award against a cigarette maker. One week later Phillip Morris raised $8.7 billion by selling 16 percent of its giant food division: Kraft Foods.

Kraft Foods was now listed on the New York Stock Exchange but it was still principally owned by Phillip Morris. In 2003 Phillip Morris changed its name to Altria, which still owned the majority of Kraft's stock. Although the judgments against the tobacco giant were reduced on appeal—the $3 billion damage award was lowered to $82 million in March 2006—more lawsuits continued to be filed against the company.

The following January, the Altria Group voted to spin off all remaining shares of Kraft Foods. A news release posted on January 31, 2007, claimed the spin-off would "enable both Altria and Kraft to focus more effectively on their respective businesses," and would "enhance Kraft's ability to make acquisitions." Kraft Foods finally became independent of tobacco on March 30, 2007. Its holdings included:

Maxwell House coffee, Philadelphia Cream Cheese, Oscar Meyer hot dogs, Nabisco cookies, crackers, and snacks, Dairylea, Terry's chocolates, and Kraft cheeses. With its complex history, Kraft, declared London's *Evening Standard* on September 9, 2009, "is a creature of Wall Street, an assemblage of businesses including General Foods and Nabisco, that were stitched together by Phillip Morris, the tobacco company during the merger mayhem of the 1980s and 1990s."

Irene Rosenfeld was appointed chairman of Kraft Foods in March 2007. She knew that despite the company's phenomenal size and range, many of its brands were established in developed markets, yielding low growth of around 4 percent to shareholders. With Cadbury's stronger footprint in faster-growing developing markets, Rosenfeld saw the potential to raise this figure to 5 percent growth.

On August 26, 2009, she flew to Luton in the Kraft company jet and made her way to the Ritz Hotel in London. The following morning, she went to see the Cadbury chairman, Roger Carr. The meeting was discreetly scheduled for his office in Centrica's headquarters in Burlington Lane (Carr is also chairman of Centrica). Carr has a reputation as a "city grandee," according to Andrew Davidson of the *Sunday Times*. "A hard man to read," says Davidson, "and as cautious and leathery as an old tortoise."

The 9:30 meeting did not take long.

Carr remembers that after about three minutes of pleasantries, "She said, 'You know, I have this great idea that we should buy you.'"

Rosenfeld told him her plans were to offer a cash and shares bid for Cadbury worth £10.2 billion ($16.3 billion).

Carr describes Rosenfeld as "clinical, distant, and quite hostile. She showed no natural warmth. . . . Her body language was driven and intense—certainly not relaxed and engaging."

Poker-faced, Carr did not hesitate and replied, "Well, first of all, this is something I will want to discuss with the board, and secondly, Cadbury is a very good business, it's doing very well as an independent, and certainly doesn't need Kraft."

After a brisk exchange, Rosenfeld said she would courier round a letter that afternoon and asked for his response by Wednesday.

"We'll give you a response when we think it is appropriate," he responded. He walked her to the elevator, "and off she went."

The meeting, he recalled afterwards, did not last more than fifteen minutes.

Later that day, Rosenfeld's letter arrived. "I very much enjoyed meeting you this morning," she began with pro forma courtesy. Her letter set out a textbook case for globalization. Kraft's purchase of Cadbury would be the logical next step as "we shape the company into a more global, higher growth and higher margin entity." The new company would have $50 billion in revenues each year, "a geographically diversified business," and "scale in key developing markets such as India, Mexico, Brazil, China, and Russia." The "strong presence in instant consumption channels in both developed and developing markets" would expand the reach of the business and provide "potential for meaningful revenue synergies over time." There was also the possibility of savings. In a subsequent letter, Rosenfeld explained how the acquisition would save $300 million in economies of scale in manufacturing, $200 million in administration, and $125 million in marketing and media.

At Cadbury's headquarters, Roger Carr and Todd Stitzer swung into action. An emergency meeting was held at Goldman Sachs offices on Fleet Street. "The mood was we will not allow these people to steal this company," recalls Carr. "Everyone had utter resolve around the board table to resist this." Carr drafted a letter rejecting the offer. The plan to bring Cadbury into Kraft's "low-growth conglomerate business," he said disparagingly, was "an unappealing and unattractive prospect." The offer did not reflect Cadbury's value or its growth prospects compared to Kraft's "less focused business mix and historically lower growth."

Rosenfeld's next move was to publish the letter she had sent to Carr, initiating what is known in the trade as a "bear hug." When letters of intent are made public, says Carr, "the predator can distress and disturb the prey whilst alerting the market to the potential for an exciting bout and quick financial gain." The audience is in no doubt "that a showdown is inevitable."

The showdown soon began. Stitzer spoke to the press in a defiant mood: "We are in half the world's fifty largest confectionery markets and we are No. 1 or 2," he declared. "We are big in Argentina, Colombia, Brazil, and Venezuela. . . . Combining with Kraft could derail Cadbury's expansion plans." The British press was equally hostile, pointing to the fate of Terry, the cherished British chocolatier, under Kraft's stewardship. Chocolate production had been moved to Eastern Europe and the historic factory in York closed in 2005. Felicity Loudon, George Cadbury's great-granddaughter, condemned Kraft as a "plastic cheese company" and voiced fears that Kraft could asset-strip "the jewel in the crown." Rosenfeld's global powerhouse was little more than "brazen imperial ambition" declared the *Evening Standard* on September 9. Kraft was caught in a static American market that "rises and falls with the waistline of Joe the plumber." The *Sunday Times* summed up the force of the British opposition: "Cadbury Gives It Both Barrels" read the headline with an image of Todd Stitzer blasting the U.S. predator.

Irene Rosenfeld did not waver. Patience, she told reporters, was her "most challenged virtue." In what was seen by many as an unnecessarily hostile move, she took her offer straight to Cadbury's shareholders. The entire future of the company would depend on the interests of the shareholders. The prospect of a takeover prompted a shopping frenzy. Hedge funds and other short-term investors piled on to Cadbury as the share price soared. What, they wanted to know, would maximize their profits?

News of Kraft's proposed takeover sent Cadbury shares soaring. City sharks and other predators began circling around the chocolate prey looking for a quick kill. The financial press was full of speculation about the possible outcome possibilities as bankers and accountants gutted the balance sheet. There was talk of carving up Cadbury's assets. Could parts of Cadbury be won for a knockdown price? Investors had their eyes on the most profitable brands, Dairy Milk and Trident gum. If the confectionery industry was about to be massively realigned, no one wanted to be left on the sidelines. Even smaller firms joined the fray.

Rumors swirled about that Hershey's management had appointed J.P. Morgan to investigate a possible bid. Finally both the trust and the company were spurred to action. Company executives were worried that Hershey would be left behind in a new world of behemoths like Kraft-Cadbury, Mars-Wrigley, and Nestlé. "They came here to the Stafford Hotel nearby," recalls Carr. "There were four or five meetings." Among the many tactical issues on the table: Could the Hershey Trust keep control with a massively reduced shareholding in a combined company? If the companies merged, how would Cadbury shareholders benefit? Hershey was half the size of Cadbury, so how could it afford the acquisition? Did Hershey have the appetite for the risk? If the two companies could resolve these and other issues, Carr was confident the merger would be "a wonderful outcome and exactly what I would have liked to have occurred."

Cadbury was under siege. Hedge funds, which previously owned 5 percent of Cadbury shares, bought 20 percent in a matter of weeks. "We had a share price of nearer £5 just before Rosenfeld bid," Carr explains. "Because she was offering around £7 per share, the market was sure any buyout would happen above that, so shares quickly ran to above £8." The loyalty of long-term investors was severely tested: If they had bought in at £4 to £5 and could see an immediate £3 profit, they were tempted to sell at least some of their holding. This opened the door for hedge funds to continue to pile in. Carr points out that British institutional investors had already turned their backs on Cadbury. At the start of the bidding process, only 28 percent of Cadbury shares was British owned, as opposed to 50 percent owned by Americans. "British investors thought it was a lacklustre business," Carr explains, "while American investors saw the stock was cheap relative to American alternatives, and they kept on buying." Now these American investors could cash in as the share price soared.

With the ownership of Cadbury changing fast, further destabilizing the company, on September 21, management asked the UK's Panel on Takeovers and Mergers to give Kraft a "put up or shut up" deadline, which required Kraft to make a formal offer or walk away.

As shareholders rushed to evaluate their options, the billionaire investor Warren Buffett, a cautious man who owned 9 percent of Kraft, spoke out. The "Sage of Omaha," as he is known to admiring investors, is one of the richest men in the world, a position earned after a lifetime of walking with care through inflammatory markets. He urged Kraft not to overpay for the British chocolate firm, and it appeared as though the Kraft management was listening.

On November 9, the day of the Takeover Panel deadline, Rosenfeld made a formal bid at the same price as her earlier offer. But because Kraft's share value had declined slightly, the bid amount was now worth less: £9.8 billion ($15.7 billion) or £7.17 per share. Once again, Roger Carr dismissed the offer as "derisory." It was beginning to look as if Kraft could not afford Cadbury.

On November 18, news broke that the Italian firm of Ferrero Rocher was joining the chocolate wars. Ferrero, the family company behind Nutella, Ferrero Rocher chocolate pyramids, Tic Tacs, and Kinder Surprise, was even smaller than Hershey with eighteen factories and 22,000 employees. Could it possibly join forces with Hershey to make a combined bid for Cadbury? Confirmation that the Hershey Trust was reviewing a possible bid for Cadbury fuelled excitement that Kraft's bid would be topped. Then Nestlé revealed it was considering joining the bidding war. Would Nestlé partner with Hershey to make a counterbid against their rival Kraft? Or would Kraft come back with a higher offer? Just two months after Kraft's opening salvo, amid speculation that Hershey—or someone else—might produce an $18 billion bid, Cadbury's shares soared by 40 percent.

On December 14, Cadbury's management issued a bullish defense. Stitzer improved profit targets and promised greater returns to shareholders as an independent with the prospect of 5 percent annual growth and double-digit dividends. These forecasts were backed up by the company's third-quarter results. Cadbury's sales were better than expected in contrast to Kraft, which had to cut its 2009 sales forecast.

After a cold and snowy Christmas, Kraft enhanced its bid on January 5, 2010. Although the total value of the deal was the same as before, shareholders would receive a higher proportion in cash. Two days later, however, Kraft revealed that only 1.5 percent of Cadbury shareholders had accepted Kraft's bid. Cadbury rejected Kraft yet again, insisting the enhanced bid was just "tinkering" and the offer remained "derisory."

Irene Rosenfeld quickly sold off Kraft's North American frozen pizza business to Nestlé for $3.7 billion. Warren Buffett was on her back: "To give up a business that makes $280 million a year for $3.7 billion," he said, "I think that's a mistake." But Rosenfeld was steadily moving closer to her goal. The sale gave her extra cash to maneuver in the Cadbury bid and made it less likely that Nestlé would join Hershey or Ferrero in an attempt to outbid Kraft. In addition, according to Adam Leyland in the *Grocer* magazine on January 23, 2010, Buffett's warnings against Kraft overpaying for Cadbury "helped Kraft shares recover, upping the value of the bid" and served to "low-ball expectations."

There was one American investor, usually vocal, who "remained uncharacteristically quiet," continues Leyland. Nelson Peltz, the activist investor who had agitated for the de-merger of Cadbury Schweppes in 2007, had at the same time taken a significant position in Kraft. Moreover, "Peltz secured a two-year deal with Kraft management not to publicly criticise the company in exchange for two independent director appointments on Kraft's board," writes Leyland. This "gagging deal" expired during Kraft's bidding process. Yet Peltz remained quiet. "By this time he had also, intriguingly, sold the majority of his shares in Kraft," says Leland. "Anyone looking for a silent player behind the scenes driving this deal should look no further than Peltz."

The week before Kraft's deadline to make a final offer on January 19, speculation rose that Hershey was about to mount a solo bid. There were anxious meetings in London hotels. "Until the very, very end, Hershey was still trying to find a way to increase the consideration in a manner they could finance appropriately," says Stitzer. "They couldn't get to a place where they needed to be." Carr was more blunt. The Hershey Company, he said later, "was paralysed by internal conflicts of opinion. There were so many schools of thought they were never able to agree on a compelling offer at the same time. It was very disappointing for Cadbury and, I believe, the Hershey Trust."

With the deadline looming, Irene Rosenfeld flew back and forth across the Atlantic. She was trying to gauge the level at which Cadbury shareholders might be tempted to sell. Short-term investors such as hedge funds now owned as much as 31 percent of Cadbury.

Carr was talking regularly to the shareholders. "Some of the hedge funds said to me, 'We've bought at £7.80—with 20p in five weeks of ownership—we'll sell for £8.' The ones that came in later, maybe they bought at £8. They'd sell for the same 20p—but the clearing price became £8.20." British institutions still held some 28 percent of Cadbury, and some of them wanted above £8.50—but they were in a minority. "A lot of the American owners said they would sell in the £8.20 to £8.30 zone for sure."

On Saturday, January 16, Rosenfeld reconvened a meeting of the Kraft board. She wanted approval to make a new offer to Cadbury.

In London, Warren Buffett's warnings not to overpay for Cadbury had been widely reported. Many investors believed that Kraft could not afford to increase its offer significantly. As the deadline approached, Cadbury shares began to fall on the expectation that the bid might fail. There was talk that Rosenfeld might be obliged to make an embarrassing retreat. Cadbury might yet get away.

But as Rosenfeld returned to London and settled into her suite at the Connaught Hotel in Mayfair, she had good reason to feel confident that she held a strong hand. "She telephoned on Sunday night at 7:00 asking for a meeting," recalls Roger Carr. It was the first time they'd spoken since their meeting in August. She assured him it would be productive to meet. "At that point I then have a duty to meet," Carr adds.

A meeting was arranged for the next morning in a private room at the Lanesborough Hotel. It was Rosenfeld's final chance to win Carr's approval for the bid, which would make the takeover far more straightforward.

Carr remembers vividly how the meeting started: "She began by saying, 'We've listened to you, we've listened to your shareholders, we know we have to pay more money, and I'm going to offer you £8.30.'"

The minute she said that, "I knew we'd lost," he said. "I knew the business was sold in the real world."

Carr left to speak to the other members of the Cadbury board. Having spoken to both shareholders and advisors, the board believed that if Rosenfeld had gone to market the following day and offered £8.30, she would have secured more than 50 percent of the shareholders immediately. She only needed 50.01 percent.

"I knew she'd got it," said Carr. "My job from that point on became to get as much value as I could. . . . The most important thing was to get it from £8.30 to £8.50, which was worth nearly another half a billion dollars for shareholders."

But did Carr and the board capitulate too soon? "By playing the heritage card so strongly in their defense against Kraft," observed Alex Brummer in the *Daily Mail* on February 2, they raised the hopes of all stakeholders "that this was a genuine defence aimed at keeping independence rather than a bluff aimed at getting the price up." Those in favor of preserving Cadbury's independence were left to wonder whether the board could have seen off the bid at £8.30 had they stood firm.

Carr doesn't accept this. "We resisted the union jack defence and focused on value. I fought for the shareholders. I'm paid by the shareholders and I delivered huge value for the shareholders with the board—that is my responsibility."

Later in the day on January 18, Carr and Rosenfeld met again at the Lanesborough. "We had a series of meetings over the course of the day to move from £8.30 to the £8.50 level," says Carr. Finally Rosenfeld offered £8.40 with a 10p dividend once the offer was unconditional. In essence, she was offering the £8.50 per share. "The board's view was that we had achieved a good price for the business," Carr says, and they were prepared to recommend the bid.

It was dark as Irene Rosenfeld and Roger Carr made their way across Mayfair to Kraft's advisors and bankers at Lazard on Stratton Street. They were joined by Cadbury's advisors from Goldman Sachs.

"The transaction was secured at around 9:00 PM," says Carr. "At that point people did shake hands." Kraft's PR people asked for a photograph of Rosenfeld and Carr shaking hands.

"I said no because I had never changed my position that I did not want to sell the business to Kraft," Carr recalls. "So why do I want to sit there having a glass of champagne on an outcome that on any other reason than value I would have preferred not to happen?" All the same, Carr felt he'd done his job: He had secured "tomorrow's price today." But there was no moment to toast. "If you've done the right thing in terms of the world in which I live, then you can continue to look in the mirror as having done the right thing—even though doing the right thing may personally leave you feeling sad and hollow." Todd Stitzer too felt "unspeakably sad." At 5:00 AM the following morning, he woke Sir Adrian with the news, anxious to reach him before the story broke.

The press was waiting for a statement. "The board of Cadbury unanimously recommends Cadbury shareholders to accept the terms of the final offer," said a weary-looking Stitzer. "The deal represents good value for Cadbury shareholders," assured Carr. The press was quick to point out that among those shareholders poised to benefit from the takeover was Stitzer himself, who reputedly walked away with an estimated £17 million ($25.5 million) in shares and options. "The strange paradox of this is that investing in the company I believe in, in the end actually was of benefit to me," he said later. "I wasn't in any way seeking an early end to my employment."

According to Carr, most shareholders "were very pleased with the price achieved." Bankers and advisors in London and New York also benefited to the tune of £400 million ($600 million). Yet some shareholders had a muted response. Legal and General Investment Management, which held 5 percent of Cadbury's shares, was "disappointed" that the price did not reflect the true value.

Others were shell-shocked by the news. Felicity Loudon saw the outcome as "a horror story" and urged people to voice their opposition to their MP and the shareholders. On fan websites, British consumers were equally angry and outraged. "There should be a national boycott of Kraft-Cadbury," urged one. Sites were launched to save the Curly Wurly and other beloved brands. There were financial analysts who thought the firm had been sold down the river. "Cadbury's exit valuation," said one industry analyst, "will rank as the lowest in the confectionery space by some margin." The two grandsons of

George Cadbury, Sir Adrian and Sir Dominic, described the news quite simply "a tragedy."

Irene Rosenfeld was all smiles. The glamorous winner in a red suit with a gold brooch, she told reporters that she felt "great." Cadbury-Kraft combined was "a global powerhouse" with worldwide sales of £37 billion (over $50 billion). "Acquiring Cadbury is a significant milestone in the history of Kraft foods," she said. "The combination of a more extensive snacking portfolio, together with an expanded global footprint and greater penetration of grocery and instant consumption outlets, creates opportunities that will truly set this company apart from its peers."

Mars and Wrigley had been knocked into second place. Rosenfeld stood at the helm of the world's number one confectionery supergiant.

21

Gone. And It Was So Easy.

The hotly contested takeover of Cadbury was one of the largest completed acquisitions in British history. For many economists this is just part of an ongoing process that has brought immense benefits worldwide. Globalization helps lift millions out of poverty and distributes a wider range of products around the world at cheaper prices than ever before. In the chocolate industry, if the rationale that Kraft used to persuade Cadbury shareholders is correct and the projected synergies between the two companies are realized, then Cadbury becomes a leaner and more efficient organization and Kraft will sell more of its products overseas, creating opportunities for all Kraft employees. Investors enjoy higher profits, and chocolate goodies are produced ever more cheaply—at least that is the theory.

Sir Adrian and Sir Dominic Cadbury warned in a letter on January 20, 2010, to the *Daily Telegraph* that a high percentage of takeovers do not live up to the bidder's claims. Kraft's record to date, they wrote, "is of underperformance and, in the case of Terry, of failing in their stewardship of the company they had acquired." The two former Cadbury chairmen pointed out that the value of a company reflects its reputation built up over a lifetime and the consumer's trust that the company and its brands are one. "Cut the tie and submerge the brands in a larger entity," they wrote, "and both present and future value will be lost."

The difficulty of maintaining the culture of a company that is taken over is linked to the acquiring company's debt load. In this case,

Kraft assumed an estimated £7 billion ($10.5 billion) of debt to fund the takeover, raising its total debt to a reported £18.3 billion ($27 billion). This staggering amount of debt generates fears that Cadbury will be asset-stripped and put to work to service this debt. Despite assurances from Kraft that this will not happen, the premise of the takeover acknowledged annual efficiencies of £412 million ($618 million). "Nobody knows whether or not they can achieve it," Sir Dominic says. "They were not obliged to show where all those savings are going to come from. They also claim the synergy with Cadbury is going to produce £650 million [$975 million], but the evidence for that is not on the table. Now if you borrow all this money and say you are going to be able to pay it off by making savings, it surely is more responsible to have a much clearer view of where those savings are coming from." Hardly surprising then that the very stakeholders whose lives George Cadbury and the pioneers were at such pains to enrich are likely to lose out sooner or later—starting with the workers.

Roger Carr himself warned that job losses were inevitable. Sir Adrian and Sir Dominic appealed to Kraft on January 20, pointing out that it had "accepted a duty to those working for the company." And they urged Kraft "to live up to that responsibility." Unite, the trade union that represents Cadbury workers, is concerned that up to 10,000 jobs in Cadbury worldwide could be at long-term risk. Under pressure to meet debt repayments, they fear Kraft will be more likely to cut jobs in Britain rather than on home turf in America. Unite claims that over the last ten years, Kraft has sacked some 60,000 workers to help pay for similar deals—a figure Kraft denies.

But just a week after sealing the deal, Kraft confirmed the closure of the famous Cadbury factory at Somerdale that makes Crunchie and Curly Wurlys. During the takeover, Kraft had said it believed it would be able to keep this site open, unlike Cadbury. But in an apparent U-turn, four hundred jobs now had to go. "This sends the worst possible message to the 6,000 other Cadbury workers in Britain," said Unite. "It tells them Kraft cares little for their workers." Union leaders and MPs were outspoken about what they saw as cynical manipulation. "Kraft has tossed away promises on jobs like a torn-up sweet wrapper," argued Liberal MP Matthew Oakeshott. "It has treated British parliament with contempt."

A House of Commons Business, Innovation, and Skills Committee was set up to investigate the U-turn, but Irene Rosenfeld failed to appear, sending Kraft's vice president for corporate and legal affairs, Marc Firestone, in her place. "I am terribly sorry," he said. He told a skeptical committee of MPs that Cadbury's plan to close Somerdale was more advanced than Kraft had initially thought. He also pledged there would be no further cuts in Kraft's UK manufacturing for two years but could provide no guarantees beyond that. The MPs' report concluded that Kraft had acted "irresponsibly and unwisely."

The effect of the merger on the workforce is not simply worry over job security. Control of the firm will now pass from London and Bournville to Chicago. In today's global village, the Bournville employees may rarely see their American management. Does this create an inspiring environment? "The danger is that people no longer see the reason for giving of their best," argues Adrian. "A business which in economic terms is doing very well can lose the drive of the very people who are in it—you lose an economic benefit let alone the social implications." It is easy to see how those whose lives are overturned by global forces beyond their control feel alienated and have low expectations. It is the opposite of what George Cadbury tried to achieve when he set out to improve a man's lot by raising his hopes and ideals.

The wider community, during George Cadbury's tenure, benefited from the generous use of chocolate wealth to funds schools, hospitals, convalescent homes, churches, housing, swimming pools, games fields, the cricket pavilion, and even such meaningful touches as the Bournville bells. These enhancements contributed to the local community's sense of unity and belonging. But in today's global village, Birmingham is fast losing its proud manufacturing heritage, and there are growing ghettos within the city that no longer convey "that eager spirit of application" so admired by the *Chambers Edinburgh Journal* in 1852. The writer and columnist A. N. Wilson, whose father helped to create village houses for the Wedgwood workforce in Staffordshire, points out that the thriving communities created by enlightened nineteenth-century business leaders "lie in sad contrast to the antisocial attitudes of modern business magnates who think only of profit and the shareholder." Writing in the *Daily Mail* on January 23, 2010, he argues, "The depression, the human redundancy in all senses of the word which has resulted from the globalisation of the market place has made us all come socially adrift," adding, "We are all victims of the 'hostile takeover' of one kind or another." Needless to say community leaders and Birmingham MPs campaigned against the sale of Cadbury in Westminster.

There was anger too at the lack of action from politicians. Prime Minister Gordon Brown stated, "We are determined that the levels of investment that take place in Cadbury in the UK are maintained, and we are determined at a time when people are worried about their jobs, that jobs in Cadbury can be secure." But he had no power to enforce his statement. The role played by the Royal Bank of Scotland was seen as a bitter betrayal. This British bank, which was 84 percent owned by the taxpayers after the government bailout during the credit crunch, joined the syndicate that funded Kraft offering a £630 million loan facility. "When British taxpayers bailed out the bank, they would never have believed that their money would be used to put British people out of work. Isn't that plain wrong?" argued the Liberal Democrat leader, Nick Clegg, in a stormy House of Commons debate on January 20.

Betrayal or not, the British government believes in an open-door policy with regard to foreign takeovers. Some economists argue this is to Britain's benefit with takeover rules focused on value and a clear financial code that leaves decisions on deals to shareholders who all have equal voting rights whether they are short-term or long-term investors. For others, like former Treasury Minister Geoffrey Robinson, this is "a one-way street," and too many British companies, especially in manufacturing, have passed into foreign hands: glass, steel, chemicals, and confectionery, to name but a few. How much closer to the truth is city columnist Anthony Hilton, who argues, "We have an economy dangerously skewed towards financial services," and "the whole nation pays the price." He points out that "investment bankers actively tout our companies around the world because one big bonanza can set them up for life." Business Secretary Peter Mandelson too questions who benefits from such deals: "The open secret of the last two decades is that mergers often fail to create any long-term value, except perhaps for the advisors and those who arbitrage the share price." The *Guardian* summed up the anger: "This is an old-fashioned Square Mile stitch-up, driven through by City short termists."

So how has this happened? For Sir Dominic Cadbury, at the heart of the issue is the changing concept of ownership inherent in our modern form of shareholder capitalism. In fact, he argues, "There's no ownership concept," at least not in the traditional sense of stewardship and long-term planning for a company that his Quaker capitalist forebears understood. The current system is far removed from the Quaker philosophy of business and "aligns too many people to be incentivised over the short-term."

"It comes back to the role of the shareholder—the shareholder is the owner of the business. But the difficulty with all this is that they are not acting as owners of the business," he says. "There are thousands of shareholders in Cadbury who would probably have said they didn't want to sell their shares and would have voted against. But they didn't have a vote, because if you are the average shareholder, you don't hold your shares personally; you hold your shares through your pension scheme or your bank. In the case of Cadbury, sixty fund managers made the decision." But fund managers are under pressure to focus on immediate gain and short-term performance targets rather than long-term wealth creation.

Hedge funds demonstrate the extremes of short-termism. "The hedge funds are 'owners' whose motivation is to see that the company disappears," says Dominic. "By definition, they have no sense of obligation and no sense of responsibility for the company whatsoever." Yet in this case, by the end of the bidding process, they "owned" more than 30 percent of Cadbury and were happy to sell for a 20p profit—a stark contrast to the dedicated Quaker capitalist founders who nurtured the company from its humble beginnings. This has to be the ultimate in the throwaway society. "One day you had the Cadbury company, the next day you didn't," says Dominic. "Gone. One hundred and eighty years of history down the tube, and I would argue 180 years of being a beacon of good practice. Something very precious got lost that day. Gone. And it was so easy."

Sir Dominic is not opposed to takeovers but questions how they are achieved. "Even the Chinese, in their Communist way, actually feel very seriously about ownership. They are not going to let ownership drift away," he says. Traditionally takeovers have been a way of removing bad management, but in this case, many argue that Cadbury's management team was more dynamic and effective than Kraft's. Todd Stitzer concedes the outcome was not consistent with his view of principled capitalism. "I felt immense frustration because this company stands for everything that is right in business," he said. "It stands for performance on the one hand in terms of reward for shareholders but also social and sustainable responsibility on the other hand." The key, he points out, is to find the right balance between short-term shareholder returns and the long-term needs of the company.

For some the takeover raised questions about the role of the company board. "Roger Carr was wrong when he said the Kraft takeover was all about price," argues Mark Goyder, the founder and director of Tomorrow's Company, a research organization. He believes the fiduciary duty of company leaders is to their company, not directly to the shareowners. "Neither the takeover code nor the general law imposes a duty on directors to recommend a bid on price grounds alone where they feel it isn't in the best interests of the company," Goyder told *Director* magazine. In a keynote speech to the city of London on March 1, 2010, Peter Mandelson, Secretary of State for Business, said that board directors should consider the interests of all stakeholders in a business: employees, suppliers, and a company's brands and capabilities. He urged directors to act more like "stewards" rather than "auctioneers" selling to the highest bidder, adding, "If this requires restating the 2006 Companies Act, then so be it."

Roger Carr, who fought for the best price for shareholders all the way through the takeover, now questions whether the current takeover rules are fair. Speaking at the Said Business School on February

9, 2010, he acknowledged that "something has happened to the system that appears to tip the playing field to short-termism. . . . Whilst capitalism is efficient, it may be unreasonable that a few individuals with weeks of share ownership can determine the lifetime destiny of many." Rather than the government "speaking from the sidelines on national interest," they could use their power "to deliver their view or at least tax measures to encourage long-term share ownership." Why not raise the acceptance for takeovers from 50.1 percent of the share register to 60 percent, he asked, "reducing the odds of deal-driven investors unduly influencing the outcome." Perhaps, he adds, shares acquired during the bid period should carry no voting rights to "ensure that short-term money does not determine long-term futures." Richard Lambert, director of the Confederation of British Industry, and many other business leaders are questioning whether short-term investors' voting rights should be curtailed. Some MPs are calling for a "Cadbury Law" to ensure that for certain "strategic" companies, two-thirds of shareholders will have to vote yes in a hostile takeover.

So why has the balance tipped to short-termism? "Greed," in the view of Todd Stitzer. "People want money fast and they don't really care. They just don't care what it takes to get it. That's what it's all about. It's disconnected. The connection between the humans who make the raw materials with the humans who make the stuff in factories, the humans who make the machines that go into the factories. It's disconnected so no one feels responsible for how it works." This disconnect, he says, leads to "people who are in it to see if they can get 20p out of you" as opposed to genuine wealth creation by innovation and increased capability.

He believes the current system can distort the notion of value and is open to abuse. "There's a game that public companies play with shareholders—with financial statements. They do things to enhance earnings, so that people who are quantitatively orientated and think that all you need to do is look at numbers and numbers relationships, say this is getting more valuable and that's going to keep going forever, but that's not true. Just not true. Brands must have brand marketing investment. They have to have science and technology investment.

You have to have machinery and equipment that's replaced on a regular cycle that's not milked and so on." He believes that process has also led to a culture of wanting higher compensation. "In the rubric of 'we want everyone to have options and identify with the shareholders,' smart people, who aren't quite as principled, figure out how to advantage themselves by manipulating the financials," he explains. "The world has borne witness to legions of company leaders doing this." The manipulation is all too easily disguised: "It's purposeful," he says. "They figure out how to fiddle with the accounting by doing certain things in the business to increase the value of their shares so they can cash in their stock options."

For Timothy Phillips, chairman of The Quakers and Business Group, which aims to promote Quaker principles in the workplace, there are wider concerns related to our modern form of shareholder capitalism. Firstly, "Shares tend to be owned by institutions rather than individuals, and they collectively become almost more powerful than governments, which are overly influenced by the growing power of the shareholder lobby." Is this truly democratic, he asks? He also questions the transparency of the process. "For example, the money that Kraft shareholders have borrowed to buy Cadbury will be repaid to the banks who funded the purchase; they in turn repay the funds they borrowed from in the first place. So what one is doing by supporting the argument that bigger is better all the time is creating essentially a global network of asset ownership on a vast scale." This has led to "a number of international well-paid jobs in powerful institutions and corporations, but it also means wealth and power is concentrated into fewer and less accountable hands."

This phenomenon has played out in the chocolate industry: A succession of smaller firms, Fry, Rowntree, Terry, and Cadbury, have disappeared into two giant corporations: Nestlé and Kraft. In the process, a myriad of middle ranking and senior positions have disappeared to create fewer, more highly paid top jobs. The credit crunch has brought with it stunning revelations about excessive pay, bonuses, and pensions for those in the upper echelons of multinational institutions and companies and a growing gap between rich and poor in the West. In the United States, the ratio of chief executive pay to factory worker pay has risen from 42:1 in 1960 to 344:1 in 2007. In real terms, the median compensation for the chief executives of companies in the Dow Jones Industrial Average was $19.8 million in 2009, well over five hundred times more than the median worker's pay of $36,000. The British press was quick to point out that in the year that Irene Rosenfeld launched a hostile bid for Cadbury, she received a 40 percent rise in compensation, bringing her total package of salary, stock, and other incentive awards to $26.3 million. By contrast, in the wake of the takeover, many Cadbury workers faced an ultimatum: Accept a three-year pay freeze or leave the final salary pension scheme.

For Timothy Phillips, who is also a director of Scott Bader, a chemicals firm owned collectively by its workforce, the astonishing differential between the highest and lowest salaries are socially corrosive and undermine the fabric of our institutions. He argues that the global village of the twenty-first century requires more aggressive international regulation—not the least to tackle glaring inconsistencies in how resources are shared worldwide. Again the chocolate industry illustrates the point. While the top executives of today's global powerhouses are handsomely rewarded, workers at the bottom rung of the ladder—in our global village, cocoa farmers in West Africa, for instance—may earn a mere $2 a day. In the worldwide race to manufacture chocolate ever more cheaply and maximize returns to shareholders, horrendous pressures remain on Third World producers. Several reports since 2001 have highlighted serious underlying concerns: the use of trafficked child labor in the production of cocoa in West Africa, especially the Ivory Coast. For these children, there is no pay at all.

The International Labour Organisation, a special UN agency that investigates labor issues, found there are more than 200,000 child laborers in the Ivory Coast of which 12,000 are estimated to be the victims of trafficking. Alarmed by the delay in improving conditions, the International Labour Rights Forum, a human rights watch group, filed a lawsuit in 2005 against Nestlé and commodity traders Cargill and Archer Daniels Midland. They claimed that Malian children were trafficked to the Ivory Coast and forced to work up to fourteen hours a day with no pay and frequent beatings. "A Cocoa Protocol is in place setting out corporate chains of accountability," said Timothy Newman for the International Labour Rights Forum. "It's outrageous that this has not been implemented." Nestlé replied that it is "committed to following and respecting all international laws and does not tolerate illegal and discriminatory practices."

Cadbury buys cocoa principally from the neighboring country of Ghana, the world's second largest cocoa producer, and has been working with the Fairtrade Foundation to try to improve labor conditions. The Fairtrade Foundation was established in 1992 by CAFOD (Catholic Agency for Overseas Development), Christian Aid, Traidcraft, and the World Development Movement to tackle trade injustices and help farmers out of poverty. Fairtrade ensures a guaranteed minimum price of $1,600 per ton to cocoa producers, even if world cocoa prices fall below this level. This stability of income helps farmers trade themselves out of poverty. In addition, no matter how high the price of cocoa rises, Fairtrade guarantees a $150 premium per ton on top to help farmers grow their business and develop their community. Fairtrade cannot rule out the possibility of child labor on its farms, but it provides better traceability and more direct contact with cocoa producers, making it possible to identify and address poor labor practices.

In 2009, Cadbury launched its leading brand, Dairy Milk, in Britain, as Fairtrade-certified, a move that tripled the sales of Fairtrade cocoa from Ghana. This was swiftly followed by the launch of all Cadbury beverages as Fairtrade, along with the global Green and Blacks organic line of chocolate bars, and Cadbury's Buttons and Dairy Milk in Canada, Australia, New Zealand, and Japan. "We were trying to make George Cadbury's nineteenth-century Quaker principle that 'Doing good is good for business' relevant to the twenty-first century," says Todd Stitzer. "We sought to do this by creating a sustainable supply of high-quality cocoa while creating a sustainable life for cocoa farmers."

On the hundred-year anniversary of William Cadbury's first initiative in Ghana, Stitzer and the Cadbury team announced the Cocoa Partnership in collaboration with the UN, Anti-Slavery International, World Vision, Care, and VSO. Cadbury made a £45 million

($79 million) commitment over ten years to enhance the lives of co-
coa farmers in Ghana, India, and the Caribbean. "The aim is to work
in a holistic way in rural communities to improve conditions," says
David Croft, Cadbury's head of sustainability. The scheme provides
funds for farmers to increase their income by investing in their farms
while also building schools and infrastructure in rural districts. Nestlé
soon followed suit. In December 2009, Nestlé launched Fairtrade Kit
Kat and promised £65 million ($113 million) for cocoa farmers over a
ten-year period.

Kraft buys most of its cocoa from the Ivory Coast and uses a different certification scheme: the Rainforest Alliance. Irene Rosenfeld
has said that Kraft has taken "a very strong stance with respect to
Rainforest Alliance coffee." In 2009, Kraft also bought 4,500 tons of
Rainforest-certified cocoa beans and plans to increase the amount to
30,000 tons. Like Fairtrade, Rainforest aims to ensure that no child
labor is employed, but its approach, with an emphasis on environ-
mental issues, is slightly different. Kraft's vice president of sustainability, Steve Yucknut, says the differences between Fairtrade and the
Rainforest Alliance are "minor" and calls both organizations "outstanding." David Croft says Cadbury chose to work with Fairtrade because they believe the scheme is "more holistic in tackling injustices
of trade" than other certification schemes and "gives more power to
farmers."

Steve Yucknut confirmed that Cadbury's Fairtrade commitments
prior to the Kraft acquisition, including the £45 million ($79 million)
commitment to Ghanaian farmers, would be respected, but he could
not guarantee that the agreement would be extended. Yucknut insists
that since Irene Rosenfeld took over, "We have elevated the importance of sustainability." He rejects "out of hand" the idea that Cadbury was doing a better job on sustainability than Kraft and points to
a wide range of company programs related to worldwide hunger relief,
promoting a healthy lifestyle, volunteerism, and a number of "green"
initiatives such as reducing the use of water, energy, packaging, and
transport.

Not everyone is convinced. Adam Leyland writing in the *Grocer*
claims, "For Cadbury, corporate social responsibility isn't the latest

faddish addition to the annual report. Doing the right thing is in the company's DNA. Kraft has a corporate reputation agenda, as all big corporates now do, but it's a box to be ticked." Alex Cole, director of corporate affairs at Cadbury, agrees: "At Cadbury we lived the values. The challenge for Kraft and others is to try to see it through." Irene Rosenfeld disagrees: "At Kraft Foods, sustainability is not just an initiative or a check-the-box exercise; it goes to the heart of how we operate as a company. In fact one of the most exciting aspects of the integration process has been realizing just how aligned our two companies are in their values." But as Kraft comes under pressure to meet performance targets that have been promised to investors, will ethical standards be compromised?

For the developed world, there is one glaring irony in all this, living as we do in a world enriched so spectacularly with cheap confectionery: The West is facing an obesity epidemic. Far removed from the Puritanical ideal of abstemiousness and self-denial, competition between global food giants has proved so successful in pleasing the public that one in four people in Britain is clinically obese. In the United States, the figure is even higher, reaching close to 40 percent of the adult population. Levels of childhood obesity in both countries have soared. No one is claiming that confectionery is the only reason for this alarming epidemic, but it certainly plays a part.

Even so, some of the most talented managers and marketers, under pressure to deliver higher returns to shareholders, are searching for ever more skillful ways to persuade us to eat yet more chocolate and candy. It is tempting to have some sympathy with the early Quaker capitalists who felt the process was somehow dishonest, and that heavy promotion was like "an assault" on the unwary consumer. In many countries where global giants have succeeded in introducing Western-style confectionery, food, and drinks, obesity has risen exponentially. Mexico, for example, is on course to become the fattest nation on earth and is currently second only to America. Joseph Rowntree would be dismayed to learn that the poorest are the hardest hit. In the slums of Mexico City, children are more obese than adults, and the epidemic is threatening to lower life expectancy. According to the *Global Post* in August 2009, this trend mirrors Mexico's switch from a local to a global economy following the North American Treaty Act Agreement of 1994, which opened the door to processed food and drink from its U.S. neighbor.

It is curious to think that the extraordinary journey for the cocoa bean began in Mexico City nearly five centuries ago. The process of chocolate manufacture has come a long way since the Aztec emperor Montezuma tried to appease the threatening conquistadors with bejewelled goblets filled with a chili-spiced cocoa drink. The legacy he bequeathed, transformed by industrialization, has become today's rich cornucopia of chocolate confections sold all over the world. The early nineteenth-century chocolatiers who created their drinks and concoctions of sometimes doubtful wholesomeness in the backrooms of shops and sheds would indeed be amazed at the vast global enterprise that their efforts have produced.

John Cadbury in his Victorian shop, wooden planks on the floor, tins of cocoa on display, would struggle to comprehend that his modest enterprise, often on the verge of failure, had evolved into a global business worth billions. Would he turn in his grave over Kraft's hostile bid? No, I don't think so. But as he sat upright in his hard back chair, true puritan conceding not one inch to self indulgence, if he listened to the language of today's deal makers and their earnest discussions of "pre-tax synergies," "revenue synergies," "vision into action," and growth in "instant consumption channels," would he recognize the spirit of what he was trying to achieve? I think not. It would be hard to see anything close to the motives that drove him and the spirit in which he and his sons founded the business in today's leaders. Would he lament that something was missing in the modern world? Yes—I believe he would.

The objectives of the chocolate Quaker capitalists like John and George Cadbury and Joseph Rowntree and the spirit in which they pursued them appear as far removed from the greed of the modern corporate world—exemplified by the worst excesses of the financial crisis—as it is possible to imagine. For them making money was a means to an end and not an end in its own right. Making a profit was important; Quaker elders were quick to point out that a failing business was no good to anyone. But it was not the only goal. The idea that wealth creation was only for the owners of the business was un-acceptable. According to Alfred Gardiner, spiritual wealth, not ma-terial wealth, was for them the enlarging force that led to "a wealth of noble living," which was the real goal of civilization. "Being" not "having" was the true test of worth. By inviting their workers to pray when faced with a difficult decision, they wanted God's guidance to make their business a force for good. Ethical and wider humanitarian decisions really did matter. It was as though, for them, God was the ultimate chairman.

The Kraft takeover represents a poignant symbolic end point to this remarkable business enterprise that had its origins in the reli-gious thinking of the English Civil War and was integral to British culture. Will Kraft act with this bigger spirit for the betterment of the world—not just the top management? Will this "global powerhouse," in Irene Rosenfeld's words, also show leadership by being a tangible force for good in our global village? It's difficult not to feel skeptical. And that's why, despite all the praise for globalization and the excite-ment of giant takeovers, it is hard not to believe that something irre-placeable and of infinite value—immeasurable in the neat columns of a balance sheet—has been signed away with a handshake.

Epilogue

Whatever lies in store for Britain's chocolate industry, the trusts created by the pioneer chocolatiers will survive. George Cadbury's Bournville Village Trust has grown into a thriving enterprise that is still run principally by the direct descendants of George and his brother Richard. The trust is responsible for more than 8,000 properties and 1,100 acres across the West Midlands and Shropshire as well as 2,500 acres of farmland to preserve the green belt around southwest Birmingham: a small piece of England that cannot be signed away.

Around the factory in Bournville, George Sr.'s utopian village has grown to 6,000 houses nestled around the original parks and playing fields. The village, however, is no longer surrounded by countryside. It lies on the fringes of Birmingham as the giant conurbation has grown out to meet it. "People still come from around the world to see Bournville," says Duncan Cadbury, chairman of the Trust's Housing Services Committee. "They've heard it is a garden village which has worked. They even come to hear the carillon on the Junior School."

The Bournville Village Trust also works to create communities in collaboration with other housing organizations: 800 homes, shops, and a school at Lightmoor village in Telford, Shropshire; 3,300 homes at Lawley in Telford; and a major redevelopment building 220 homes at Shenley, part of the Bournville estate. "The Trust is much more than just the houses," says Duncan Cadbury. "We still maintain George's vision of creating mixed communities with houses for the

315

very poorest alongside those who can afford to buy their homes." The Bournville estates team is always on hand to fulfill the English dream of cottages and trees surrounding the eternal village green.

Other legacies bequeathed by family members have fared less well. Travelling out of Birmingham on the Bristol Road, I went in search of George Sr.'s manor house, which was donated to Birmingham University. As I drove up the once tree-lined lane past student housing, suddenly the rambling old house came into view. At first it was hard to believe it was the same house, its ancient multifaceted shape peeping out between concrete shrouds and wooden boards. Its fate was entwined with the vagaries of modern administration. An extension to the original house was added for student housing with huge wings on each side, which give it the appearance of a prison. Now abandoned, George Sr.'s cherished gardens long since vanished, the house appears to belong to a twilight world of a distant century. Nearby, Manor Farm Park, once the annual retreat for 25,000 excited children to enjoy a break in the country, and Pocklington Place for the Blind have suffered a similar decline. Both sites were donated to the local council, and estimates for upgrading the buildings to comply with modern regulations proved prohibitive. Peeping through the boards at the windows, the neglect is a sad indictment: These philanthropic gifts to the community were once supervised effectively by one man and his team. They have failed under public stewardship.

The remains of the once lively British chocolate industry have also left their mark. Terry's gargantuan works, now closed, stand a poignant mausoleum to past glories, the telltale broken glass in the yard a symbol of disinterest. Could this be the fate that lies in store for Bournville under Kraft's management? Michael Mitchell, head of Kraft's corporate affairs, declined to make any commitment: "Guarantees are not the right word—if you're asking us about guarantees we're never going to get there."

The sweet aroma of chocolate still wafts over the suburbs of York and down Haxby Road to Joseph Rowntree's original factory, which is owned today by Nestlé. The factory lies behind metal railings and is patrolled by security. There is one visible reminder of the company founder in the Joseph Rowntree lodge—now derelict—near the main entrance. As I pressed my face to the window to glimpse the empty rooms inside, I saw little more than gathering dust and papers scattered on the floor—and then a guard with a dog came to move me on.

Like George Cadbury, Joseph Rowntree's voice still carries into the twenty-first century thanks to the trusts he established. His original three—the Village Trust, the Charitable Trust, and Social Service Trust—have been modified by the trustees to adapt to modern times. True to the analytical spirit of their founder, the trusts today remain heavily involved in investigating causes of social problems. The Village Trust—now known as The Joseph Rowntree Foundation—bestows more than £10 million annually and is one of the largest foundations in England. Research projects cover a wide range of issues, including the causes of persistent poverty, building public support to end poverty, and—in an intriguing full circle—the effects of globalization on poverty. In keeping with Rowntree's commitment to the temperance cause, there are also research projects underway to help people suffering from alcoholism. Lastly, the Joseph Rowntree Housing Trust, established in 1968, manages housing projects across Yorkshire, including the village of New Earswick, which has grown to 2,500 homes.

Fry's chocolate works in Bristol suffered a more extreme fate than its Quaker rivals. The business transferred to Somerdale in the 1930s. Union Street was hit in a bombing raid in the Second World War and Fry's great citadel was severely damaged. Today the Fry business, which once held proud claim to being the largest chocolate company in the world, has been reduced to boxes of archives at Bournville, Somerdale, and the Bristol Records Office.

And what of the Quaker movement that inspired this great chocolate enterprise and proved such an astonishing force in the early industrial age? I went in search of their headquarters in Euston in central London. Leaving the vast, anonymous station, it seemed improbable that anything to do with the Quakers could be found here in the Euston Road with its thundering traffic and heavy fumes. I was looking for Friends House, built in the 1920s with contributions from the Cadburys and other Quaker families. After the Edwardian revival of the early twentieth century, the roll call of family dynasties that subscribed to the movement has fallen away. The Quaker movement has not been able to maintain its role as a guiding force in business. I was unsure what to expect as I made my way down Euston Road.

Suddenly, I noticed a rose garden on the other side of the road. It seemed incongruous—a garden cast in deep shadow from tall buildings on either side. Despite the bitter October day and the dirt from passing lorries, incredibly the roses were still in bloom, luminous in the wintry light. With traffic obscuring my view, it was hard to tell if the garden was connected in any way with Friends House. Remembering George Cadbury's passion for roses and his belief that no child should play where a rose could not bloom, I took a closer look. It was a few minutes before I could cross the road, but sure enough, the small rose garden led to the entrance to Friends House.

Stepping inside was like stepping into a different world. A sudden hush prevails, creating a totally different atmosphere from the one outside. Beyond the stone-clad hall, lined with straight-backed benches puritan in their simplicity, are corridors leading to a shady courtyard. It is easy to picture forbears and business leaders gathering here for passionate meetings to discuss the pressing issues of the day.

I met Helen Drewery, head of the international department of the Society of Friends. "People are surprised to discover that we exist," she said. There was a time when one in ten people in Britain were Quakers, but today there are only 15,000 members. "Quakers don't put very much store on dogma or church hierarchy," she said. "We put our energy into trying to make the world a better place." Inside the neatly kept archives was plenty of evidence to support her point: the antislavery movements of earlier centuries, the Kindertransports that relocated Jewish children before the Second World War, numerous famine relief programs, and, more recently, support for setting up the Child Poverty Action Group and Oxfam. Today, Drewery explains, Quakers have a presence in the world's greatest trouble spots. There are Quaker offices in New York and Geneva to work through UN agencies. She described an "accompaniment project" on the West Bank, which she calls "a ministry of presence" to help people caught in conflict zones feel that "the world has not forgotten about them" and to facilitate communication between opposing sides. People say, she continues, that "we punch above our weight, but that never feels like quite a comfortable phrase to use—not for a Quaker."

Helen Drewery believes that many people feel a hunger for something meaningful in their lives, and because Quakers don't have a specific creed, "In a way, we are a good space for people to explore what that deeper kind of life is about." She insists that "everything you do in your life can be for the good. You can reflect on every action you take, what you buy in the shops, the way you speak to each person: Every movement, every action, every word can be for the better or the worse." The aim "is to nurture something in ourselves—maybe something people would call their conscience, but that seems an inadequate word—a wellspring that early Quakers called 'the seed' that touches the ultimate mystery."

A force for the good surely, a quiet sane voice still there for those who want to hear it in this noisy century, putting the case for ending conflict between cultures and religions and nurturing peace. In today's material world, where the breathless glamour of celebrity culture holds the public in thrall, the Quaker message has become stifled, shut out from the boardrooms in the City of London just a mile away. It is hard to imagine today's business leaders giving more than a passing thought to the extraordinary claim of George Fox that the inner light is within us all. But those nineteenth-century entrepreneurs who made this their quest did succeed for a brief period in putting the remarkable Quaker movement in the spotlight. In the process they illuminated a different work ethic on a more human scale between master and man.

Acknowledgments

I was fortunate to receive help from a great many people who made this account of the chocolate Quaker dynasties and their rivals possible. For expert knowledge on the chocolate branch of the Cadbury family and the history of the company, I would particularly like to thank Sir Adrian Cadbury, one of the firm's longest serving chairmen. It was an inspiration to discuss the historical research and visit key locations with such a welcoming and informed guide; an experience that I will always look back on with great pleasure. Thank you, too, to former chief executive and chairman Sir Dominic Cadbury for his insights into a critical era in the firm's history from the 1960s through 2000 and for his patience in dealing with follow-up queries.

I owe a great deal to two members of my family who are no longer living. When I was young, my father, Kenneth Cadbury, and my uncle, Michael Cadbury, provided wonderful accounts of Quaker forebears in the chocolate branch of the family. Perhaps unknowingly, they each embodied different aspects of Quaker culture and helped to inspire this account. My cousin, Duncan Cadbury, chairman of the Bournville Village Trust's Housing Services Committee, provided invaluable assistance with research into Quaker history and the numerous family trusts. Many others in the wider Cadbury family shared compelling insights into the characters and history, which I have distilled into this account. Any views expressed in the book are my own and do not represent a unified Cadbury view.

For events at Cadbury since 2000, when family members were no longer members of the board, I am grateful to the last chief executive, Todd Stitzer, for discussing his period of leadership, the takeover, and his thinking on principled capitalism. I am also indebted to Cadbury's last chairman, Roger Carr, for his fascinating account of the takeover and the issues it raised. David Croft, Cadbury's head of sustainability; Alex Cole, global corporate affairs director; and others at Cadbury provided a wealth of information. Thanks are also due to Sarah Foden, the information manager, and Jackie Jones at the Cadbury archives in Bournville. Sarah provided generous assistance with numerous queries and gave up valuable time to comment on the manuscript.

At Kraft Foods, I am indebted to Steve Yucknut, head of sustainability, Michael Mitchell, head of external communications, and Becky Tousey, head of archives, for answering my questions relating to the company's history and the takeover. At Nestlé, archivist Tanja Aenis in Vevey, Switzerland, and Alex Hutchinson at Nestlé's Confectionery Heritage in York investigated historical questions bearing on the early years of Nestlé and Rowntree. Tammy Hamilton at the Hershey Community Archives provided invaluable assistance with the project. At Altria, John Marshall in corporate communications fielded queries pertaining to tobacco litigation. For insights into Mars and other chocolate companies, I received excellent support from a number of specialist archives and have credited them in the bibliography.

At the Society of Friends, I would particularly like to thank Helen Drewery, General Secretary of Quaker Peace and Social Witness, for her perspective on the Quaker movement. Timothy Phillips, chairman of The Quakers and Business Group, raised key questions about the modern business world and changing ethical values. In the library of the Society of Friends, I am indebted to Josef Keith, Joanna Clark, Tabitha Driver, Beverley Kemp, Jennifer Milligan, and Julia Hudson for responding to queries over many months, and I was particularly touched when they traced the unpublished "family book" written by Richard Cadbury in the 1860s, which provides a vivid insight into the early years.

There are so many others who helped during the months of re-search that it would be impossible to name them all, but I would like to acknowledge Timothy Newman at the International Labour Rights Forum in Washington, D.C.; Dave Goodyear at Fairtrade; Hugh Evans for discussing aspects of Fry history; Adam Leyland, editor of the *Grocer*; and John Bradley.

At PublicAffairs in New York, it was a pleasure to work with Clive Priddle, and I have appreciated his skilled editorial judgment and ad-vice at each stage in the production of the manuscript. I am also grateful to Melissa Veronesi and Nancy King for their thoughtful comments on the text and to Scott McIntyre at Douglas McIntyre in Canada for his continued support. At Curtis Brown, Gordon Wise's insights and encouragement on the project over many months proved invaluable.

Lastly, I would like to express my thanks to Julia Lilley without whom this book would not have been written. Her generous support for and great faith in the project has, as ever, kept me going through the long months of writing.

Bibliography

ARCHIVES

From the Library of the Society of Friends, Friend's House, London:
Cadbury, Richard. "Family Book," Temp MSS 996, 1863.
Fry, Joseph. Records 1727–1787, MS Vol S272.
Fry, Joseph Storrs. Correspondence MS Box 16/4/28.
Fry, Joseph Storrs. Correspondence. Temp MSS 668/1.
Successive editions of the Quaker Book of Discipline:
    Christian and Brotherly Advices, Manuscript version, 1738–1749.
    Extracts from the Minutes and Advices of the Yearly Meeting of Friends 1783.
    Rules of Discipline of the Religious Society of Friends, with Advices, 1834.
    Extracts from the Minutes and Advices of the Yearly Meeting . . . held in
        London . . . relating to Christian Doctrine, Practice and Discipline, 1861.

From the Cadbury Archives, Bournville, Birmingham, England:
Bournville: A Descriptive Account of Cocoa and its Manufacture. 1880.
Bournville Works Magazine, 1900–1970.
Bridge Street Album. 1830–1900. 010 003250 AZ1.
Cadbury Brothers Fancy Boxes and artwork.
Cadbury Brothers overseas records. 030–090.
Cadbury and Fry company publications.
Fry Company papers. 910–918.2.
Fry's Works Magazine, 1922–1929. 910.2 001687.
Fry, J.S. & Sons., *Bicentennial Issue: Fry's Works Magazine 1728–1928.* Broadmead,
    Bristol: Partridge and Love, 1928.

Industrial Record: A Review of the Interwar Years, 1919–1939. Cadbury Bros./ Pitman, 1945.

Somerdale magazine, 1961–1968. 910.2 001696.

Thirty Years of Progress: A Review of the Growth of the Bournville Works. 1910.

From the Cadbury Papers Collection, Birmingham City Archives, Central Library, Birmingham, England:

Cadbury, Barrow. Letters and notes/gift from employees. UBL MS 466/211–221.

Cadbury, Benjamin Head. Richard Tapper, and others. Family letters, vols 1– 3. UBL MS466/85 1.

Cadbury Brothers. Bull Street and Bournville early images. UBL MS 466/41/ 1/2/3/8/

Cadbury Brothers. Business Affairs: Ledgers and Accounts. UBL MS 466A 39.

Cadbury Brothers. Business Affairs: Wages from 1859–1864. UBL MS 466A/ 1–10.

Cadbury Brothers. UBL MS 466A/163–165.

Cadbury Brothers. December 16. UBL 1910 180/2.

Cadbury, Candia. Letters to her sons John and George, including "A Mother's Affectionate Desire for Her Children." UBL MS 466/97 1–53; 466/98; 466/99/1–8; 466/100/1–2.

Cadbury, Elizabeth. Journal. UBL MS/466/ 431–434.

Cadbury, George. Letters. UBL MS 466/209/1–13 and 209/219.

Cadbury, William. Correspondence. November 1907. UBL 1907: 180/365.

Cadbury, William. Miscellaneous personal album. UBL MS 466/32.

Cadbury, William. UBL 1903 180/336.

Notebook. UBL 1909 299–300.

From the Rowntree Papers Collection, Borthwick Institute of Historical Research, University of York, England:

Information on Tanner's Moat site in the 1890s, including insurance documents, plans for new Haxby Road site, and other documents relating to Rowntree's factories. HIR 2 10–12 Archive 398.

Reports on the Van Houten process. HIR1/5–13 & HIR 2 1–7.

Rowntree, Joseph. Personal notebooks, correspondence, business memoranda, drawings, etc. Ledger HIR/1 Sections 1–4.

Rowntree, Joseph. Undated agreements on work, wages, machinery, etc. HIR 2 8–12 Archive 376.

MANUSCRIPTS

Fry, Theodore. "A Brief Memoir of Francis Fry." Unpublished typescript. British Library, London: 1887.

———. *History of J.S. Fry and Sons*. Unpublished typescript.

The London Commodity Exchange. Unpublished typescript from The London Stock Exchange, 1961. City Library, London: FO PAM 1486.

Strong, L. A. G. *The Story of Rowntree*. Unpublished typescript. 1948

Wallace, Paul. The Wallace manuscripts, typescript for the Hershey Trust, 1955.

BOOKS

Acheson, T. W. "The National Policy and the Industrialisation of the Maritimes." In *Canada's Age of Industry, 1849–1896*, edited by M. S. Cross and G. S. Kealey, 62–94. Toronto: McClelland and Stewart, 1982.

Alexander, Helen. *Richard Cadbury of Birmingham*. London: Hodder and Stoughton, 1906.

Barclay H. F., and A. Wilson-Fox. *A History of the Barclay Family*. 1934.

Barringer E. E. *Sweet Success: The Story of Cadbury and Hudson in New Zealand*. Dunedin Cadbury Confectionary Ltd., 2000.

Bartlett, Percy W. *Barrow Cadbury: A Memoir*. London: Bannisdale Press, 1960.

Beable, W. H. *Romance of Great Businesses*. London, 1926.

Beckett, Stephen T. *The Science of Chocolate*. Cambridge, UK: Royal Society of Chemistry Publishing, 2008.

Benson, S. H. *Wisdom in Advertising*. London: John Murray, 1901.

Bradley, John. *Cadbury's Purple Reign: Chocolate's Best-loved Brand*. Chichester, UK: John Wiley and Sons, 2008.

Braithwaite, William C. *The Beginnings of Quakerism*. London: Macmillan, 1912.

———. *The Second Period of Quakerism*. York, UK: Sessions of York, 1979.

Brayshaw, A. Neave. *The Quakers: Their Story and Message*.

Brenner, Joël Glenn. *The Emperors of Chocolate: Inside the Secret Worlds of Hershey and Mars*. New York: Random House, 1999.

Briggs, Asa. *Social Thought and Social Action: A Study of the Work of Seebohm Rowntree, 1871–1954*. London: Longmans, Green and Co., 1961.

———. *Victorian Cities*. London: Penguin, 1963.

Broekel, Ray. *The Great American Candy Bar Book*. Boston: Houghton Mifflin, 1982.

———. *The Chocolate Chronicles*. Wallace Homestead Book Co., 1985.

Cadbury Brothers. *Cocoa and Its Manufacture*. Carlisle, UK: Hudson Scott and Sons, 1880.

_____. *Industrial Challenge: The Experience of Cadburys of Bournville in the Post-War Years*. London: Pitman Publishing, 1964.

Cadbury, Christabel. *Robert Barclay: His Life and Work*. London: Headley Brothers, 1912.

Cadbury, Edward. *Experiments in Industrial Organisation*. London: Longmans, Green and Co., 1912.

Cadbury, Edward, and George Shann. *Sweating*. London: Headley Bros., 1907.

Cadbury, Edward, George Shann, and Cecil Matheson. *Women's Work and Wages*. London: T Fisher Unwin, 1906.

Cadbury, George. *Conurbation: A Survey of Birmingham and the Black Country*. Birmingham, UK: West Midland Group, 1948.

Cadbury, Richard. [Historicus, pseudo.]. *Cocoa: All About It*. Birmingham, UK: Sampson, Low and Marston, 1892.

Cadbury, William. *Labour in Portuguese West Africa*. London: Routledge, 1910.

Carnegie, Andrew. *The Gospel of Wealth*. London: Penguin, 1889.

Carr, David. *Candy Making in Canada*. Toronto: The Dundurn Group, 2003.

Chernow, Ron. *Titan: The Life of John D. Rockefeller*. New York: Vintage Books, 1999.

Chinn, Carl. *The Cadbury Story: A Short History*. Studley, Warwickshire, UK: Brewin Books, 1988.

Church, Roy A. *The Great Victorian Boom: 1850–1873*. London: Macmillan, 1896.

Clarence-Smith, William Gervase. *Cocoa and Chocolate: 1765–1914*. London: Routledge, 2000.

Coady, Chantal. *Chocolate: The Food of the Gods*. San Francisco: Chronicle Books, 1993.

Coe, Sophie D., and Michael Coe. *The True History of Chocolate*. London: Thames and Hudson, 1996.

Cook, L. Russell. *Chocolate Production and Use*. New York: Books for Industry, 1972.

Crosfield, J. F. *A History of the Cadbury Family*. 2 vols. Cambridge: Cambridge University Press, 1985.

Crutchley, Geo. W. *John Mackintosh: A Biography*. London: The National Sunday School Union, 1921.

D'Antonio, Michael. *Hershey: Milton S. Hershey's Extraordinary Life of Wealth, Empire and Utopian Dreams*. New York: Simon & Schuster, 2006.

Diaper, Stefanie. "J. S. Fry and Sons: Growth and Decline in the Chocolate Industry, 1753–1918." In *Studies in the Business History of Bristol*, edited by Harvey Charles and Press Jon, 33–53. Bristol, UK: Bristol Academic Press, 1988.

Duffy, James. *A Question of Slavery*. Cambridge, MA: Harvard University Press, 1967.

Emden, Paul H. *Quakers in Commerce*. London: Sampson Low, Marston and Company, 1940.

Fergusson, Niall. *Empire: How Britain Made the Modern World*. London: Penguin, 2003.

Finch, R. *A World Wide Business*. Birmingham, UK: n.d.

Fitzgerald, Robert. *Rowntree and the Marketing Revolution: 1862–1969*. Cambridge: Cambridge University Press, 1995.

Folster, David. *Ganong: A Sweet History of Chocolate*. New Brunswick, Canada: Goose Lane Editions, 2006.

Fraser, W. H. *The Coming of the Mass Market: 1850–1914*. London: Macmillan, 1981.

Fry, J. S. & Sons. *Fry's of Bristol Established 1728*. Bristol, n.d.

Fry, J. S. & Sons, and Cadbury Bros Ltd. *The British Cocoa and Chocolate Co. Ltd.* 1948.

Gardiner, Alfred G. *Life of George Cadbury*. London: Cassell & Co., 1923.

Grivetti, Louis E., and Howard Shapiro. *Chocolate: History, Culture, and Heritage*. Hoboken, NJ: John Wiley and Sons, 2009.

Harris, J. H. *Dawn in Darkest Africa*. London: Smith, Elder and Co., 1912.

Harwich, N. *Histoire du Chocolat*. Paris: Editions Desjonqueres, 1992.

Head, B. *The Food of the Gods: A Popular Account of Cocoa*. London: Routledge, 1903.

Heer, J. *World Events 1866–1966: The First Hundred Years of Nestlé*. Lausanne, Switzerland: Imprimeries Reunies, 1966.

Hewett, C. *Chocolate and Cocoa: Its Growth and Culture, Manufacture and Modes of Preparation for the Table*. London: Simpkin, Marshall and Co., 1862.

Hinkle, Samuel F. *Hershey: Far Sighted Confectioner, Famous Chocolate, Fine Community*. New York: Newcomen Society, 1964.

Hobsbawm, Eric. *The Age of Capital: 1848–1875*. London: Weidenfeld and Nicolson, 1975.

Hodgkin, J. E., ed. *Quakerism and Industry [Record of the Conference of Employers at Woodbrooke April 1918]*. London, 1925.

Howard, Ebenezer. *Tomorrow: A Peaceful Path to Real Reform*. London: Routledge, 1898.

Knapp, Arthur W. *Cocoa and Chocolate: Their History from Plantation to Consumer*. London: Chapman and Hall, 1920.

———. *The Cocoa and the Chocolate Industry: The Tree, the Bean, the Beverage*. London: Pitman Publishing, 1923.

Markham, Leonard. *York: A City Revealed*. Gloucestershire, UK: Sutton Stroud, 2006.

Marks, W. *George Cadbury Jr*. Birmingham, UK: n.d.

Mathias, Peter. *The First Industrial Nation: The Economic History of Britain, 1700–1914*. London: Methuen, 1969.

Milligan, Edward H. *Biographical Dictionary of British Quakers in Commerce and Industry*. York, UK: Sessions Book Trust, 2007.

Murphy, Joe. *New Earswick: A Pictorial History*. York, UK: Sessions Book Trust, 1987.

———. *The History of Rowntree's in Old Photographs*. York, UK: York Publishing Services, 2007.

Nevinson, Henry W. *A Modern Slavery*. New York: Schocken, 1968. First published 1906 by Harper and Bros.

Nickalls, John L., ed. *The Journal of George Fox*. Philadelphia, PA: Religious Society of Friends, 1997.

Othnick, J. "The Cocoa and Chocolate Industry in the Nineteenth Century." In *The Making of the Modern British Diet*, edited by Derek T. Oddy and Dereks Miller, 77–90. London: Croom Helm, 1976.

Pfiffer, Albert. *Henri Nestlé: 1814–1890*. Vevey, Switzerland: The Nestlé Corporation, 1995.

Richardson, Paul. *Indulgence Around the World in Search of Chocolate*. London: Little Brown, 2003.

Richardson, Tim. *Sweets: A History of Temptation*. London: Bloomsbury, 2002.

Roberts, Jane S. *Drink Temperance and the Working Class in Nineteenth-Century Germany*. Boston: Allen and Unwin, 1984.

Rogers, T. B. *A Century of Progress: 1831–1931*. Birmingham, UK: Cadbury Bros, 1931.

Rosenblum, Mort. *Chocolate: The Bittersweet Saga of Dark and Light*. New York: North Point Press, 2006.

Rowntree, Benjamin Seebohm. *Poverty: A Study of Town Life*. London: Thomas Nelson and Sons, 1901.

———. *The Human Needs of Labour: Land and Labour*. London: Thomas Nelson and Sons, 1910.

Rowntree, C. Brightwen. *The Rowntrees of Riseborough*. York, UK: Ebor Press, 1989.

_____. *The Way to Industrial Peace and the Problem of Unemployment*. London, 1914.

Rowntree, John Stephenson. *A Memoir of Joseph Rowntree, 1801–59*. Birmingham, UK: privately printed.

Rowntree, Joseph, and Arthur Sherwell. *The Temperance Problem and Social Reform*. London: Hodder.

Rowntree, Joseph. *Pauperism in England and Wales*. 1865.

Rowntree and Co. *Industrial Betterment at Cocoa Works*. York, UK: 1905, 1910, 1914.

Rowntree and Son. *A Century and a Half of Progress*. 1930.

Satre, Lowell J. *Chocolate on Trial: Slavery, Politics and the Ethics of Business*. Athens: Ohio University Press, 2005.

Schwarz, Friedhelm. *Nestlé: The Secrets of Food, Trust and Globalisation*. Ontario, Canada: Key Porter Books, 2002.

Sharman, Cecil. *George Fox and the Quakers*. Richmond, IN: Friends United Press, 1991.

Shippen, Katherine, and Paul Wallace. *Milton S. Hershey*. New York: Random House, 1959.

Smith, Page. *The Rise of Industrial America*. New Haven, CT: Yale University Press, 1986.

Snavely, Joseph. *An Intimate Story of M. S. Hershey*. Hershey, PA: privately printed, 1957.

Sprüngli, Rudolph R. *150 Years of Delight Chocoladefabriken Lindt & Sprüngli 1845–1995*. Schweiz, 1995.

Stranz, Walter. *George Cadbury: An Illustrated Life*. Aylesbury, UK: Shire Publications, 1973.

Taylor, Alan J. *Progress and Poverty in Britain: 1780–1850*. London: Harper.

Teiser, R. *An Account of Domingo Ghirardelli and the Early Years of the D Ghirardelli Company*. San Francisco, CA: D Ghirardelli Co., 1945.

Terrio, Susan J. *Crafting the Culture and History of French Chocolate*. Los Angeles: University of California Press, 2000.

Terry, J. & Sons. *Terry's of York: 1767–1967*. Privately printed by Newman Neame.

Townsend, Richard F. *The Aztecs*. London and New York: Thames and Hudson, 1992.

Turner, Earnest S. *The Shocking History of Advertising*. London: Michael Joseph, 1952.

Urquhart, D. H. *Cocoa*. London: Longmans, Green and Co., 1955.

Vernon, Anne. *A Quaker Business Man: The Life of Joseph Rowntree 1836–1925*. London: Allen and Unwin.

Wagner, Gillian. *The Chocolate Conscience*. London: Chatto and Windus, 1987.

Walvin, James. *The Quakers: Money and Morals*. London: John Murray, 1997.

Whitney, Janet. *Elizabeth Fry: Quaker Heroine*. London: George Harrap and Co., 1937.

Wild, Anthony. *Black Gold: A Dark History of Coffee*. London: Harper Perennial, 2005.

Williams, C. T. *Chocolate and Confectionary*. London: L. Hill, 1953.

Williams, Iolo A. *The Firm of Cadbury: 1831–1931*. London: Constable & Robinson, 1931.

Wood, Stephen. *A History of London*. London: Macmillan, 1998.

Woolf, Virginia. *Roger Fry: A Biography*. London: Bloomsbury, 1940.

Worstenholm, Luther. "Joseph Rowntree: 1836–1925." A typescript memoir and related papers. York, UK: Sessions York, 1986.

ARTICLES

It would not be possible to list all articles consulted. This is a guide to the key articles:

Banks, Myron. "Mars to Expand Factory." *Chicago Daily Tribune*, April 6, 1958.

Burtt, Joseph. "How America Can Free the Portuguese Cocoa Slave," *Leslie's Illustrated Weekly*, October 14, 1909, 368–369.

———. "My Success in America." *Leslie's Illustrated Weekly*, December 16, 1909, 608.

Chase, Al. "Standard Set by Mars Plant Built in 1928." *Chicago Daily Tribune*, November 15, 1953.

Daily Mail (on outbreak of Boer War), October 11, 1899.

Dombrowski, Louis. "Candy Makers Unspoiled by Sweet Smell of Success." *Chicago Daily Tribune*, January 5, 1961.

Elwood, Berman. "Mars Embattled over Succession." *Chicago Daily Tribune*, June 10, 1959.

"The Factory in a Garden." *Cosmopolitan*, June 1903.

Ferguson, Richard. "At Mars, Sweet Success." *The Times*, May 8, 1953.

Gross, Alan. "Sweet Home Chicago." *Chicago* magazine, February 1988.

Gussow, Don. "Forrest Mars." *Candy Industry and Confectioners Journal*, 1966.

Hobhouse, Emily. Letter to the editor. *The Times*, June 27, 1901.

Kessler, Ronald. "Candy from Strangers." *Regardie's* magazine, August 1986.

Lippman, Thomas W. "The Mars Empire: How Sweet It Is." *Washington Post*, December 6 and 7, 1981.

Nevinson, Henry. "The New Slave Trade." *Harper's Monthly Magazine*, August 1905–February 1906.

Poe, Tracy. "Sweet Home Chicago: Candy Makers Made City Their Capital." *Chicago Tribune*, July 16, 1997.

Saporito, Bill. "Uncovering Mars's Unknown Empire." *Fortune*, September 26, 1988.

_____. "The Eclipse of Mars." *Fortune*, November 28, 1994.

"The Sweet, Secret World of Forrest Mars." *Fortune*, May 1967.

"Where Happiness and Health Go Hand in Hand with a Great Enterprise." *Business World*, June 1903.

Young, James C. "Hershey Unique Philanthropist." *New York Times*, November 18, 1923.

Index

335

About the Author

Deborah Cadbury is a writer, award-winning documentary producer for the BBC, the author of seven books, and a relative of the famous Quaker family who gave their name to one of the world's most famous brands of chocolate.